LF

MODERN FRANCE

Theories and Realities of Urban Planning

Peggy A. Phillips

UNIVERSITY
PRESS OF
AMERICA

LANHAM • NEW YORK • LONDON

University Press of America,® Inc.

4720 Boston Way
Lanham, MD 20706

3 Henrietta Street
London WC2E 8LU England

Printed in the United States of America

British Cataloging in Publication Information Available

Library of Congress Cataloging in Publication Data

Phillips, Peggy A., 1952-
Modern France.

Bibliography: p.
Includes index.
1. City planning—France—History—20th century.
I. Title.
HT169.F7P48 1987 307.1'2'0944 86-28225
ISBN 0-8191-6037-7 (alk. paper)
ISBN 0-8191-6038-5 (pbk. : alk. paper)

All University Press of America books are produced on acid-free paper which exceeds the minimum standards set by the National Historical Publication and Records Commission.

For John and Eileen Phillips

I wish to acknowledge the role played in shaping this study by former Mayor Paul R. Soglin of Madison, Wisconsin and many, many other urban activists in the United States and France. My colleagues Harvey Goldberg, Edward T. Gargan, Stanley Schultz and John B. Sharpless assisted with the early versions of the manuscript. Dozens of archivists at INSEE helped bring the study to its final form. I also want to thank Mrs. Patricia Stango for typing the manuscript. Thanks also to my husband Bob and my son Joey for peace, quiet and patience.

TABLE OF CONTENTS

Preface

This volume has tried to answer questions that owe a great deal to the municipal radical movement in the United States and France during the late 1960s and early 1970s. To urban activists, this author included, the politics of urban life was an intensely ideological question and seemingly technocratic and neutral institutions like land use planning came under severe criticism. Who controlled the planners? What social class vision did they etch into the urban environment for the whole community? Was not the real issue in land use the relationship of the individual's autonomy to the collective self interest? Was not the idea of property at the core of all decisions in France? The long established doctrines of the traditional critics of property--the Socialists and Communists in France--failed to satisfy the critics from the New Left. Too much Stalinism had destroyed the appeal of Marxism for many in both the United States and France, and too much reformism had dulled the Socialist bite. Moreover, the protection of individual rights over collective restraints seemed to have received its most serious consideration among conservative social theorists and that great *bête noir* of the organized French left, the anarchists. In France, I believe the failure of the established opposition parties to offer an intellectually satisfying analysis on these important issues led an entire generation to abandon the historic left parties which in turn has produced the first signs of the death rattle of the French Communist Party.

This volume unravels the origins and some of the mysteries of modern French urban design within its political and ideological context. Far from being a technically neutral and apolitical process *urbanisme* is a powerful reflection of contemporary French theories about the uses of property. The intention has been to go beyond an institutional history and to answer some of the broader questions that underpin modern town planning in France. My intention has been to make history useful in the present.

September 1986
Miami

Introduction

Historians often have referred to urbanization as a fundamental characteristic of modern Western Europe. In the early modern period urbanization began as a spontaneous growth of towns and cities, but by the twentieth century urbanization has become a deliberate process. As such, it embodies all the complex social and political philosophical choices of contemporary European history.

French urbanization in the twentieth century differs qualitatively from all previous types of urban growth in the country. Contemporary urbanization takes place within a consciously specified paradigm which shapes the choices of the entire urban community. That paradigm known as *urbanisme* has been created by urban planners and implemented by the State. While the process of guiding modern urban development has on the whole been a largely anonymous and bureaucratic phenomenon, one individual has clearly left a personal legacy to French cities. In twentieth century France, Le Corbusier's name has become synonymous with *urbanisme* and French conceptions about modernity. From his birth in 1887 until his death in 1965 the life and times of Le Corbusier circumscribe the most critical period in the evolution of modern town planning in France.

Like Le Corbusier's personal life, the development of modern French town planning fell into two distinct periods: The era of theory to 1939, and the age of implementation after 1946. From the *révolution des maires* in the mid-1880s which brought urban reformers to the helm of French local government through the depression years of the late Third Republic, urban planning remained a vague predisposition on the part of social reformers and town engineers without precise intellectual or legal definition. *Urbanisme* was merely a sketch on the canvas. After Vichy and the crisis of conscience it represented for France, the political environment changed and openly embraced planning in a wide variety of areas. Corporatism the ideology of many of the wartime leaders and the Keynesian economic theory of the post-war leaders, both played a critical role in shaping new national strategies for implementing town planning. After the Second World War, urban planning began to take on substantive form as something more than a handful of experiments in the Parisian suburbs. At the base of the new urban planning system lay philosophical principles just as intricate as the engineering diagrams themselves. The first chapters in this volume will examine the historic development of urban planning during the early twentieth century. The second part of the volume will explore the most important aspects of planning policy within the political history of the two post-war republics.

In _L'Espace vital_ (1984), the leading French urban critic Jean François Gravier assessed _urbanisme_ against the broadest possible sweep of European historical development. His global treatment of the subject began with the Gallo-Roman days, inorder to offer a vivid background for the examination of contemporary land use. In contrast, this volume has focused on the more immediate intellectual and political history of the same urban environment from the 1880s through 1965 during the life and times of Le Corbusier. In important ways, the findings in this study have complimented the analysis by Gravier. The literature on specific problems of urbanization during the Third Republic is vast, and there are many episodic treatments of Le Corbusier's work. Yet with the exception of Gravier and a few other analysts, urban planning after the Second World War has been treated as an almost apolitical process by historians and other social scientists. I believe the failure to produce a broad synthetic treatment of the subject has stemmed from the highly ideological character of the process of urban planning which at the same time was propounded by architects and engineers like Le Corbusier who claimed to be apolitical and even anti-political. While several excellent studies of the mechanics of French urban planning after the Second World War have been published such as by Ann-Marie Hackett-Walsh in 1963 and by J. E. Godchot in 1958, these studies offer a depoliticized view of what was in fact an intensely political phenomenon. My study provides a more complete picture of the deep political divisions within the history of French urban planning.

Property and the social institutions that govern it are at the core of the urban political process just as they stand at the heart of the urban engineering problem. Le Corbusier and the urban planning cadre that he attracted were essentially propagandists for a powerful reconceptualization of the ideas about property in modern France. The Third Republic rested squarely upon the natural right of private property in the Declaration of the Rights of Man and Citizen of the late eighteenth century which was also the foundation stone of the modern middle class political parties. But since Le Corbusier's youth the primacy of property in France had been under profound challenge from both the right and left of the political spectrum. Socialists blamed the institutions of property for the widespread poverty in French society which to them made a mockery of the other civil and political guarantees of the Declaration and the Republic. Extreme leftists called for the outright abolition of property and the institutions that had created it. On the right, the crypto-fascists also quarreled with the unchecked private control of property. Both poles of the spectrum saw the competition among national monopolies and trusts as the prime cause of the Great War. To these critics the moral and physical devastation of the First World War demonstrated the bankrupt nature of nineteenth century capitalism as well as the concepts of private property and Republicanism. Some of these critics became the early Communists and others the fascists of France in the 1920s. Both ends of the ideological debate during the inter-war period repudiated the old institutions of private property in Republican.

It is critical to see the origin of Le Corbusier's ideas about urbanisme within this early twentieth century political context in order to fully appreciate the nature of the conflict over the alternative urban development strategies in France after the Second World War. The differing models for urban planning, including the refusal to plan at all, became code words for larger philosophical positions on the nature of property and the institutions that should govern it. Three basic conflicts formed the essence of the urban planning political problem in modern France as elsewhere. (i) Collective governance of land can foster collective and sometimes individual prosperity, but that same collective governance by definition alienates a portion of individual proprietary control over property. (ii) Intellectuals with special skills, an internal vocabulary and perhaps a self-serving elite philosophy use urban designs to produce unified plans for collective land use which can not effectively be modified by members of the subject community. Le Corbusier assumed that the rational economic man naturally wanted to live in a rational economic urban environment which planners can discover and precisely specify. Dissent will violate the assumption of rationality, hence represents a danger to the whole system. (iii) Planned communities only can function according to artificial or induced equilibrium much like the economic model of John Maynard Keynes. That presumption of induced equilibrium makes urban planning self-perpetuating within the modern State.

The historical evolution of these three philosophical components of modern urban planning in France was hardly an unbroken march of determined urban reformers to a certain body of principles. Instead, the flow of events saw sharp setbacks, and considerable failure to persuade national and local political leaders of the efficacy of the new view of property and the institutions that should govern it. Le Corbusier's own career best illustrated the perils of these urban propagandists. In the 1930s, he abandoned the old Republican tradition entirely and flirted with Mussolini's fascism. During the Second World War, he worked for Pétain in the collaborationist government. Le Corbusier hoped that the wartime regime would give him a free hand to carry out his ideas on urban planning in the Reconstruction of the north east during 1940 and 1941. After 1945, the new French government held Le Corbusier's collaborationist past against him. He was excluded from participation in the next wave of Reconstruction planning during the late 1940s.

Le Corbusier wanted to erase the road ways, sewer lines, the distribution of infrastructure like schools, hospitals and post-offices, and begin again with empty space and unencumbered property. Barring that costly project, he suggested creating New Towns rather like the old Garden Cities of Ebenezer Howard, which spring into being as completely planned urban communities. But better than the early Garden Cities, Le Corbusier's New Towns were intended to be compact new communities in the center of the old crumbling cities like Paris. Skyscrapers would house an entire new community in one unified structure. Instead of following Le Corbusier's vision, the reconstruction planners decided to rebuild the existing communities within existing boundaries and from existing infrastructure, while concentrating capital expenditures on basic industry, intra-urban communications, and energy delivery. Post-war planners, however, did build millions of residential units in large apartment complexes that borrowed directly from Le Corbusier's early ideas about cities within single buildings. These new communities came under intense political scrutiny during the 1950s and 1960s. By the Fifth Republic of the 1960s, the Reconstruction era town plans came under strong criticism by planners who demanded a more coherent, easier to manage urban environment. Under Gaullist style corporatism, Le Corbusier received full rehabilitation and open endorsement, which was reflected in the town plans of the 1960s.

Urbanisme and Le Corbusier's city designs stand at the core of modern corporatism in France. During the inter-war years, the ideology of corporatism attracted followers throughout Europe because it provided a cogent rebuttal to the chaos and brutality of the Great War. The rugged Individuals who launched the war were, of course, politicians roughly the age of Le Corbusier's father. For Le Corbusier's own generation those Europeans slightly too old to go to the front in 1914, corporatism initially appeared to be a culmination of the social scientific search of the nineteenth century for a lower risk model of society and economic behavior. Thus theorists such as Le Corbusier hoped to give the returning war veteran a more rational, perhaps safer, philosophical system that in its mature form became corporatism. Soldiers returning from the Great War in France as well as in England, Italy and Germany proved to be highly receptive to the notion of replacing chaos and waste with order and prosperity. However, in France it took another twenty five years for the new philosophy to become established. In the victorious countries the generation of Le Corbusier's father continued at the helm of government until the eve of the next war. To this older group of politicians, corporatism was both alien and bound up in the old bitter quarrels over religious education. In nineteenth century France clashes over education had brought nearly all the Republics to the brink collapse, thus even in the 1920s this issue remained the great bête noir of French politics.

Le Corbusier proposed a corporate urban scheme in his designs of the 1920s and 1930s. In these urban plans, Le Corbusier drew upon the earlier ideas of Garden City. Ebenezer Howard designed his Garden City to combat the disease and disorder of late nineteenth century London. Le Corbusier rejected Howard's suburbs as wasteful of greenspace, but appropriated the concept of completely integrated physical and political land use planning for the urban environment. That combination of physical layout with a high powered political philosophy was the essence of the urban corporatist model of Howard. Le Corbusier called his Parisian skyscrapers "vertical Garden Cities." After the Second World War these skyscrapers became the massive suburban apartment complexes, *les grandes ensembles*, and the most important corporatist symbols of the French school of Modern Architecture.

What did corporatism offer to modern European societies? Moreover, what is the special nature of the contemporary relationship between corporatism and *urbanisme* in France? Corporatism appealed to both the right and the left political movements in France because it claimed to explain the weaknesses of nineteenth century capitalism and to provide concrete solutions to the problems of economic distress. In France, capitalism in its nineteenth century form had many opponents on the Royalist right and the Socialist left. Twentieth century corporatism (often called neo-corporatism to distinguish it from the mediaeval practices) promised to place economic matters in the hands of experts devoted to the common well-being, by taking property rights away from the selfish Individuals of *laissez-faire*. Like the old guild masters, the new corporate managers were supposed to act to ensure full employment, fair prices and just marketing practices. These new corporate managers were to adopt policies according to a clear social compact that governed economic and social relationships. In mediaeval Europe this social compact was known as the convention of the "just price" which fixed the prices of consumer good to the social station of the producer within a rigid social hierarchy. The modern compact never received complete definition in France, but certainly included the promise of stable employment and the end social class rivalries.

Modern French theories of corporatism, in large part, came from the ideas of Pierre Joseph Proudhon in the mid-nineteenth century. Following Henri Saint Simon and Auguste Comte, Proudhon demanded that the economy be placed under the rule of law. Economic regulation by specially trained managers in the great Peoples' Bank formed the core of his modern corporatist theory. In some descriptions of the new economy Proudhon also saw the rule of law devolving from legislatures to simple contracts between employers and workers. He viewed this transformation as a means of taking law making away from the narrow upper middle class elite which dominated French government in the nineteenth century. The theories of Proudhon, as well as Le Corbusier and his Modern Architecture Movement have defied easy ideological assessment. When generous, Marxist historians have viewed Proudhon as a fanciful, utopian Socialist, and when less sanguine as a proto-fascist. Le Corbusier has received the same treatment. The failure of historians to offer a political history of French urban planning can be credited precisely to the difficulty in providing a satisfactory explanation of the ideologies behind the politics of property holding under modern corporatism in France.

Corporatism and its application in city life urbanisme form the critical components of the modern Welfare State that emerged in France after the Second World War. While the code words in the French political debate have changed since the time of Proudhon and since the inter-war years, the essence of the dialogue remained intact. At the same time, it must be recognized that a new factor entered the debates when it became clear that this form of corporatism in France worked and worked very well during the 1950s and 1960s. No longer did discussions rest on mere speculation, the Growth Miracle provided evidence about the success, if not the wisdom of corporate style economic management in a modern European nation. After the defeat of the fascist powers in the war, the key to the revival of corporatism was Keynesian economics and urbanisme which recast the logic of corporatism within the seemingly apolitical language of planning. Le Corbusier's concepts of physical planning for urban land use became the most visible and graphic symbols of the widespread implementation of corporatist regulation in France.

When de Gaulle created the Fifth Republic around his new constitution of 1958, the new form of regulation was secure in French society. The early

Fifth Republic merely refined the existing structures. The central planning bureaucracy made important concessions to the demands of regional and local elites for more control of land use planning. These adjustments, however, failed to foreshadow the explosion of May 1968. Rebellious Parisian students and the young workers in the countryside raised dozens of issues, but the central theme of the protests seems to have been the anonymous character of modern life. The corporate model under the Fifth Republic appeared to have set the categories for regulation very narrowly. To these rebels, Le Corbusier's great skyscrapers reduced homes to standard cubicles, workplaces to production units, and people to the size of ants. That argument was also the substance of the earlier humanist critiques of Positivism and corporatism during the inter-war years.

This study presents this history of the French debate over the wisdom of urbanisme in the image of Le Corbusier.

CHAPTER ONE

Municipal Taylorism (1880-1939)

The period from 1880 through the 1930s were Le Corbusier's formative years as an architect and planner. Those years were also the era of municipal Taylorism in France.

Municipal Taylorism

Modern French town planning originated with the attempts to foster housing reform under the early Third Republic during the 1880s and 1890s. Town planning, however, only took its present form in the early twentieth century, when new economic philosophies made *urbanisme* not only a cure for serious urban problems but more importantly a vehicle for the reform of capitalism itself. Only after the Second World War, when Keynesian economic principles gained general acceptance in France, did town planning's great potential to change the environmental physical as well as society and culture come to be fully realized. The new Keynesian macro-economic theory taught that national prosperity was partly a function of the actions of the State as the purchaser of last resort. According to the new theory, in peacetime, States traditionally have purchased public works: Roads, schools and in France public housing, the basic components of the infrastructure of towns. Thus the pre-war development of the ideology of *urbanisme*, housing reform movement and Keynesian economic principles formed the foundations of the urban management practices of the 1950s and 1960s.

The Origin of Urbanisme

Urban planning began with the introduction of the mass-produced brick in the 1880s which dramatically changed home construction methods and urban growth patterns. This technological innovation created a need to control the new suburban areas of housing construction. Between 1870 and the outbreak of the First World War in 1914 the population of French large cities more than doubled with a full ten percent of all Frenchmen coming to live in the Paris region. Most new Parisians found housing in the suburbs and not in the city proper. At that time, traditional home construction in European large cities generally fell into two categories: Massive, expensive single family homes, _grandes maisons_, and large blocks of small rental units for the remainder of society. In both cases, the nature of the buildings required the owner to invest a large sum of capital in the construction. In turn, owners demanded the most durable construction materials, using stone, and building the house to stand for three hundred years.

But after 1880, when construction replaced agriculture as the major employer of non-industrial labor in France, mass-produced brick replaced hand-hewn stone. This made it possible to produce housing with a far lower initial capital investment.(1) No longer did the cost and durability of the chief raw material dictate that dwelling be built of stone. It was now possible to put up dozens or even hundreds of modest brick _pavillons_ in the suburbs on cheap land, each to last fifty years or so. This change in construction materials and techniques led to a rediscovery of the small capitalist in the French housing market: The small borrower of Proudhon's Peoples' bank, or equivalent in England, the Penny Bank. The prospect of thousands of scattered _pavillons_ also raised important questions for French local public authorities, who were obliged to provide basic utilities and worried that costly urban services spread over large areas would be unmanageable.

These _pavillonaires_ became in a sense, the most dynamic and rapidly expanding market in France as the newly developed suburban zones around the older large cities created concomitant need for a wide variety of goods and services.(2) Distance and thin densities in the suburbs generated a demand for individual means of transportation in place of the big city rail systems. The geography of the expansion, similarly created a need for every type of public service from enlarged road networks to expanded energy utilities. Automobile manufacturing and the electric industry (which in France was tied closely to the older coal industry) at the turn of the century grew and prospered as the suburbs expanded. These turn of the century growth industries were among the first to accept new Taylorite methods of production, non-classical forms of finance, and town planning.

Bringing a greater level of order to the new areas of home construction in the suburbs of major cities led to a significant change in the way the French State regulated private property. The term Municipal Taylorism referred to the attempt to place such troublesome ideological issues in the hands of technocrats who could stand as public servants above the competing private interests and create urban order from chaos. Maxime Leroy, a political economist, coined the phrase in 1927, borrowing from Fredrick Taylor. In his classic study of the ideology of *urbanisme*, Jacques Dreyfus correctly has pointed out that far from being neutral, or above private interests, town planning from the beginning consciously reflected the image of the politically and culturally dominant forces of the Third Republic.(3) Municipal Taylorism, or early *urbanisme*, stood at the center of the conflict between *communal* needs to regulate urban growth and private desires to guarantee the rights of property under the Liberal traditions of the Third Republic. Difficult and even irreconcilable ideological conflicts between property rights, civil liberties and communal well-being at the end of the century passed into the hands of expert urban technicians, the *urbanistes*. These were generally well intentioned men, well educated and from good families: Architects, civil engineers, and public health physicians.(4)

Their ideas about *urbanisme* had deep roots in the determinist and Positivist social philosophies of the mid-nineteenth century. Blending Comtean faith in immutable, inexorable laws of social behavior with pseudo-Darwinian assumptions about the progressive natural evolution of society to higher forms of organization, the new social philosophy of the late nineteenth century exuded an optimism and a confidence in the future that cut across the ideological spectrum from the Socialist reformers to the industrialists of the great monopolies and cartels.(5)

August Comte (1798-1857), the intellectual heir of Claude Henri de Saint Simon and Isaac Newton, gave social philosophy natural and regular assumptions like those ascribed to the Universe in the famous Newtonian law of gravity. Like the natural view of the Universe, man made laws, and even divine right injunctions could not alter the behavior of the cosmos. It followed in Comte's explanation that after the natural laws of human social behavior have been revealed the only remaining task is to modify the laws of parliament in keeping with the conclusions of the social scientists. For Comte, social scientists played an active role in history and Liberal institutions like parliament held only residual roles in governing society. To the extent that _urbanisme_ stood upon these Comtean assumptions, it rejected the humanist traditions of Liberal thought which saw the creation of law and of legal social behavior as the result of a Rousseauean social contract among consenting members of society. To Rousseau, the right to private property stood as inviolate as the Republic that made the social contract that recognized it, while in contrast private property only could be valid in Comte's framework if it were demonstrated to be a natural, immutable form of human behavior. Many _urbanistes_ by the turn of the twentieth century had come to doubt the scientific validity of individual private property rights as defined by social class and geographic space. Social scientists and political economists from Frédéric Le Play, to Ebenezer Howard, to Frederick Taylor gave specific applications to these Comtean assumptions about the nature and regularity of human behavior.(6) Later, Le Corbusier, the architect, synthesized the work of the earliest _urbanistes_ within his new functionalist approach which came to dominate French urban designs for most of the twentieth century.(7)

The first _urbanistes_ who subscribed to this broad determinist and Positivist social philosophy saw themselves as the coordinators of all the diverse elements that make up social behavior itself from the engineering problem of laying out new roadways to revitalizing a market district to remaking and replenishing human capital through the creation of healthy comfortable dwellings for the laboring classes.(8) In this broad sense, town design, _urbanisme_, came to mean the charting or calculating of all the likely patterns of interaction between all members of a society and their daily activities and then allocating all those patterns in physical space. Fundamentally, the idea of _urbanisme_ stood upon the assumption that a planner as a social scientist could discover regular norms and patterns of human behavior that accompany the activities of work, leisure, food gathering and so forth, then use that standardized information to alter the physical environment in order consciously to make some of those patterns of behavior more efficient and more pleasant. Just as Taylor dissected the movements of workers shovelling coal into a blast furnace into a dozen micro-motions in the productive process, the urban engineer delineated the different types of trips between residences, work sites, shopping and civic activities for members of the community and then allocated the local roads accordingly.

To a very great extent, the definitions of standard of normal social behavior in urbanisme reflected the cultural practices of late nineteenth century middle class. While these behaviors and values received sharp criticism from socialists who were frozen out of the benefits of middle class prosperity in the nineteenth century, there is little substantial evidence that these cultural norms did not represent in many ways the actual aspirations of broad segments of French society.(9) Secure, well paid, regular employment, with both personal satisfaction and material reward stood at the base of the middle class vision of proper society. A financially secure foyer with a devoted housewife and an couple of obedient children completed the domestic circle as a caricature with more than a touch of reality about it. For society at large, good education, adequate modern utilities, roads in proper repair, access to theatre and church, and above all security and order in society finished the picture. These social concepts can be found in bold relief in the Garden City design of Englishman Ebenezer Howard, which swept the world at the turn of the century. In France, the early efforts to create low cost housing for workers provided a ready vehicle for the encorporation of the Garden City formula in French urbanisme. Garden City was important for the clarity of its vision of middle class aspirations and for the simplicity of its implementation.

Comtean, social scientific assumptions, also strongly influenced Keynes and his general theory of 1936. Instead of analyzing the individual in the marketplace, as in Classical theory, Keynes postulated the propensities of groups to follow predetermined behavior patterns. It was collective behavior in the marketplace that counted, and not the householding choices of the individual. Yet Keynes still made the proper nineteenth century middle class assumption that a certain portion of income was saved and those savings can be counted upon for investment in new ventures. The thought that income earners might dis-save in aggregate, ineffect contract personal debts that greatly exceeded assets was not considered to be a likely behavior nor the source of economic problems. The similar social philosophical foundations of Keynesian theory and French _urbanisme_ permitted the close integration of these ideas in policy making after the Second World War.

To the extent that the new social scientific assumptions contradicted those underpinning older liberal political institutions, it followed that the acceptance of _urbanisme_ and Keynesian theory required considerable changes in the institutions of government in France. The rivalry between the _Commissariat Général du Plan_ after 1946 and the parliaments of the Fourth and Fifth Republics reflected the shift of decision making power towards the central, appointed and civil service, bureaucracy and away from elected representatives of France.(10) Under the Third Republic, the balance between private individual property rights and collective controls on property had thrown the Chamber of Deputies into unresolvable and interminable conflicts that effectively stalemated the State's ability to govern, especially during the 1930s. In the immediate years after the Second World War, this primary conflict over social philosophies did not become a salient point for political disagreement because the success of the growth miracle effectively discredited and dwarfed the older _laissez-faire_ arguments. However, with the unraveling of the miracle in the 1960s, the old clash of social philosophies reemerged with new vigor and the relationship between representative institutions and the planning bureaucracy became the focus of political conflict.

French Housing Reform and the Garden City Idea

Before the First World War, much housing demand went unmet in France, despite the change in construction materials and methods. Investors at the powerful finance houses, the _Crédit Foncier_ and the _Caisse des Dépôts et Consignations_ found the risks unacceptably high and the profits far lower than competing opportunities to invest in industry and colonial commerce. While largely remaining faithful to the balanced budget doctrines of economist Léon Walras and the Classical School, however, the Third Republic fostered a modestly funded public housing program in an effort to entice private capital into building housing for the working class.(11) By most measures, the public housing programs of the Third Republic failed to produce much additional housing for France, yet the early legislation was not without consequence. As State initiated, quasi-public works projects, public housing programs kept alive under the Third Republic the tradition of flexible capital mortgaging principles of the Saint-Simonians of the Second Empire. While the collapse of the urban renewal projects of Baron von Haussman in the 1860s gave State deficit spending and long term debt schemes a well deserved bad reputation at the great finance houses, the idea of spreading the costs of large scale construction projects over a period of years in the future, appealed to urban reformers.(12) The counter-policy, which actually dominated fiscal decision making under the Third Republic, required the State as in any prudent business to save from tax revenues over a period of years and then spend to initiate a large public works project such s building a block of working class housing, or to limit the scale of projects to only modest proposals that could be serviced out of current tax revenues. As a consequence State initiatives in housing and in public works remained modest under the Third Republic.

The new Third Republic's first National Assembly in 1871 failed to agree on most major issues though it reached a working consensus on the need to ameliorate working class living conditions in order to diffuse Socialist criticism.(13) In the law of August 23, the Chamber created the initial framework for public housing in France under the program for cheap housing, _les Habitations à Bon Marché_ (HBM).(14) In many ways, the Chamber modeled HBM on the limited liability corporations, the _sociétés anonymes_ of the Second Empire and the Empire's experimental housing projects for workers in Paris.(15) The first provision of the law allowed private developers to form limited liability companies for the purpose of building working class housing, and the second provision authorized the State to set aside funds to initiate small scale housing projects and to guarantee the mortgages. Individual workers, private developers, even towns or local parishes made the down payment to start up the construction. Then the State secured the remainder of the mortgage against a special pool of funds set aside to induce the Caisse des Dépôts et Consignations and Crédit Foncier to make these loans that they normally found too risky.(16) Loan guarantees by the State shielded the finance houses from the risks of loaning capital to small individual borrowers who might suffer from unemployment and unstable incomes or to a larger developer who faced the same uncertainties in collecting rents from the working class.

The public housing program used the organizational model of a mixed economy development corporation, structured like those that would become popular after the Second World War and would be the backbone of the French growth miracle of the 1950s. Mixed economy corporations usually retained the fundamental premise of private ownership of the means of production and in the actual organization of work, while accepting a high degree of public regulation of a wide range of business activities from the financing of expansion, to the quality, quantity and type of goods produced, to the terms of labor contracts, to the share of the industry in the domestic market.(17) In many ways, the mixed corporation represented a hybrid of the old private firm of de Wendel for example and its anti-thesis the nationalized firm like Air France.

While HBM built very little housing, slightly more than 100,000 units between 1871 and 1936, the supplemental HBM legislation played a key role in defining the role of State in the process of creating residential space, and this sphere of State action became critically important in shaping the urban environment in the twentieth century. Rightists in the Chamber tauted the HBM program as the means to bring the virtues and social controls of respect for private property to the working class as each family became a petty property holder. Social stability, and even the potential improvement of the low birth rate, figured prominently in the debates over HBM as the program became more carefully delineated in the 1880s and 1890s, and as the thorny problems over the transfer of HBM properties between generations became the focus of debate. Provisions were added to HBM in 1889 which specified that when the male head of the household died before the mortgage was redeemed the property would pass to his heirs and not revert to the State, though it remained unclear how the bereft family would continue to make the mortgage payments on the property. Similar inconsistencies crept into the program as provisions were added to give preference to families with many children, while at the same time HBM houses remained limited to two or three bedrooms with strict guidelines to limit crowding.(18)

Under HBM, a small amount of inexpensive housing went up in the Paris region, mostly concentrated in the eastern part of the city. In the mining districts of the northeastern departments, however, HBM provided an attractive tool for the creation of company towns out in the bleak coal fields. Coal mining by its nature as an industry required the mining companies to concentrate their industrial work force in essentially a rural area, away from readily available housing, shopping and social activities. In the late nineteenth century the rapidly expanding coal industry turned to the State HBM program to assist in the construction of their company towns. The weak and rudimentary housing program led to the building of the type of company town that provided the site for Emile Zola's grim novel *Gérminal*.

In the 1890s, the financing of HBM at the national level became even more closely tied to the national industrialization and development policies often in direct collaboration with major cartels. The Siegfried Law of 1894 regularized the relationship of the State and business by requiring every department to establish *Comités des Habitations à Bon Marché* composed of employers and housing reformers to encourage the development of housing for workers living primarily on their own labor. The law went further, permitting employers to draw from a special reserved pool of capital at the *Caisse des Dépôts et Consignations* to initiate housing projects.(19) Departmental HBM committees under the Siegfried law, stayed firmly under the control of the Ministry of Commerce and Industry which appointed a full one-third of the departmental committees, and reviewed the appointment of the remaining members, who by law were to be drawn from the town councils, mayors, chambers of commerce and manufacturing associations. And as a final precaution against any overly ambitious departmental committee, the *Caisse* retained strong veto rights over any departmental initiatives.(20)

The only serious opposition to the early HBM program came from the Marxists under Jules Guesde, who founded his *Parti Ouvrier* in 1876. Guesde warned against the dangers of class collaboration and denounced the exploitation of workers in company towns but his appeals were generally ignored by the ill housed workers of France who desperately wanted better conditions for themselves and their families. In 1882, Paul Brousse broke with Guesde and formed the Possibilist Party around a strong commitment to municipal reform. Standing upon the Joffrin Municipal Programme of 1881, Brousse and the Possibilists called for municipal or public housing for poor workers, arguing that this type of housing, like public utilities, water and sewer, street light and so forth, was leading society on a predestined path to a more harmonious, communal, socialist state by regulating the individual's use of private property. Brousse's vision of socialism did not promise the destruction of the bourgeois State in a bloody revolution, but rather the slow, gradual reform and eventual control over the State and the economy by the popular classes.(21) In the debate with the Guesdists, Brousse stood firmly in the tradition of Proudhon within French socialism and from the 1880s a close association developed within the Possibilist movement (and its non-Marxist successors) between urban reform, and syndicalism. While there certainly was a period in the 1870s when some syndicalists sought the violent destruction of the Third Republic by the end of the century Socialists in the reformist tradition had become faithful defenders of many liberal concepts of civil rights and popular sovereignty.

In the local elections of 1878 and resoundingly in those of 1881, the Reformist Socialists and Radicals scored impressive victories, coming to control 20,000 out of the 36,000 communes in France and securing majorities on 66 of the 87 departmental councils. Radical and Socialist control over local government sparked a mood of experimentalism and high expectations among urban reformers in the areas of housing, public health and education in the following two decades. Under the swelling tide of Radical Republicanism, Jules Ferry reorganized municipal government in 1884, making it an integral part of national administration and politics for the remainder of the Third Republic. From the mid-1880s, deputies in the Chamber commonly held concurrent positions in local government, often as deputy mayor or justice of the peace in the most important town of their assembly district. These interlocking political positions raised municipal concerns to the national level, which on some occasions resulted in the careful attention to the problems of renovation of the national roadway system, but on other occasions focused national political passions on petty, parochial disputes. Ferry's Reform Law of 1884 also authorized the direct popular election of town mayors throughout the provinces, though the mayor of Paris continued to be appointed by the central government as did each departmental prefect.

On the whole, these local reforms attracted a large body of moderate grass roots support for the institutions of the Third Republic and for the Radicals and Reformist Socialists. By demonstrating competence in local decision making and in local administration, these partisans of the Third Republic tried to establish their very modern ideas that governmental legitimacy should be derived from functionalism and from public service. According to their proponents, these benignly technocratic notions stood outside of the historic ideological clash between the class of the property holders and those without property.

Boulanger's challenge to the Third Republic in the spring of 1888, the elitism of Pope Leon XIII in the Rerum Novarum of 1891 as well as the recession of 1893 pushed the supporters of the Third Republic even closer to their municipal roots. Part of the strength of the early Republic can be attributed to the pervasive and curiously depoliticized municipal reform movement of the late nineteenth century.

Reformist Socialists in the urban movement rejected the Marxist vision of devastating unresolvable class conflict infavor of evolutionary social change. Equally, Radical Party members in the reform movements gave up some part of the prior and exclusive claims to individual property ownership in agreeing to such useful and beneficial public services such as compulsory sewer connections for every dwelling. These fundamental compromises on the part of the Socialists and the Radicals formed a critical foundation stone of the Third Republic and these position were consistent with the long run development of French political institutions in the twentieth century.

At the turn of the century, the English Garden City Idea provided the means to integrate the faltering French housing program within a broader social philosophy of functionalism and public service that attracted the Socialists and Radicals of the urban reform movements. Garden City brought a new vitality and scope to municipal government. Ebenezer Howard developed his Garden City concept in England during the 1890s and published his comprehensive summary of the plan in 1898 under the title To-Morrow: A Pathway to Real Reform.(22) With the patronage of the wealthy British philanthropist and chocolate baron Cadbury, Howard supervised the creation of one model town at Bourneville using his principles of design and social organization. Urban reformers across the world heaped enthusiastic praise upon Howard and his town as a prime example the potentials of urban renovation and control. Howard, however, was interested in more than pilot projects. He insisted that the ideas of Garden City and socialism were inseparable and that his principles of urban design represented a step in the rational and progressive movement of society to a future with greater material prosperity and social harmony.(23) Howard drew his own definition of socialism from the work of Russian anarchist Peter Kropotkin, the heir of the anti-Marxist tradition of Bakunin, and from American tax reformer Henry George. Howard stressed the intrinsic value of social harmony and slow progressive economic change. He assumed that the greatest amount of social harmony grew from the opportunity for all in society to have successful and secure employment, a comfortable home and easy access to education, religious institutions and recreation. At the same time, Garden City maintained substantial social segregation by income and social class, though Howard wanted these distinctions to be less than in his own society and to be reduced over time. He believed that his type of socialism would come about without a radical change in the civil guarantees associated with Liberal government. Rational town planning, Howard saw as simple steps in the evolution of a form of socialism that was to prevail over capitalism through the justness of its cause, rather than through violent revolution.(24)

While seeking to extend social harmony and to promote greater egalitarian prosperity, Garden City's charter did so at the expense of such cornerstones of nineteenth liberalism as democratic suffrage, representative government, and the legitimacy of private property. The social and economic organization of Garden City was thoroughly and explicitly corporatist in design.(25) According to Howard, four men of "responsible position and of undoubted probity and honour" governed Garden City "in trust for the people."(26) These four gentlemen were obliged to follow the community's constitution, "modeled upon that of a large well-appointed business."(27) Commerce and industry also came under the control of the four gentlemen who granted monopolies to "fair and honest" tradesmen and employers that charged just prices and maintained satisfactory relationships with their workers. If a particular shopkeeper exploited his monopoly to the disadvantage of the community, the four gentlemen would invite a competitor into the town to ruin the unscrupulous businessman, which according to Howard "will have the effect of converting competition from an active into a latent force."(28) No one in Garden City voted, or even discussed the administration of the town, and, of course, no one could choose to open a new book store, for example, if one already existed.

Within Garden City the spatial arrangement of employment set clear and distinct boundaries of movement for each social class, and maintained a high level of class segregation in the daily routine of the community. Howard located the noxious industries, like metal working and food processing, along the outer ring within walking distance of a large area of small homes and gardens. A middle ring of small commercial establishments and the promenade, Grand Avenue, separated the working class zone from the much smaller group of large homes near the center of Garden City. Middle class employment at the library, the museum, the shops, the college and in the administrative complex formed the heart of the town. For planners the message of Howard's model was clear: Social class distinctions must be incorporated into the successful design of residential and occupational space within a town plan. The daily movements between home and work rarely permitted social contact between the working class and the middle class in Garden City.

When examining an unplanned town, such social segregation can be attributed to the anonymous distributing power of the marketplace. In a planned community, however, these spatial assignments must be seen as reflections of the values and judgments of the planners who designed that specific urban space. Howard's sketch of 1898 was the first significant statement of the conscious use of town planning to replicate the urban social divisions in nineteenth century bourgeois society. In the rural zone of Garden

City contained those groups rejected by the norms of the urban center and the cultural system that it represented. Hence, Howard exiled the insane, those with dreaded public diseases, like tuberculosis, and those who do not inherit property, the orphans, to dwell among the cows in the countryside. Curiously enough, the new industrial schools have also been placed in Howard's sketch in the rural zone far from the sites of actual industrial employment and far from the homes of the working class.

French Garden Cities, known also as the *villes nouvelles* received legislative approval under the Strauss Law of April 12, 1906 and became encorporated within the HBM program in the reform laws of 1908 and 1912 which permitted the grouping of HBM units within a Garden City design. The early Garden City advocate, Georges Benoît-Lévy, however, failed to obtain new funds for the construction of additional HBM-Garden City units.(29) Since virtually all previously authorized HBM units had been allocated to replace isolated units in disrepair, and for unplanned *lotissements* in the Paris suburbs, the Strauss Law remained without immediate effect. Yet Strauss Law represented a breakthrough for the urban reform movement, since it recognized the need to develop urban infrastructure along with the simple building of new houses. Later under the Bonneway Law of December 23, 1912, departmental HBM committees received permission to directly contract for the creation of Garden Cities by private developers and funds were set aside for that purpose at the *Caisse des Dépôts et Consignations*. In general, the developers of low cost, brick *pavillons* in the suburbs of Paris stood to benefit enormously from the new commitment to Garden City expansion plans since it brought the prospect of extending roads, public services and utilities and cultural institutions to the vast disorganized suburbs of Paris and other major cities. But not all suburban developers greeted the Garden City-HBM reforms with enthusiasm, since the housing reform legislation by 1912 contained a large number of restrictions. Stiff requirements for quality in construction materials and restrictions on the size and the number of units per hectare, both limited the ability of developers to squeeze profits out of what remained a high risk venture. Since most of these requirements could be enforced only when the State provided some or all of the financing for the housing project, developers often refused to cooperate with the public housing programs.

Slowly, Paris and the other major urban centers developed suburban rings, les ceintures noires, composed of bidonvilles, shanty-towns for the virtually homeless; low quality pavillons for the working class and slightly better quality homes for the lower middle class, but all without adequate infrastructure, even in the most basic areas of public health, education, utilities and transportation.(30) Then the outbreak of war in 1914 brought virtually all housing construction, private and public, to a halt for the next five years.

HBM may have built very little housing in France but the financial reforms of the public housing system on the eve of the First World War provided a blueprint for the financing of the war itself. Alexandre Ribot sponsored the HBM Reform Law of February 26, 1912. This generated the extra funds for new Garden City-HBM projects by establishing a new mortgaging principle that freed HBM funding from the Classical and tight fiscal controls of the early governments of the Third Republic. Before 1912, the revenues allocated to HBM came from each budget and required a balancing of accounts between projects authorized and projects completed during each fiscal year. In contrast, the Ribot Law of 1912 permitted the State to issue longer term bonds and to use current and future tax revenues to redeem these debts. This approach to budgeting was an attempt to return to the flexible policies of the Saint-Simonians under the Second Empire, a point not lost on contemporary critics of the plan. Even under this scheme, HBM funding remained low with less than 20,000,000 francs being raised (and even less spent) before the outbreak of war. The Crédit Foncier and the Caisse des Dépôts et Consignations remained highly skeptical of the financial logic which had brought Paris to utter financial ruin in the previous generation.(31) The First World War, however, changed minds.

Ribot became the first Premier under the presidency of Raymond Poincaré in the 1914 national unity government, la union sacrée, with the Reformist Socialist Alexandre Millerand as Minister of War. After the initial shock of the successful German invasion in the fall of 1914, France settled into a long protracted struggle, and Ribot was forced to confront the economic hemorrhage that the war was creating in the State budget. Ribot dealt with the problem by issuing war bonds, redeemable after the conclusion of hostilities in order to meet the immediate need for revenues to conduct the war. The measure received strong approval from the broad based war-time coalition. Collaboration between the Socialists and the more conservative parties of the Republic reached its peak during the fifth cabinet of Aristide Briand who held office from October 29, 1915 to December 12, 1916 when the left was represented by Marxist Jules Guesde, and the moderate Socialists by Marcel Sembat and Albert Thomas. In Briand's last cabinet, governing from December 12, 1916 to March 20, 1917, only Thomas remained in his post as Armaments Minister. He left in September of 1917.

As Minister of Armaments and therefore deeply concerned about the economic management of the war, Thomas lobbied hard for the principle of paying for the war with long term financing than one crushing burden of new taxes during wartime which was the policy demanded by the devotees of the Classical system. Thomas also found great merit in the strong economic guidance where planned production schedules and careful allocations would optimize the meager stockpiles and in good Taylorite fashion minimize waste. Instead of direct nationalization of industry, a cumbersome and complex task, Thomas saw greater efficiency in the indirect manipulation of industrial production through the traditional methods by which governments influenced the marketplace as the purchaser of goods. Thomas also advocated a careful policy of planned State and private investment which would attempt to minimize duplication and other wasteful uses of capital. He certainly did not abandon the idea of nationalization as corrective to the arrogant and abusive wielding of private capitalist power, rather, he merely argued that direct national control of production carried the serious potential for high levels of inefficiency. For Thomas, national economic planning held the key to national survival in the war years, and he raised the argument after the war that it was the basis for peacetime prosperity.(32)

As Minister for Reconstruction after the war, Louis Loucheur applied the Ribot formula to precisely the task suggested by Thomas: Domestic economic development. Before the war, Loucheur worked for the Thompson industrial empire which held extensive investments in the coals, rails and fast growth electric industries, where the HBM funded company towns had been welcomed. The majority of these holdings slipped into German hands as the northeastern departments were occupied during the early phase of the war. In 1915, Loucheur joined the war effort and participated in the implementation of the new war bond based production plan. Given the Ministry of Reconstruction at the close of hostilities, Loucheur returned to the industrial northeast to find enormous losses in manpower and in productive capacity. Almost one quarter of the active male work force had been killed, wounded or displaced, and over half a million homes and factories had been destroyed in the industrial heartland of France. To repair these horrendous damages, Loucheur asked for the Reconstruction Law of October 27, 1919 which continued the long term bonding practices of the war, which frankly confronted the inability of the French economy to meet the costs of recovery out of current tax revenues under a balanced budget.(33) At the same time, Loucheur proposed a Russian redevelopment corporation that would also issue extraordinary long term bonds and enable the French to profit from the rebuilding of the Soviet Union. While this proposal was genuinely unpopular with virtually all segments of the French political community, it foreshadowed the operations of the Banks of China and Indo-China in the late 1920s and early 1930s.(26) The Bank of China provided the worldly financial training for Jean Monnet, who would create the Commissariat Général du Plan in 1946 and use it to reconstruct France after the next war.(34) The Bank of Indo-China also played a role in the financial training of inter-war industrialist and admirer of Nazi economic theories, Pierre Taittinger, who would rule Paris under the Occupation.(35) Edmond Giscard d'Estaing, father of the future president of the Fifth Republic, also was associated with the innovative strategies of the Bank of Indo-China before the Second World War.(36) The Ribot-Thomas-Loucheur principles of flexible financing during the war and their application to the peacetime economy as well, anticipated some of the logic of Keynes' general theory.

What ideological force held together neo-rightist civic and business figures like Loucheur and Giscard, Reformist Socialists like Thomas and fascist fellow travellers like Taittinger?(37) All rejected the laissez-faire assumptions about the inherent viability and optimization capacity of the unregulated marketplace, and saw the activist State as the appropriate vehicle for intervention in the economy.(38) In the middle of the nineteenth century, Proudhon had also argued for the model of strong central regulation of the marketplace within a society composed exclusively of small property holders, with the whole society found under consentual contracts among the members.(39) In the inter-war years, neo-corporatists demonstrated that Proudhon's two propositions were actually independent assumptions and that regulation of the marketplace need not be accompanied by any leveling of the existing distribution of wealth and power. On the contrary, the experience with corporatism in Italy, for example, seemed to reenforce the patterns of wealth holding from the nineteenth century.

The corporatist basis of Howard's Garden City and the attractiveness of the flexible, non-Classical financing schemes after the First World War produced a flurry of new public housing construction in France. Between 1919 and 1939, almost 85,000 units went up in the Paris region alone under the auspices of the public housing programs. HBM under the new financing built 64,000 units, with the remainder being built under other public formulas. Of the HBM dwellings, 26 percent of them were allocated by the HBM-*Office Départemental de la Seine*, under Henri Sellier to the development of six Garden Cities. Half the units available were built in the showcase model town at Suresnes where Sellier served as mayor.(40)

Yet, urban reformers like Sellier and even the trend setting architect Le Corbusier frequently found their efforts at urban renovation blocked by the fiscally conservative majorities in the Chamber who clung to the concept of a properly balanced budget. The severe economic crises of the inter-war years seemed to reinforce the wisdom of the injunctions of the Classical economists to manage the State's budget like any prudent household budget, or beware of the frightful consequences for the economy as a whole. The short lived cabinets of the 1920s struggled to achieve stability in the franc and to pay off the gigantic national debt which carried a debt service charge that reminded some of the last years of the Old Regime. Between 1923 and 1926, France took a severe battering on the currency markets which in turn threw both export and domestic industries into a slump that only abated with the Poincaré stabilization of the franc in late 1926 and was finally resolved with the devaluation of 1928. The traditional right and even the moderate left attributed most of these grave national difficulties to the failure of successive governments to balance the State budget and to redeem outstanding State debts that sparked high interest rates and reduced the ability of private business to borrow for new plants and equipment. All this, of course, was complicated by the continued impoverishment of Germany who was unable to resume normal trade relation with France.

The home construction market closely reflected the failure to achieve monetary stability. Housing starts returned to near pre-war levels by 1924, only to fade very badly in the following twenty-four months. The _Cartel des Gauches_ won the elections of 1924, but Eduoard Herriot's new government stood on a shaky coalition of reformist Socialists and Radicals. The Socialists remained as wedded to the old economic logic of balanced State budgets as any of the conservative parties and demanded an extraordinary capital levy to balance the budget and to redeem the reconstruction debts. These measures failed to win approval in the Chamber and economic policy drifted in an even more conservative direction in the next governments. As Finance Minister from November 28 to December 15, 1924 under the Briand cabinet, Louis Loucheur immediately called in all possible taxes to which the government could lay claim and used the revenues in a desperate attempt to balance the budget and to pay off immediate debts. While Loucheur had proposed some of the most innovative financial measures under consideration during the 1920s, including deficit spending for major but isolated projects such as the reconstruction of the northeast, he too supported the fundamental principle of a balanced State budget. But his tax program in the winter of 1924 failed to improve the situation of the Treasury as debts continued to outdistance revenues. The measure merely reduced the capital available for new construction projects without appreciably improving the financial health of the State.

In July 1926, Loucheur's successor at Finance, Raymond Poincaré brought stability to the franc with a policy that devasted the domestic housing market. Still keeping faith with the principle of balancing the State budget, Poincaré attacked the problem from another direction, aiming his policies against high interest rates and bond overextension in a far more direct and draconian manner. Poincaré abandoned the idea of maintaining the pre-war parity of the franc and consequently allowed it to fall below its real value. Poincaré's policy created an almost embarrassingly large gold flow towards the stabilized franc: Capital fleeing the weaker mark and pound. By the end of the decade, almost one-third of the world's gold reserves had been transferred to the Bank of France. The influx of new capital helped cushion the domestic impact of devaluation to some extent, and even limited the impact of the major crisis of the 1930s. Yet for the holders of State securities, pensions, savings and other notes backed by bonds and the overvalued currency, the effects of devaluation were devastating. The holders of such debts saw their accumulated assets reduced by nearly eighty percent along with the corresponding reduction in the State debt. Poincaré balanced the budget in 1928 at the cost of a ruinous deflation for many small capitalists. It was effectively the last time in this century that the budget was balanced.

The recession in the home construction industry in the wake of the Loucheur and Poincaré policies bottomed out in late 1928, when home construction fell almost seventy percent below the level of 1923. The growing capital reserves returned some strength to the construction market in late 1928 and the National Assembly passed the Loucheur Law for inexpensive middle class and publicly financed housing. It authorized new Garden City projects as well as setting aside funds for the expropriation and renovation of the Beaubourg slum in central Paris (a project contemplated by municipal reformers since the cholera epidemic of 1832). But the collapse of the American economy in 1929 drastically cut short the period of business recovery. Americans stopped buying European goods and began to call their capital home. As the economic crisis deepened in 1933 and 1934, French governments from that of conservative Eduoard Daladier to reformist radical Eduoard Herriot remained unwilling to give up the idea of a balanced budget though that goal effectively eluded all regimes. At the same time, support grew across the political spectrum for some measure of national economic governance though that only came to France after the Second World War.

Despite the uncertainties of the home construction market, housing reform remained the focus for urban reformers in the inter-war years. As the socialist mayor of Suresnes, a western suburb of the capital, Henri Sellier spearheaded the reform movement in Paris and actively shaped the town management policies of the whole country. Sellier began his career as a syndicalist, editing La Revue Syndicaliste with Albert Thomas before the First World War. The catastrophe of the war and the Bolshevik coup in 1917 radicalized Sellier.(41) After the Congress of Tours in 1921, when the socialist movement split into two competing factions: la Section Française de l'Internationale Ouvrière (SFIO) and the new Parti Communist Française (PCF), Sellier joined the fledgling Communist Party. He was promptly expelled for his right wing deviations. In the years immediately following the war, Sellier wrote exhaustively on the crisis of housing in the capital which he saw as a consequence of the rapidly growing city population, the out dated and crumbling nature of the housing stock and the deeply diseased nature of the historic core of the city.(42)

In the Saint Merri quarter of the Old City, the Beaubourg slum represented the worst example, to Sellier, of the degenerate and destructive nature of the old capitalist system within urban life. He saw Beaubourg as a symbol of the deeply flawed nature of the societies that had launched the destruction of the Great War. In Beaubourg, tuberculosis claimed an extraordinary number of victims in the area shown on Map One.(43) City health rolls listed two hundred and fifty out of the two hundred and seventy-six buildings as uninhabitable due to tuberculosis contamination. The death rate in Beaubourg ran as high as forth-two per thousand when the comparable city-wide rate had declined to a mere ten per thousand.(44) In one of his most extensive examinations of the housing problems of the capital, La Crise du logement et l'intervention publique (1921), Sellier cited the description of fellow urban reformer George Cachan who saw "all around the Church of Saint Merri, almost on its doorsteps the most hideous hovels: Long alleyways with decrepit facades and lines of garbage, some doorways have been covered with grating that looks like chicken wire, the stench and filth are pervasive . . . . On the rue Quincapoix, one unfortunate hotel has seen more occupants die [of tuberculosis] than were registered on the list of residents over the past ten years."(45) The population density on the worst two block yeilded a

Map Two
Beaubourg Slum

ASSAINISSEMENT D'ILOTS INSALUBRES

riverains des rues St Martin, des Etuves St Martin, Beaubourg, de Venise, Simon le Franc

Echelle de 2 millimètres par mètre

Tableau indicatif des propriétés à exproprier

Nos du plan	Situation des propriétés	Noms, prénoms et demeures des propriétaires: Tels qu'ils sont inscrits à la matrice des rôles	Tels qu'ils résultent des renseignements pris sur le terrain	Tels qu'ils résultent des renseignements fournis par l'enquête	Surfaces à exproprier (mètres carrés)	Observations
206	Rue des Etuves St Martin, 19; Rue Saint Martin, 138	Postel, Auguste, Félix	Fourcade, 33 allée Lamartine, à Pau (Basses Pyrénées)	Postel, Amélie, Marie, épouse de M. Fourcade, allée Lamartine, 33, Pau (Basses Pyrénées)	301,00	
207	Rue des Etuves St Martin, 17	Chambon, Anne, née Tissier, d'Orléans, rue Croix de la Pucelle n° 4	Vve Chambon, à Anney, par Tonnay (Nièvre)	Tissier, Marie, Jeanne, Amélie, Pauline, Vve Chambon [illegible]	50,80	
208	Rue des Etuves St Martin, 15	Gasset, Anatole	Gasset, 15 rue Michel Ange	Epoux Gasset, 15 rue Michel Ange, élisant domicile chez M. Latour, 116 rue de Rivoli	72,40	
209	Rue des Etuves St Martin, 13; Rue de Venise, 16	[illegible]	Bachelas, 3 rue Turbigo	[illegible]	242,50	
210	Rue des Etuves St Martin, 11	Savart, Pierre, Louis	Savart, 4 rue de Rosny à Montreuil (Seine)	Savart, Edouard, 4 rue de Rosny à Montreuil (Seine)	90,10	
211	Rue des Etuves St Martin, 9; Rue de Venise, 10	Coulaud, Léonard	Coulaud, 16 rue Nicollet, Chaumes en Brie (Seine et Marne)	1° Coulaud, Léonard, 16 rue Nicollet à Chaumes en Brie (Seine et Marne); 2° Coulaud Léonard Eugène, 3 rue Beaubourg, Paris; 3° Coulaud, Henri, [illegible] élisant domicile chez M.M. Jouguet et Bourgeois, 62 boulvd de Sébastopol	86,40	
212	Rue des Etuves St Martin, 7; Rue de Venise, 8	Gouhier, Henri	Gouhier, impasse Montferrat 11	Gouhier, [illegible] élisant domicile chez M.M. Jouguet et Bourgeois, 62 boulvd de Sébastopol, Paris	62,80	
213	Rue des Etuves St Martin, 5; Rue de Venise, 6	Mallet, Jean Louis, époux Boissonade	Mallet, 134 avenue du Maine	La Ville de Paris	63,40	acquis par contrat du 22 novembre 1928
214	Rue des Etuves St Martin, 3	Bero, Pierre	Consorts Bero, propriétaires; Mme Hiel, née Bero, gérante, 13 rue des Gâtines	[illegible]	47,80	
215	Rue des Etuves St Martin, 1; Rue Beaubourg, 11	Rabot, Marie	Mlle Rabot, 37 rue du Renard	Mlle Rabot, Marie, 37 rue du Renard	53,50	
216	Rue Saint Martin, 136; Rue de Venise, 24	La Ville de Paris	La Ville de Paris	La Ville de Paris	125,30	
217	Rue de Venise, 22	Derousteau, Eugène, Adolphe	Vve Derousteau, 131 bd Voltaire	Vve Derousteau, 131 boulvd Voltaire, élisant domicile chez M.M. Jouguet et Bourgeois, 62 boulvd de Sébastopol	62,60	
218	Rue de Venise, 20	Bulleau, Camille, Léon, Alphonse	Bulleau, à Pontgouin (Eure et Loir)	1° Bulleau, Camille, Léon, Alphonse, à Pontgouin (Eure et Loir) [illegible]	77,30	
219	Rue de Venise, 18	Riols, Calixte	Riols, 23 rue Maret	[illegible]	62,60	
220	Rue de Venise, 14	Bourguion, Alexandre, Antoine	[illegible]	[illegible]	26,10	
221	Rue de Venise, 12	Huet, à Neuilly	Huet, propriétaire; Michel, gérant, y demeurant	Huet, propriétaire, [illegible] à Neuilly sur Seine; Michel, y demeurant, gérant	45,60	
222	Rue de Venise, 4	Mallet, Jean Louis, époux Boissonade	Mallet, 134 Avenue du Maine	La Ville de Paris	23,50	acquis par contrat du 22 novembre 1928
223	Rue de Venise, 2; Rue Beaubourg, 9	Flandin, Paul, François	Flandin, 54 rue Bobillot	[illegible]	64,70	
224	Rue de Venise, 19; Rue Saint Martin, 134	Gaudebert, Joseph, Louis	Gaudebert, propriétaire; [illegible], gérant	[illegible]	99,80	
225	Rue Saint Martin, 132	Dufour, Jean, François, Eugène	[illegible]	[illegible]	85,00	
226	Rue Saint Martin, 130	Germilhac, Antoine	Germilhac, 4 rue de la Grande Truanderie	[illegible]	85,00	
227	Rue Saint Martin, 128; Rue de Venise, 13, 15, 17	[illegible]	La Ville de Paris	La Ville de Paris	639,00	
228	Rue Saint Martin, 126	Gabchet, [illegible]	Gabchet, 38 boulvd de Sébastopol	[illegible]	50,70	[illegible]
229	Rue Saint Martin, 124	d'Aubigny de Ferrières, [illegible]	La Ville de Paris	La Ville de Paris	126,30	
230	Rue Saint Martin, 122; Rue Simon le Franc, 52	Duceing, Albert	Duceing, 52 rue [illegible]	[illegible]	40,40	
231	Rue Simon le Franc, 50	d'Aubigny de Ferrières, [illegible]	La Ville de Paris	La Ville de Paris	57,80	
232	Rue Simon le Franc, 48	Félix, Marcel	Félix, propriétaire	[illegible]	83,30	
233	Rue Simon le Franc, 46	Paschaux, Armand, Barthélemy	Paschaux, 7 rue d'Abbeville	Paschaux, 7 rue d'Abbeville, élisant domicile chez M.M. Jouguet et Bourgeois, 62 bd de Sébastopol	79,80	
234	Rue Simon le Franc, 44	Barrial, Blaise, [illegible]	Barrial, Mur de Barrez, Aveyron	[illegible]	77,30	
235	Rue Simon le Franc, 42	Lefèvre, Ernest	Lefèvre, 7 rue Le Regrattier	Epoux Lefèvre Ernest, 7 rue Le Regrattier	65,80	
236	Rue Simon le Franc, 40	Liandier, François	Liandier, à Blesles (Haute Loire)	[illegible]	86,00	
237	Rue Simon le Franc, 38	Saint Paul, Victor	Vve Saint Paul, Victor, à Mur de Barrez (Aveyron)	[illegible]	92,60	
238	Rue de Venise, 11	Sauton, Jules, Adolphe	La Ville de Paris	La Ville de Paris	46,90	
239	Rue de Venise, 9; Rue Simon le Franc, 36	d°	La Ville de Paris	La Ville de Paris	270,60	
240	Rue Simon le Franc, 32, 34	Judrin, Paul, François	Judrin, 3 rue du Départ	Epoux Judrin, Paul, François, 3 rue du Départ	162,00	
241	Rue Simon le Franc, 30	Rigal, Jean	Mme Quillié, ex veuve Rigal, avenue des Tuileries, à Saint Cirq [illegible]	[illegible]	63,20	
242	Rue de Venise, 7; Impasse de la Baudroirie	Judrin, Paul	Judrin, 3 rue du Départ	Judrin, Paul, François, rue du Départ	65,50	
243	Rue de Venise, 3, 5; Impasse de la Baudroirie	J. Dragicevics, Auguste, Jules; E. Violet	La Ville de Paris	La Ville de Paris	209,10	
244	Rue Simon le Franc, 28	Laborde, Philippe, Prosper	Mme Laborde, M. Dillie, notaire gérant	La Ville de Paris	139,40	acquis par contrat du [illegible] juillet 1928
245	Rue Simon le Franc, 26	Loubergue, Louis	Loubergue, y demeurant	Epoux Loubergue, y demeurant	139,40	
246	Rue de Venise, 1; Rue Beaubourg, 7	Dages, Jean, Léon	Mme Dages, 6 rue de la Villette	La Ville de Paris	73,10	acquis par contrat du 2 juillet 1928
247	Rue Beaubourg, 5	Guyot, Louis, Auguste	Guyot, y demeurant	Guyot, Louis, Auguste, 5 rue Beaubourg	67,10	
248	Rue Beaubourg, 3	Vincent, Charles, Eugène	Vve Vincent, 3 rue de Bois Colombes, la Garenne	[illegible] élisant domicile chez M.M. Jouguet et Bourgeois, 62 boulvd de Sébastopol	147,90	
249	Rue Beaubourg, 1; Rue Simon le Franc, 24	d°	d°	d°	119,80	

Rue des Etuves Saint Martin
Rue de Venise
Rue Saint Martin
Rue Quincampoix
Rue Beaubourg
Rue Simon le Franc
Rue du Renard
Rue Geoffroy
Rue Brisemiche

per capita living space equivalent to the size of a telephone booth. Beaubourg had been targeted for clearance for decades, but expropriation and demolition of the houses only came under the auspices of the Popular Front government in 1936 when Sellier served as the Minister for Public Health.(46)

The ancient and deep misery of slums like Beaubourg led Sellier and many fellow urban reformers essentially to abandon the old European cities and to concentrate their energies on the still salvageable suburbs. Here the Garden City Idea proved immensely useful for organizing suburban expansion. The spate of housing legislation that left the Chamber between 1922 and 1928 aimed at regulating and regularizing the contracts for privately financed *pavillons* and for controlling the spatial arrangement of these small single family *lotissements* in the suburbs of Paris. Private developers, in general, refused to respect the new laws that merely reminded them to obey the existing laws governing the quality of construction materials and building codes. Like the pre-war Bonneyway legislation, the new housing laws in the 1920s sought to control private development by extending the fruits of public cooperation to those developers who voluntarily respected required levels of quality for housing. To ease cooperation between the housing program, departmental officials and private developers, the HBM program received a thorough administrative reorganization in November and December of 1924. The Chamber carefully consolidated the several varieties of HBM programs that had emerged during the previous half century and placed a new super administrative board over the entire national public housing effort. Out of the eleven seats on the new national oversight committee, five went to representatives from the Public Offices of HBM (the administrative corps), three to the old limited liability companies *sociétés anonymes de HBM*, two to the newer public *sociétés coopératives de HBM* and one final place was reserved for the representative of the *Conseil d'Etat*. In April of the following year, the reorganized HBM program received formal permission to plan and execute Garden City projects. After decades of work, the first Garden City opened in 1928 in the north western suburb of Suresnes.(47)

Henri Sellier, mayor of Suresnes and political architect of the model town, persuaded the HBM *Conseil Supérieur*, which he chaired, to build the first full scale experimental town in France adjacent to his suburb. The achievement brought him enthusiastic praise from housing reformers across the political spectrum. On the Social Catholic right, Pierre Lhande lauded Sellier's model town as a true "Socialist and materialist marvel," going further to rhapsodize about "the Garden Cities [which] crown the [Social Catholic] movement like a magnificent work by Ozanam, responding not only to the urgent needs for actual shelter but to the exigencies of material and religious assistance. They put in the hands of the traditional benefactors of the poor classes the master weapon by which they can combat the scourge of hovels, civilize and Christianize the working masses."(48) As it turns out, upon assuming the office of mayor of Suresnes in 1925, Sellier had the famous town statute of Emile Zola, which had been cast from two bronze church bells during the Paris Commune, unceremoniously hauled from the town square and deposited in the municipal closet, which secured him the good will if not the complete trust of the Church. From the political center, the _Journal de la Société de Statistique de Paris_ called Sellier the "Haussman of the western suburbs," and a wide spectrum of leftists from Léon Blum to Jacques Doriot to Marcel Déat heralded Sellier as political architect of a new urban era.(49)

While the Social Catholic movement and Reformist Socialists sought to bring the benefits of good quality housing to the working class in the suburbs of Paris, the actual model town at Suresnes quickly developed into a solid middle class community. Construction of the new town began under the auspices of the reformed HBM, but the community was completed and embellished under the Loucheur Law that created _les Habitations à loyer modéré_ (HLM).(50) Appropriately enough, on the day before that great bourgeois holiday, Bastille Day in 1928, the Chamber created the new public housing program that extended to the middle classes and intellectuals the same type of mortgage guarantees that HBM had offered to the working class. After the Second World War, HLM became the major housing program for all publicly assisted housing.

During the late 1920s and early 1930s, the model town at Suresnes quickly became a highly attractive bedroom suburb for Parisian bureaucrats who commuted into the capital via the specially designed autopark. The careful contours of Sellier's model town sharply contrasted with the cramped and wasteful lines of the

Map Two

New Town at Suresnes

CITE-JARDINS DE SURESNES

Architecte M. Maistrasse

Plan d'ensemble

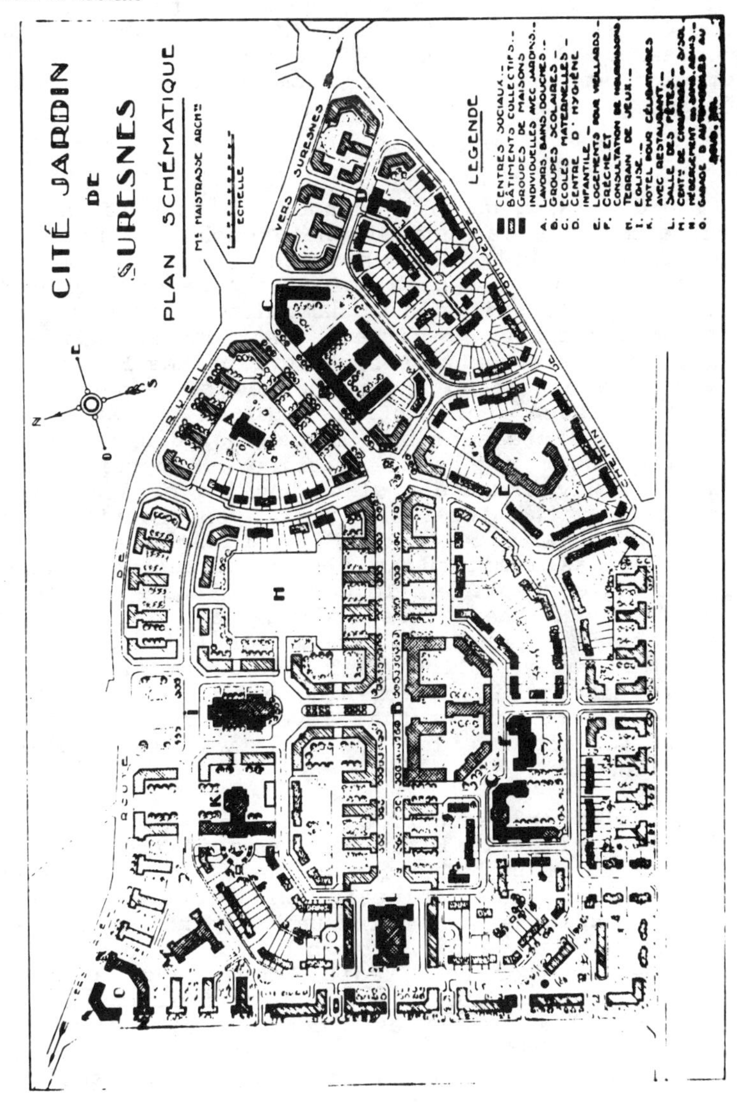

two blocks in the Beaubourg slum in historic Paris. In his little volume on the Garden City Idea, Howard predicted that the proliferation of model towns in the suburbs of London eventually would drive down the value of land in the historic core of the old city to the point where the virtually worthless property also could be redeveloped into pristine, healthy and low-density Garden Cities.(51) In the case of the Beaubourg slum, the clearance zone remained vacant for an entire generation with renewal only coming under the Fifth Republic.

The declining quality of housing stock in the city of Paris and the failure of the French housing market to generate a supply of housing that could accommodate the migrants to the region before the Second World War has been attributed to the dampening effect of rent controls on the housing market by Anthony Sutcliffe and others.(52) Rent controls began during the First World War and were continued under the law of March 1918 in peacetime. These rent controls limited the ability of landlords to increase rents in new buildings and also restricted their rights of eviction. According to F. Marnata's study of middle class housing conditions and rents, during the inter-war years construction costs jumped by 692 percent.(53) Clearly, a keen competitiveness remained in the construction industry despite rent control. While working class Parisians by the 1930s found themselves spending as little as ten percent of their household income for lodging, it does not automatically follow that rent control were the dominating factor in determining either the supply of housing stock not the actual level of rents. Renters paid less for lodging, but the quality of their housing also declined.

Far greater attention must be paid to the availability of capital for mortgages in the inter-war period, which Michel Lescure as well as Alfred Sauvy before him, saw as completely sufficient to generate far greater numbers of housing units than were actually built during the period, but blocked due to the low risk preferences of the _Crédit Foncier_ and _Caisse des Dépôts et Consignations_.(54) Sutcliffe and Lescure found the finance houses' conservative investment policy old-fashioned to the point of seeming irrationality. But that was not really the case. Both the arguments of Sutcliffe and Lescure missed the most critical feature in the inter-war market picture: The fact that however inadequate the housing construction was in terms of relieving the terrible overcrowding in the capital, a great deal of new housing was actually built. In the suburbs of Paris, the number of dwelling units more than doubled between 1870 and 1939, though most were very humble. In the city proper, the filling up of vacant lots in the outer arrondissements and the addition of new floors in the older districts increased residential space by about 15 percent.

It follows that the real value of the existing housing in the suburbs fell by at least half, and in the city by around 15 percent, thus the declining returns on capital invested in housing reflected the actual loss of value in real property during the period. Of course, while other shifts in the marketplace such as the extension of rail service into the suburbs offset some of the impact of the declining value of the existing pool of housing, it still remains clear that the decline was large enough to influence the policies of mortgage lenders. Seen in this light, the attempts by the _Crédit Foncier_ and _Caisse_ to restrain the building process were entirely rational, they had the most to lose from the declining real value of housing. That this type of financial policy coincided with the same formulation by Proudhon hardly should be surprising since it was not only the syndicalist left that found his theories compelling but also the neo-right.(55) Gross overcrowding, intensive competition for housing, and subsequent rent controls more accurately reflected the great ability of the French credit institutions to limit the expansion of housing in accord with their own long run interests. In this context, it should be emphasized that the large gold reserves brought to France under the Poincaré policies of 1926, made the same financial community far stronger in resisting the proposals of 1935 and 1936 for massive public works programs, based on large scale deficit spending by the State (and its corollary, large scale borrowing from the _Caisse_). The far weaker banking systems in the United States, Scandinavia, Italy and Germany succumbed to State pressure for a radical change in economic philosophy, in part because of their own vulnerability to ruin under the rules of Classical theory.

The management of the urban environment of Paris was only in its infancy during the inter-war years, yet some acute observers of the process, like Maxime Leroy, clearly understood the inherently corporatist character of the early French attempts at urban planning.(56) Like Sellier, Leroy was initiated into syndicalism and the local government movement in the years before the First World War, when he served as the justice of the peace in Colombes, a working class suburb of Paris. After the war he left the world of political practice for that of theory, and accepted a university appointment in political economy. Eventually, under Vichy, he instructed the new generation of bureaucrats in the ideological bases of corporatism at the prestigious Ecole des Sciences politiques.(57) In his Vichy period lectures, Leroy spoke at length about the common elements in neo-corporatism, the anarcho-syndicalism of Proudhon and Saint Simon's technocratic theories. Leroy provided in effect a cogent argument for the inherently French roots of the social and economic theories of fascism.

In his key work on the ideological content of urban planning, La Ville française (1927), Leroy insisted that the strong spatial segregation of the urban environment which separated the wealthy of the First Arrondissement and the dangerous classes of the Beaubourg slum, and, the concommitant social turmoil, came from the historic suppression of the corporations or craft guilds and their mode of production which included strong internal social controls. For Leroy, the old corporate structure automatically ensured a high level of economic, social and political cohesion and order which made the task of governing the whole nation much simpler, and much more efficient for the State. Leroy also believed that the age of laissez-faire capitalism which had destroyed the harmony of the older type of society in the name of the individual, was passing. In the early twentieth century, Leroy was convinced that he saw a great structural shift beginning to resegregate society into distinct occupational corps within the industrial cartels and large trade union federations. The task for town developers, then, was to enhance and extend that process by regrouping housing into work related communities where the physical arrangements would reinforce the controls over social behavior that were generated in the workplace.(58)

Leroy's Municipal Taylorism or town planning as a modernizing force only served the needs of the progressive elements in society: The middle classes and workers.(59) Like Marx, Leroy viewed attempts to aid the marginal or backward poor as foolish and wasteful of scarce resources. Slum dwellers in Beaubourg to Leroy were a _lumpenproletariat_ destined for historic obliteration. Leroy saw the Garden City as a marvelous vehicle for the corporatist remaking of French society, and Benoît-Lévy of the Garden City Association also recognized the strong connections between municipal corporatism and model towns. In 1927, Benoît-Lévy, proposed subdividing the space of Garden City into "hamlets each to represent a specialty: There will be a hamlet for the iron-workers, for the carpenters, and for the men of letters."(60) (Social Catholic urban reformer, Lhande, in contrast, Lhande merely wanted to exclude from model town "Socialists, Protestants, _mouscoutaires_ . . . the poor devils, undesirables, the Turks, the Serbs, the Czechs and the Arabs," as he put it "these Sioux.")(61) Benoît-Lévy gave the concept of Municipal Taylorism or town planning its fully corporatist character when he denounced the "inadequacy of a democratic regime in such affairs . . . [and] the regrettable absence of a Napoleon III . . . or Mussolini, telling the mayor of Rome: 'Governor, in five years I will have razed the entire heart of the Old City and the model town Rome-Ostié will be built.'"(62) In France, the Beaubourg slum at the heart of Old Paris disappeared leaving behind cleared lots that stood vacant for a generation and the new town at Suresnes went up in the suburbs, subject to the faltering slowness of public funding for housing and urban renewal that deeply frustrated reformers like Benoît-Lévy and Sellier.

To cut through the democratic and parliamentary encumbrances in France, Leroy offered a series of suggestions: That reformers rely more heavily on sub-national grouping of leaders, of town managers who functioned as a _corps_; and that they persuade the State to devolve real powers to groups such as _l'Union des villes et des communes de France_. Eduoard Herriot and Henri Sellier were charter members of the national coordinating council of the local government league. Sellier held the position of General Secretary for the regional branch, _l'Union des maires de la Seine_. The good government leagues met periodically to share new ideas about controlling urban growth, they planned joint lobbying strategies on behalf of urban legislation in the Chamber, and sent delegations to investigate the advanced experiments in urban design in Italy, Germany and Scandinavia. In the leagues, local leaders came together to discuss problems of management and not governance, and operating fully as the technocratic elite in Saint Simon's New Christianity or like Howard's four men of great probity.(63)

Conclusion

The early years of the Third Republic before the Great War were an era of reform and speculation. Urban organization models still stood between the dreams of utopian artists and the handful of legislative experiments during the heyday of the urban Radical movement. After the grim tragedy of the war, urban planning came to be seen in a new context, within the search for a fundamental restructuring of European life that might preclude another war. These years gave Le Corbusier's urban art a focus and a social purpose.

CHAPTER TWO

Le Corbusier's Early Urban Art (1887-1945)

Charles-Edouard Jeanneret was born in 1887 to a middle class family headed by a watch-engraver living in La Chaux-de-Fonds, Switzerland. Later in the 1920s, Jeanneret took the pen name Le Corbusier. At the time of his birth, La Chaux was a small, rather isolated and idyllic community caught between the French border on the west and Lake Neuchatel to the east. The French town of Besançon, Fourier's home and Proudhon's birthplace, stood just across the border. Artists and writers flocked to the community for its peaceful beauty. The small town boasted of a fine arts academy with a high reputation.

Political and religious dissent viviated the intellectual atmosphere in La Chaux as far back as the persecutions of the French Huguenots during the sixteenth century. More recently, La Chaux had attracted a thriving anarchist movement, founded by the Russian Mikhail Bakunin and continued by Prince Petr Kropotkin during the nineteenth century. Jeanneret's paternal grandparents seem to have been among Bakunin's followers, and both grandfathers fought in the Swiss 1848 Revolution.

This family political tradition, however, did not immediately place the Jeannerets on the left in Charles-Edouard's own time. Mid-nineteenth century European anarchism owed much of its intellectual vision to Pierre Joseph Proudhon and through him Henri Saint Simon. These so-called utopian socialists had, of course, been vigorously denounced by Karl Marx. Their followers had been virtually driven out of the organized Social Democratic movements by the turn of the century. Anarchists were socialist heretics. Le Corbusier's later urban plans, such as _The Radiant City_ have often been attributed in part to the old anarcho-syndicalist social philosophy of his grandparents' generation at La Chaux, and rightly so. La Chaux and the Radiant City (like the English Garden

City) remained faithful in their social designs to the anarchist and Saint Simonian ideal of a Council of Newton for regulation collective and individual rights for the purpose of obtaining the maximum amount of social harmony and material prosperity. Who stood at the apex of the Council which resembled Plato's Republic in many respects? Artists and poets. The vision of the spiritual superiority of art in organizing society remained a constant in Le Corbusier's work throughout his life. But the Social Democratic followers of Marx had a very different model for social organization, where the dictatorship of the proletariat played the lynchpin role that Saint Simon had assigned to the artists and poets. Thus Le Corbusier's vision, at its base, stood diametrically opposed to the ideological premises of Social Democratic political movements and their heirs such as the French Communist Party and the Marxist-wing of the Socialist Party. From the Social Democratic perspective, his art, his philosophy and his buildings were bourgeois or worse.

Jeanneret began art studies in La Chaux in 1900 at the age of thirteen. As a talented young artist and voracious reader, Jeanneret quickly completed his studies at the academy with high marks. In 1907, he left school for an extended tour of Northern Italy and Austria. Jeanneret explored the vast variety of architectural styles and cityscapes associated with different cultures and societies outside little Chaux. Architecture, like Darwinian biology, seemed to him to be evolving towards new uses and jettisoning old encumbrances. While on the tour, Jeanneret visited the Monastery of Ema outside of Florence, with its simple, highly functional, cubic cells. The simplicity of the monastery contrasted sharply with the ornate decorative style that had been popular at the arts academy in his home town.

In 1908, Jeanneret moved to Paris to work and continue his studies of art and architecture under the direction of Auguste Perret. Paris before the Great War was home to an optimistic and intense generation of artists, writers and political exiles. Jeanneret thrived in the new urban environment, and for the first time he dealt with the immediate issues of large scale urbanization, as in a major European capital such as Paris. Perret's firm introduced the first concrete steel reinforced buildings in France with their accompanying, definitively rationalist style. At this point, apart from his art studies, Jeanneret became thoroughly immersed in the elitist literature of his day reading with admiration Hippolyte Taine among others. His choice in the humanistic literature was diametrically opposed to the socialist-humanist school of Jean Jaurès who had written his great opus on the 1789 Revolution in order to refute Taine. (It was Jaurès, of course, the great pre-war socialist leader who gave definition to the whole socialist movement in France.) Jeanneret extended his readings to include engineering and the physical sciences. The work of Fredrick Taylor, the inventor of time-motion studies, caught his attention. Two years after arriving in Paris, Jeanneret left to join Peter Behrens architectural firm in Berlin.

When the job in Berlin failed to work out, Jeanneret returned to Chaux in 1912. He remained in Switzerland for five years, leaving for Paris towards the end of the war. These last years in Chaux were generally unpleasant ones for Jeanneret. His business ventures failed, his plans went unbought. Beyond continuing his personal studies of engineering and modern technology, he taught briefly at the arts academy and organized a small, quarrelsome artists collective, known as the Section Nouveau. In both activities, Jeanneret encountered the wrath of the local Social Democratic establishment which fired him from his teaching post for having corrupted young minds with new ideas, and harassed his art circle for their indecent ideas. Opposition from the Social Democratic movement plagued Jeanneret for the rest of his career. Over the years, Le Corbusier became increasingly embittered by the rejection of his artistic and philosophical concepts by the nominally progressive portion of the political spectrum.

At the end of the Great War Paris offered few luxuries and then only at scandalously high prices. So, Jeanneret settled for modest lodgings at 20, rue Jacob in the Saint Germain des Prés district with its solid bourgeois ethos. He lived in the domestic quarters of a seventh floor walk-up in a seventeenth century aristocratic apartment which was far from comfortable and functional in the twentieth century. Aside from the constant struggle to earn a living, Jeanneret devoted his energy to clarifying for himself and eventually for the rest of Europe the essence of functional architecture in the world of modern technology.

Renewing his connections with the architectural firm of August Perret, Jeanneret reentered the circle of artists and intellectuals around Perret. The chief influence on his work of this period was the Cubist painter, Amédée Ozenfant, whom Le Corbusier met in 1917. Their tempestuous friendship and collaboration yielded several paintings and the provocative essay Après le Cubisme. Ozenfant pushed Jeanneret further towards a clear definition of functionalism.

Le Corbusier's first systematic exposure to modern urban planning came through the writings of Georges Benoît-Lévy, the head of the French Garden City Movement. Long passages from the last volume of Benoît-Lévy's La Cité-Jardin (1913) appeared in Le Corbusier's notebooks from the war years and after. The basic principles of Garden City resurfaced in Le Corbusier's designs during the remainder of his career. Specifically, Le Corbusier borrowed from the Garden City Idea, the principle of locating housing in park-like settings within a clearly defined social system. He added the notion of large scale collective units, and rejected dispersed single family homes, in order to conserve space that might be devoted to collective use in greenways and parks. He further borrowed the inter-urban highway, giving it elevation and a more rational, mathematical layout. In effect, Le Corbusier extended the Garden City Idea with the new physical options in design which could be carried out with steel reinforced concrete: The techniques of Auguste Perret. Le Corbusier transformed the turn of the century English garden suburb to the modern suburb of twentieth century France. At the same time he accepted the elitist portions of the social ideology underlying the Garden City: Class segregation and authoritarian city planning. For him expert artists and engineers should not sacrifice the artistic integrity of their designs to the presumably ignorant criticism of the community.

By 1920, peacetime life had been resumed in France, and Jeanneret, now using the name Le Corbusier, obtained financial backing for his first major architectural magazine, L'Esprit Nouveau. Together with Amédée Ozenfant and Paul Dermée, Le Corbusier published the magazine which attempted to popularize functional architecture among the community of architects in France. By the second year of publication, L'Esprit Nouveau began reaching beyond France, finding avid readers throughout Europe and

America. During the three short years between 1922 and 1925, Le Corbusier produced an avalanche of articles, building plans and city designs which firmly established his reputation as a major innovator in architecture and a literary force.

His plans were exhibited in the studio that Le Corbusier opened with his cousin Pierre Jeanneret at 35, rue de Sèvres in the fashionable Seventh Arrondissement of Paris. The exhibition of his plan _A Contemporary City for Three Million People_ at their Salon d'Automne drew widespread acclaim. Le Corbusier followed the exhibition of his Contemporary City with his slender volume entitled _Vers une architecture_ (sometimes translated as _Towards a New Architecture_) where he synthesized the arguments which had been advanced in piecemeal form in the pages of the architectural magazine of early 1920s. Le Corbusier published a second volume in 1925 known under the title _Urbanisme_ (and _The City of To-Morrow_). In his essay of 1925, he struggled to integrate functional buildings with functional land uses. The volume also reflected his growing frustration with the time consuming and contradictory urban management practices of the late Third Republic.

In 1925, Le Corbusier also produced his _Voisin Plan for Paris_ which was shown at the Salon d'Automne. The sweeping dimensions of skyscrapers for central city Paris tickled the imagination of fellow architects, but was less well received among the Parisian city fathers and general populace. Implementation of such a drastic overhaul of historic Paris was beyond the comprehension of the political regimes of the inter-war Third Republic. So Le Corbusier turned his attention to three smaller projects: _La cité universitaire_; a Parisian housing project, known as _la cité Audincourt_; and finally, La Pessac near Bordeaux. The cellular home at La Pessac set the mode for future development in France and around the world. La Pessac was the first modern apartment building.

Le Corbusier also competed for the contract to design the League of Nations headquarters in Geneva. Ostensibly, the design was rejected for not being submitted in India ink as the competition required. A more likely reason for the rejection, however, was the flood of unfavorable articles written in La Chaux by a Social Democratic journalist, and repeated in the highly social democratic Geneva, which was also the home of the International Labor Organization and the Second Socialist International. Old controversies from the days of the Section Nouveau resurfaced and fueled the criticism of Le Corbusier's work in Switzerland and in France. Undaunted, Le Corbusier extended his efforts in the international arena where he sought a broad constituency among both architects and political leaders. His concern with the world-wide movement for functional architecture led to the founding of the International Congresses of Modern Architecture (CIAM). As a founder of CIAM, Le Corbusier visited South America during 1929 to popularize the movement in Buenos Aires, Montevideo, Sao Paulo and Rio de Janeiro. He returned to Paris with copious designs for the renovation and modernization of these American cities as well as embarking on a redevelopment plan for the Porte Maillot in the western suburbs of Paris. The Stock Market Crash of October 1929 and the subsequent world-wide economic contraction, of course, brought all Le Corbusier's projects to a standstill.

He closed the decade by becoming a French citizen in 1930, and by marrying Yvonne Gallis, a fashion model from Monaco and his long-time mistress. With French citizenship and marriage to Yvonne, Le Corbusier settled into a more properly bourgeois life-style during the 1930s, when the very institutions of bourgeois Republicanism seemed near collapse. During the decade of grave economic suffering for most French, Le Corbusier's well established reputation brought him personally to a higher standard of living than he had previously known. By 1934, Le Corbusier could build himself a model apartment that demonstrated the boldness of his techniques. He now gave even greater amounts of his time to international propaganda on behalf of the New Architecture of functionalism. Finding responsive customers in the fascist countries, as well as in France, Le Corbusier designed a wide range of government and private buildings, though few were actually constructed. Even so, his reputation as an architect grew enormously and by the 1930s, his name had become synonymous with contemporary architectural design.

When private building declined dramatically during the Depression, Le Corbusier turned his attention towards city planning. Like the Stockholm School economists and John Maynard Keynes, Le Corbusier recognized the relationship between public works projects for unemployment relief and urban design.

Jumping to take advantage of this unexpected spurt of urban renovation, Le Corbusier revived his Garden City concepts from the 1920s.

Contracts for large scale public building projects, however, constantly eluded Le Corbusier's grasp. First, there had been the League of Nations failure, and then in 1931, Stalin rejected his design for the Palace of Soviets. Instead, his advice was sought in Mussolini's Italy. The combination of central place, as in the old Roman forum for public events, and public control, with monastery like cells of individual residential apartments from medieval Europe fit very well with Mussolini's brand of fascism. The Algiers Viaduct project of 1932, for example, was derived from this basic Le Corbusier formula.

Much confusion exists over Le Corbusier's relationship to fascism. Mussolini, the senior fascist during the 1920s, came out of the international socialist movement from the pre-war years. In its first decade at any rate, Mussolini's National Revolution in Italy was more than nationalist. Instead Mussolini promised to recapture the imperial grandeur of ancient Rome to compensate for the great catastrophe of 1914. Like Lenin, Mussolini wanted to build his new nation using modern technology like electrification, and new management concepts like mass production. His scenario in many respects was close to the grand designs of Bonapartism, thus familiar in French culture as well. With Mussolini's vision also came the old Roman desire to build: Roads, cities, the foundations of an empire.

For Hitler and the Nazi movement of the 1930s, fascism was somewhat different. Their empire was that of Spengler's "barbarians" who ruled the Holy Roman Empire of mediaeval Europe. Biology ruled the human empire not material goods. Modern technology to the mediaeval age had been the fearful magic by which capitalists and industrialist corrupted the idyllic harmony of the world where every hungry peasant had his lonely chicken and his divine deliverance. Moreover, it was that modern technology was the beast which had consumed the generation of 1914. To prevent the corruption of the soul and, ostensibly, the destruction of another generation, in Nazism the State took hold of new technology and distributed it in a highly controlled and sanitized form. Hence, the Nazi ideologues had a primary quarrel with Le Corbusier's head long dash into functionalism and the New Architecture in the hands of individual architects and developers. Le Corbusier felt much more at home with Mussolini.

One of Le Corbusier's closest collaborators, Walter Gropius took the plunge to close the gap between the two varieties of fascism by placing his services as an architect at the disposal of the Nazi State. For his own part, Le Corbusier walked a narrow line between outright support for Mussolini and his lingering Republicanism. He came closest to Mussolini in 1934 when Le Corbusier gave a series of lectures at Il Duce's personal invitation in Rome. Back home, in Paris, his ideas about pre-fabricated dwellings--the application of the cell to mass production--were bitterly denounced by both the established contractors and their Socialist or Communist unions who feared grave new problems of unemployment as the building trades became automated. Le Corbusier responded with denunciations of the old capitalist system which were so vociferous that he was invited by a personal friend in the Communist Party, Paul Vaillant-Couturier, to lend his name to the anti-fascist Popular Front political campaign of 1936. He declined.

Vichy France, that somber wartime regime of Marshal Pétain, found Le Corbusier among the handful of architects of the first rank in service to the collaborationist government. While many other architects in the new movement for functionalism went into the Resistance, Le Corbusier joined his old mentor Auguste Perret in Reconstruction planning during the fall of 1940 and the spring of 1941. In May, Le Corbusier became the director of the Reconstruction Committee for housing and general urban redevelopment. In that post he worked with the prominent French fascist intellectual, François de Pierrefeu. They co-authored a short book on corporatist doctrines and social theory behind urban design and its applications to contemporary France. A falling out with others on the Reconstruction Committee led Le Corbusier to resign. In 1942, Vichy reassigned him to Algiers, where he also failed to get along with the local government officials and even quarreled with the local architects in the Algiers branch of CIAM. After the frustrating assignment in Algiers, Le Corbusier returned to private life in France.

Like many, he spent 1943 and 1944 awaiting the judgment of the victors. Both the left-leaning Liberation Government of 1945 and the Americans with their Marshall Plan dollars, firmly refused to consider the Reconstruction projects of Le Corbusier. He was lucky, other collaborators like de Pierrefeu were shot.

Le Corbusier's Philosophy of Planning

Like Howard, Le Corbusier believed that the fundamental purpose of town design was to stabilize society. By combining the economic and social functions of town space, Howard's Garden City Idea had provided architects with parameters within which to set their own artistic creations. After the Second World War, Le Corbusier's work gave France the *grandes ensembles* those massive public housing projects of the 1950s in the suburbs of Paris which broke down the Garden City concept into its most elementary functional components of residence, employment, transportation and socialization. By stating the architectural problem in these terms, Le Corbusier believed that he made it possible for planners to create a rational urban physical environment that could meet the needs of the rational economic man as simply as solving a quadradic. The origins of the *grandes ensembles* lay in Le Corbusier's work during the 1920s, when the most modern and progressive architectural symbol was certainly the Manhattan skyline. Skyscrapers represented the most powerful contemporary experiments in producing immense, multi-functional edifices containing the most sophisticated economic and cultural activities of the age.(1) The penthouse provided a luxurious, almost Napoleonic view of the metropolis; the intermediate floors housed the new mode of production, the paperwork industries; the street level shops served the commercial needs of both residents and employees with convenience; and finally, the elevators: Were they not like flying within a building in the 1920s? How vivid was the contrast between the new world of the skyscraper and the crooked lanes of uncertain direction in the heart of the Old City, where even from the fifth floor a Parisian could not see beyond the court yard six feet away.

Like Leroy, Le Corbusier had spent much of the First World War studying Taylor's writings and gleaning from them a deep appreciation for both functionalism and the natural tendency towards an immense growth in the size, scope and complexity of productive activities.(2) For Le Corbusier mass production on a gigantic scale dominated the new historical stage, and in his designs, he intended "to illustrate how, by virtue of the selective principle (Standardization applied to mass production), industry creates pure forms, and to stress the intrinsic value of this pure form of art that is the result of it. Secondly, to show the radical transformations and structural liberties reinforced concrete and steel allow us to envisage in housing--in other words, that _a dwelling can be standardized to meet the needs of men whose lives are standardized_."(3) In his design of 1925, _Pessac: La Maison standardisée_, Le Corbusier featured the cell, as the basic component of either the dwelling or the office.(4) In the Pessac design, Le Corbusier posed the "problem of a house plan, of finding a method of standardization, to make use of walls, floors and roofs conforming to the most rigorous standards for strength and efficiency and lending themselves to true taylorite-like methods of mass production . . . [my] method: Standardization, industrialization, taylorized production."(5) Also drawn in 1925, the _Plan Voisin de Paris_ collected the individual cells into a series of immense skyscrapers that Le Corbusier suggested for the center of the Old City of Paris to replace the crumbling, diseased slums like Beaubourg. He wanted to provide a "free description of an actual town-planning and architectural project which has been based on concrete statistics, the proven reliability of certain materials, a new form of social and economic organization, and a more rational exploitation of real property."(6) The great buildings supposedly gave its army of "400,000 clerks" the opportunity to look down upon "a mass of serried trees swaying beneath them," a dubious proposition from the scale of the tall skyscrapers in the sketch.(7)

Le Corbusier charged his architectural students with the duty to continue his functionalist philosophy in their own designs, and much of the town planning in France after the Second World War flowed from his injunction "_Normaliser, standardiser, mesurer, proportioner_."(8) According to his functionist school "the four functions of _urbanisme_ . . . are: To house, to employ, to socialize, and to transport, functions intertwined with the unfolding of every twenty-four hours, with the changes from activity to rest, of motion to sleep, the rhythm of life in our world forever. If the journey across the twenty-four hours is broken by disorder and disequilibrium," he wrote, "then our entire lives will be in disequilibrium and disorder, and society equally."(9) Like Benoît-Lévy and the socialist urban reformers, Le Corbusier frequently found his grand schemes bogged down by the fiscal tightness of State fiscal policies and by the old prerogatives of private property.

In his sketch book from 1934, Le Corbusier carefully underscored the political implications of his "modern architecture [which was] born about 1803 in Paris, became bolshevist in Geneva, fascist in the Paris Humanité and petty bourgeois in Moscow (where gable and column have again come to style), recognized but by Mussolini (see his speech to the young architects in June 1934)."(10) Franco-Italian collaboration in architectural design reached a high point during the Fifth International Congress of Modern Architecture (CIAM) in 1936, when the meeting, hosted by Le Corbusier, drew the participation of such prominent Italian designers as Gino Pollini and Piero Bottoni. The Congress demanded a radical change in European laws governing private property. The group proposed "nationalisation pure et simple. Notre solution qui est celle de techniciens purement et simplement est: LIBERATION ET MOBILISATION DU SOL."(11) While the proposal shocked or annoyed most traditional supporters of the Third Republic who clung tightly to the ideals of private ownership, it was a proposal that was highly consistent with the contemporary doctrines of Italian corporatism. Fascism under Mussolini categorically rejected the individualism of the eighteenth century in favor of a new form of authoritarian State and equally rejected the natural right of property.(12) It was precisely that conflict between State authority and private property that stood at the crux of the dilemma facing the French in the urban reform movement before the Second World War.

For all their old anarcho-syndicalist memories, by the 1930s members of the French Socialist Party stood firmly in the camp of Third Republic parliamentarism and reform under Republican institutions. While the Socialist Party programme also called for the nationalization of industry and land, the party had no intention of abandoning the Enlightenment heritage of natural, individual civil liberties and popular sovereignty. Many Socialists including the leader of the Popular Front Government Léon Blum favored the indirect economic controls which Thomas had proposed over direct State operation of industry. These moderate socialists only sought to limit private property rights not to abolish them. As for the other party most clearly associated with the urban reform movement, the Radicals under the leadership of Herriot and Daladier held an absolute terror of rejecting the principles of 1791 and especially the guarantees to private property.(13) The Radical Party programs under the Third Republic, carefully and consistently defined their support for urban reform and such public activities as regulation of housing through building codes as measures permitted under the police powers of the State when necessary to maintain public health and well-being. Implicit in the Radical view was the notion that whatever authority was conceded to the State under these practices required a correspondingly great degree of vigilance on the part of the representatives of the Republic to check any abuses of the powers granted to the State.

The New Economics: Regulation, Planning, Corporatism

Many economists and politicians have labored to draw distinctions between the concepts of regulation, planning and corporatism since the inter-war years when the first term was chosen as the economic policy of Roosevelt's New Deal, the second as the foundation for Stalin's Five Year Plans and the third as the economic philosophy of fascism. While some very important distinctions among these concepts can be usefully debated the differences are not so great as the common elements. Fundamentally, the new economic systems of the inter-war years rejected the Classical idea that the economy and society functioned better without State intervention. In France, the adoption of interventionist economic policies by the State provided the essential mechanism to transform the fragile experiments of the urban reformers of the Third Republic into the massive programs for the *aménagement du territoire* in the post-war period. State governance of the economy represented the fulfillment of Saint Simon's predictions. It was the outcome of political power shifting from old, individualistic elites of the nineteenth century tradition towards a specialized elite of managers. In the societies that had suffered the most casualties in the Great War in Russia and Italy, the erosion of the cultural heritage of the nineteenth century was most severe. For the victors in the war, the new philosophy of an activist State was forced to make an accommodation with the older tradition of individual civil liberties and popular sovereignty. France, the United States and England retained parliamentary institutions. The courts also continued to apply precedents drawn from the earlier tradition of individual civil liberties including the right to private property ownership.

Yet even such staunch defender of Liberal parliamentary institutions as Keynes found a strong common link between his own views and the new concepts of a governed economy in Russia and Italy. In his insightful little essay A Short View of Russia (1924), Keynes saw very clearly the passing of the old economic order and its replacement in both Russia and Italy by a far different philosophy when he playfully quipped about "Il Duce who is a rake susceptible of being reformed, and the President [Calvin Coolidge] a decent person whose salvation is out of the question."(14) Later in his world shaking General Theory of Employment, Interest and Money (1936), Keynes explicitly dealt with the consequences of his formulations about the nature of market equilibrium for liberal political institutions, when he recognized that "the central controls necessary to ensure full employment will, of course, involve a large extension of the traditional functions of government . . . . It is not the ownership of the instruments of production which it is important for the State to assume. If the State is able to determine the aggregate amount of resources devoted to augmenting the instruments and the basic rate of reward to those who own them, it will have accomplished all that is necessary. Moreover, the necessary measure of socialization can be introduced gradually and without a break in the general traditions of society." Keynes continued "thus I agree with [Silvio] Gesell that the results of filling in the gaps in the classical theory is not to dispose of the 'Manchester System,' but to indicate the nature of the environment which the free play of economics requires if it is to realize the full potentialities of production."(15)

It is highly significant that Keynes drew upon the theories of Silvio Gesell, one of the truly important but obscure economists of the twentieth century, as well as the theories of French Socialist Albert Thomas. Both of these political economists shared a deep fundamental agreement with Proudhon's deconcentrated schemes for governing a modern economy. Like Proudhon himself their views were fundamentally antagonistic to the centralized and unitary vision of Marx.(16) During the Great War, Thomas favored the regulation of production over the direct nationalization of plants. The reluctance to nationalize lay at the heart of the post-war quarrel between French Socialists and Communists. The latter were committed to a rigorous expropriation and nationalization policy. Bowing to the strength of nineteenth century and even Enlightenment traditions of private property holding, like Gesell Keynes retained the ownership of property as a strong positive cultural value that conferred a sense of free and independent action in political life. While Proudhon and Thomas as socialists saw great injustices and perils to the civil liberties of the common people from the grossly unequal distributions of wealth in nineteenth century French society, at the same time the idea of the ownership of some wealth, perhaps the family _foyer_, by all citizens was their key to a free and fair distribution of power in society.

As early as 1926, Keynes indicated that corporations then currently being revived in Mussolini's Italy, provided the best vehicle for the deconcentrated management of the economy rather than direct nationalization or the benign neglect of Manchester economists. In _The End of Laissez-Faire_ (1926), Keynes wrote that "progress lies in the growth and the recognition of semi-autonomous bodies _within the State_ . . . . I propose a return, it maybe said, towards medieval conceptions of separate autonomies. But in England at any rate, corporations are a mode of government which has never ceased to be important and is sympathetic to our institutions."(17) Writing in 1863, Proudhon made the same argument in defining his famous principle of mutuality, or deconcentrated coordination. Proudhon insisted that his idea of mutuality was "is seen in welfare organizations, then in chambers of commerce, guilds of arts and crafts, and workingmen's associations, in exchanges and markets . . . in what the English call self government."(18)

In the French town planning theory of Le Corbusier and in the urban administrative tradition of Leroy, towns took on the functions of a corporation within the national economy. The planned town became the funnel through which the State introduced public works into the economy in order to stimulate the creation of new jobs. The first experiments in the new economics of the 1930s came in the United States, Sweden, Germany and Italy.(19) In France, the notion of State induced prosperity or even simple economic balance through an active public works program only took hold during the post-war reconstruction period under the leadership of Jean Monnet. He worked closely with Keynes on the war finance boards in London during the Second World War. While the desirability of governing the economy ran through much of nineteenth century French socialist thought, only in the early 1930s did the idea of a national economic plan receive attention in the National Assembly. The depression fighting proposals of Henri de Man the Belgian _planiste_ went before the Assembly under the sponsorship of the socialist deputies most closely linked to the _Confédération Générale du Travail-Force Ouvrière_, the trade union wing of the Socialist Party.(20)

Neo-rightists, at the helm of the French business community also began to look towards some form of State aid in resolving the extraordinary crisis of the 1930s. Under the Flandin and Marchandeau ministries of 1935, for instance, Louis Renault's nephew and general manager of the giant autoworks, Lehideux sat on the crisis committee formed by the _Conseil d'Etat_ to suggest new methods to cope with the high unemployment and general economic distress. Moderate Socialists, Robert Marjolin and Jules Moch also participated in work of the crisis commission.(21) While the commission reached a consensus that an active national policy of public works would create badly needed jobs, it failed to persuade the Chamber of Deputies or even the Marchandeau government that it made economic sense for the State to contract a large debt in order to purchase all these proposed public works projects. The principle of prudent and balanced State budget pushed French fiscal policy in the opposite direction from the proposals of either the _planistes_ around de Man or the extraordinary commission of 1935.

Elsewhere in America, in Scandinavia and in the fascist countries, however, public works project became the compelling proof of the viability of the new non-Classical economic theories of Keynes, Gunnar Myrdahl and their Continental counterparts. And public works were the backbone of town planning, they were the infrastructure of the Garden City. At its base, the Keynesian formula for economic management required the State to become the consumer of last resort and purchase the normal goods that States buy in peacetime:

Roads, dams, school houses and the like.(22) Moreover, the new way of viewing the operation of the marketplace taught that the production of new tangible goods was a general stimulant for the economy that increased the capacity to produce as well as reducing the number of unemployed. As part of the construction industry, public works predominantly employed unskilled or semi-skilled labor that suffered higher levels of unemployment in the recession than the skilled occupations. While the reasonableness of an active public works program appealed to the small circles of neo-rightists and _planistes_ in France, the ideas failed to impress the financial community. The _Crédit Foncier_ became increasingly reluctant to loan capital for housing or public works projects as the depression deepened in the mid-1930s. Public housing programs ended in 1936 and private construction dropped to the levels of wartime.

A small and extremely disenchanted segment of the urban reform movement followed the strategies of former Socialists Jacques Doriot and Marcel Déat in repudiating the Third Republic and a full acceptance of fascist style corporatist ideas. As mayor of the militant working class suburb of Saint Denis, Doriot broke with the French Communist Party in the late 1920s, while Déat as mayor of the Twentieth Arrondissement of Paris made his move towards corporatism in the early 1930s. During the Depression, both mayors remained active in the municipal reform movement, and maintained relationships with Socialist and Radical reformers. In 1934, for example, Sellier staunchly defended Déat from charges of fascist sympathies in his speech inaugurating the new public school at Colombelles. Both Sellier and Déat worked together in support of public works spending and saw it as the key to breaking the grip of Depression. Sellier joined the Popular Front government in 1936 which attempted to slow the rise of French fascism, while Déat went along a different and founded his fascistic _Parti Unique_ in 1942 around a strong corporatist program of public works and urban reform.(23)

Vichy enacted a series of new municipal laws which in theory devolved certain decision-making powers to regional prefects and to local civic committees. These measures attempted to integrate urban life within the explicit corporatist vision of the Pétain regime. The reconstruction laws of October 11, 1940 and the subsequent decrees of February 7 and May 26, 1941 required regions and localities to draw up formal reconstruction plans, that were in effect regional and municipal master plans, under the direction of the regional prefect and with the advice of committees of *notables*.(24) In regions like Brittany, with a long history of separatist agitation, the *Comité consultatif* played a powerful role in gaining initial support for the Vichy government among the local civic and business leaders. Over the course of the war, the *Comité* in Brittany became a cohesive and experienced group which agreed among itself on a full range of careful development plans for everything from urban expansion to economic renovation to the promotion of tourism. Vichy's acceptance of long standing regionalist demands for the introduction of *breton* history and language into the school curriculum gave the Occupation government a measure of strong support among those who sought cultural autonomy.(25) *Notables* from the duc du Rohan, a dynastic rival to the Bourbons, to separatists like Yann Fouéré to autonomists like Joseph Martray actively participated in the work of the *Comité*, though many members became increasingly disenchanted with the authoritarian drift of the regime at Vichy. Some like Martray broke with Pétain and swung into the Resistance. These disaffected Vichyites and a new generation of leadership emerged in the post-war years and reformed the *Comité* to continue its programmatic work under the name *Comité des Etudes et Liaisons des Intérêts de la Bretagne* (CELIB).(26) In 1954, CELIB produced the first regional master plan in France generated from local and regional initiatives. In most respects it was the same plan drawn up by the *Comité* during the war.

Conclusion

American aid for European recovery under the Marshall Plan required the implicit adoption of the New Deal faith in Keynesianism by the Europeans. Some Frenchmen like Jean Monnet received the credit terms for reconstruction with genuine enthusiasm, for he was from that small part of the neo-rightist financial community that sincerely believed in an activist State economic policy. Keynesian ideas also found a sympathetic reception among the reformist element in the French Socialist movement, who drew their traditions from Saint Simon and Proudhon. And French Communists buoyed by the Liberation struggle pushed hard for massive nationalization and a highly centralized, Stalin style planning system. Le Corbusier also looked to the new Republic to support his ideas for urban France. In this political climate the troubling linkages between increasing State powers and the potential threats to individual civil liberties receded from political debates, much as did the Radical Party.

Keynesian assumptions about the nature of economic life were so pervasive that in the field of urban economics, the leading French theorist Claude Ponsard attempted to weave together the econometric models of August Lösch and the Keynesian system.(27) Lösch who had subscribed to the adamantly anti-Saint Simonian economics of Léon Walras would certainly have found such a marriage of ideas outrageous. After all, in his classic work on urban economics of 1946 he denounced both Keynes and the American New Deal as thoroughly degenerate. That, however, did not stop the new generation of urban technicians at the _Commissariat Général du Plan_ from extending these econometric models into actual policy making. It was only after the fall of the Fourth Republic in 1958 at the hands of General Charles de Gaulle, that serious opposition to nationally directed policies for the economy and for the towns emerged. Regionalists and Gaullist nationalists reacted against the centralization planning system and the Americanism of the ideology. And the socialists now out of power, rediscovered the dangers to civil liberties and parliamentary institutions from the highly powerful, well organized State.

CHAPTER THREE

The Urban Growth Miracle (1945-1958)

After the Liberation in 1944, France found it impossible to completely shake off the political rivalries that had deadlocked the Third Republic. Le Corbusier also had great difficulty in providing an apology for his inter-war and Vichy era activities. Yet his early work served as the intellectual blue print for post-war urban reconstruction. The Liberation Government barred Le Corbusier as a collaborationist from directly participating in the task of rebuilding. France's Fourth Republic (1946-1958) provided the vital transition from the ephemeral and theoretical world of municipal Taylorism to the comprehensive, philosophically integral system of urban management.

Political instability played a critical role in the original design of French urban planning institutions and policies during the late 1940s. In communities across France, local conservatives who had collaborated with the Pétainist regime lost their positions in municipal government at the end of the war. Many times the leaders of the local Resistance forces replaced the old notables (elites) at the helm of the community. Three factions dominated the Resistance in France: The Communists, the Socialists and the Gaullists. In some communities, each faction claimed a share in local power similar to the tripartite agreement for the national government in Paris. But in most communities only one faction emerged with effective political control. Like the municipal revolution of the Radicals in the 1880s, these new local governments brought profound changes throughout France.

As might be expected, the new Communist and Socialist municipal leaders rarely enjoyed much support from the displaced old town elite. Local businessmen often distrusted, even feared them. Moderate and pro-Catholic Gaullist local leaders, on the other hand, more easily mobilized the disenfranchised but potentially powerful wartime local leaders. Leftist town officials balanced their local isolation by linking themselves tightly to the central regime in Paris. Because many town businesses rejected their leadership, leftist municipal officials could not organize effective local initiatives to build housing, to lay roads or to develop new factories. Gaullist officials managed to foster modest, very parochial plans for local growth with the cooperation of the banished Vichy municipal officials and town business leaders.

At the national level, the newly created Commissariat Général du Plan (CGP) attempted to integrate all the specific development policies of the equally new Fourth Republic within one comprehensive national strategy. But as a creation of this unsettled political climate of the Liberation period, the CGP struggled with its own political contradictions. As a concept, it was the invention of the Keynesian Liberal financier Jean Monnet, and as a State institution it was the handiwork of a National Assembly dominated by the Communist and Socialist movements. They chose the title Chief Commissaire for the head of the planning agency because many deputies believed that their planning bureau was initiating a peaceful transition to a Stalinist style of economic governance in France. Like the chief planning bureau in Russia, the new French planning commissariat was intended to be highly centralized and powerful enough to make a reality out of Lenin's dictum to govern the heights of the economy. A vast array of nationalizations during this early period brought many basic industries under State control, and under the direct guidance of the new planning commissariat.

Dissension among the three political movements springing from the Resistance broke up the Tripartite Goverment by the end of the 1940s. In left dominated towns the shocks from the national level reverberated when local Communists went into the opposition and abandoned their places in municipal government. Slowly, across the next decade local Socialists and left Radicals also lost their positions at the town level as well as in the National Assembly. Gaullists from the Resistance movement and rehabilitated Vichyites assumed the posts the the left vacated. By the end of the Fourth Republic in 1958, local special interests began to test the central powers of the national planning agency in a variety of ways, and found that the illusion of a soviet style planning program had completely vanished along with the left partisans of the Resistance. In its place stood a very solid national planning agency dedicated to the modernization and promotion of capitalism.

Urbanism and Republicanism

From its moment of inception in the Constituent Assembly of 1945-6, the Fourth Republic rested upon a vital compromise. In 1945 the Communist Party gave up its opposition to Republicanism in France, by agreeing to the restoration of a Liberal government based upon the old principle of private property holding in the Declaration of 1790. In exchange for the peaceful reestablishment of Republican institutions, the Gaullists, Socialists, Radicals and moderates in the first assembly consented to the establishment of some form of national economic planning. In the late 1940s Communism in France was Stalinism, and Stalinism in Russia was the Five Year Plans. But the compromise on the question of private property holding precluded any suggestion of a true soviet style plan. So France embarked on a method of planning that drew its practical theory from Keynesian and Social Democratic models for guided economic growth yet looked towards the highly centralized Stalinist plans also. Planned economic growth in this Western tradition stood squarely upon the simple strategy of inducing full employment by building public works. Urban infrastructure was indirectly a key component of the whole scheme for managing prosperity. Le Corbusier saw the connexion and bitterly resented his exclusion from participating in the actual implementation of the new French system of planning.

What were the elements of Le Corbusier's _urbanisme_? Function, mutability, mass scale conceptualization. All these fascets, of course, had been present in his inter-war sketch books, and in the early structures such as the cellular house at Pessac. Two forces ensured the acceptance of architecture designed with these qualities during the late 1940s and early 1950s. France looked for large scale development from scarce resources: A seemingly stagnant population, living in all the wrong places, little modern industry and safe markets under challenge in

Africa and Asia. New buildings needed to meet new uses of the occupants whether as residences, workplaces or public offices, while decorative facades remained a luxury.

The new architecture was also reinforced by the massive shift in the balance of the population from rural to urban during the course of the Fourth Republic. Although a great deal has been written about significance of the movement away from a nation of vigorously independent peasants to a country of congested urban dwellers, the consequences for urban design have not been well understood. After the Second World War, France became a nation with an urban majority. Towns with 2000 residents were regarded as urban and their town designs came under new philosophical pressure as well as actual physical changes. Rural France had a strong tradition of owner occupation of farmsteads, and even residences in small villages. In contrast, during the early twentieth century in major cities like Paris urban households rented their homes. Urban planners in the 1940s and 1950s expected this urban pattern to continue. Many former peasants, however, continued to demand direct ownership. Popular preferences for home ownership created a major, largely unanticipated drain on nation capital resources during the Fourth Republic as the new urbanites sought mortgages. Finding urban prices high and capital expensive, urban dwellers turned in large numbers to the pre-fabricated, standardized cell-like apartments of Le Corbusier's _grandes ensembles_. This mass movement to condominiums had another consequence. The new living arrangements forced apartment dwellers to confront basic conflicts between traditional individual private uses of property and collective needs of the community in the new urban complexes. For many the shift from the highly particularistic, and individualistic life-style of rural France, to the more communal urban setting was troubling. For others the new collectivity brought freedom, or anonymity, from the narrow circle of the village elites. Whatever the case, the result was an important change in the way in which many Frenchmen lived, and more importantly in how they perceived people should live.

Urbanisme, like other forms of social planning spoke to the ostensible need to organize and rationalize social relationships in these rapidly growing urban areas. Like the _révolution des maires_ in the 1880s, the _révolution des urbanistes_ of the 1950s brought a new ideas about the nature of the State itself. Where the localist revolt in the late nineteenth century fostered reformism in the name of public safety and clean cities, the _urbanistes_ of the 1950 sought to more broadly distribute the public fruits of prosperity, such as roads, schools, energy and modern communications, ineffect urban infrastructure.

While the _urbanistes_ of the Fourth Republic plunged ahead with implementation of stripped-down versions of Le Corbusier's designs from the inter-war years, he concentrated his own work in the international sphere. Le Corbusier's domestic projects, Saint Dié in 1945 and the Unité d'Habitation apartment complex in Marseilles were plagued with political troubles. The Saint Dié design for a civic center followed the Pessac model from the 1920s. It became a prototype for the Boston Government Center. Despite the project's artistic value, all elements of the governing coalition Gaullists, Socialist and Communists rejected Le Corbusier's Saint Dié proposal. But two years later in a more conservative political climate, following the departure of the Communists from the Tripartite Government, Le Corbusier obtained the commission to build 360 residential units outside of Marseilles. Known as the Unité d'Habitation, this project became his chief post-war statement in domestic design. And like his earlier efforts, disputes and bitter wrangling hampered the project for over five years. He placed the apartment building on enormous cement legs, in an absurdly defiant stance that angered many. Le Corbusier called his last architectural style the New Brutalism.

After the very the difficult period of the late 1940s, Le Corbusier's fortunes brightened somewhat. In 1950, he received an offer to design a chapel in eastern France, using his new brutalist style, in slightly muted fashion. The Ronchamp Chapel went up between 1950 and 1955, which coincided with the political rehabilitation of many ex-Vichyites. These years also saw the rapid spread of the _grand ensemble_ design throughout urban France. In all parts of France, New Towns sprang up around the massive apartment blocks.

While working on the Ronchamp Chapel, Le Corbusier completed his design for the General Assembly hall at Chandigarh in East Punjab. Designed to celebrate the emergence of an independent South Asia (or the death of the British Empire, here Le Corbusier was cryptic) the Assembly was the only major public building that the architect ever actually built. Construction began in 1953 under his own direction but quickly drifted into other hands as the project bogged down in delays from work stoppages and halting financial support. The final complex lacked many amenities in the original design, and the grounds were never finished in Le Corbusier's lifetime.

Between 1956 and 1965, Le Corbusier drifted into a period of semi-retirement where his time was devoted as much to painting, writing, friends and his public role, as to his designs. He designed two major buildings during this last decade. The Youth and Cultural Centre at Firminy was drawn in 1956 and completed in the mid-1960s. Finally, the Centre Le Corbusier in Zurich was begun in 1963, and served the depository for many of his sketch books and painting after the architect's death in 1965.

Like the Fourth Republic, Le Corbusier's work was seemingly completed by the mid-1950s. France at last tolerated Republican rule, and appeared willing to accept much of the Radical tradition. Ironically, the depth of this transformation in France could be seen in the withering of the Radical political parties. Their agendas and voters slipped away to other parties over the next decade. _Urbanisme_, became defined by new _urbanistes_ like Jean-François Gravier, who wrote his arresting tract _Paris et le désert français_ in 1947. A regular system of physical land use planning no longer shocked conservatives, nor seduced those to the left. It was merely accepted like the Republic itself. Schemes for urban renovation within general fiscal policy making as advocated by academics such as Claude Pönsard and Alfred Sauvy became incorporated in standard government policies. France jettisoned the make shift experimentation of the early years of municipal Taylorism. A more comprehensive urban planning took the place of early reformism. New ideas about control over regional development challenged the old provincial elites. The great apartment complexes threatened the concept the single family home of rural France. Big businesses absorbed small ones. Planned urban growth, of course, gave the disrupted in French society a specific entity the planning process to blame for those changes. Urban planning's inescapable authoritarian facet still remained strong under the

Fourth Republic. Le Corbusier's old assumption that freedom was the product of the rational harmony of careful, purposeful physical layouts of community life deeply influenced urban planning. Urban sociologists such as Chombart de Lauwe began to worry in these years, about the sterility of rational design, about the seeming explosion of anti-social behavior and mental illness among the new urban French of the huge apartments complexes.

Le Corbusier's post-war contribution to planning was largely indirect. Yet at the same time, it was substantive. Le Corbusier had placed great faith in the wisdom of the designer to foresee the needs and desires of a community just like Ebenezer Howard. Now the State gave these urban artists the authority to build their invented towns. In France, Le Corbusier believed four great needs dominated all others. He told planners that they must decongest the centers of old cities by introducing efficient new road networks and by creating new buildings. These new businesses, government offices and homes needed to take advantage of height and to avoid cluttering up valuable ground space. Next designers must drastically increase the densities of activity in central cities inorder to keep the areas vital. Le Corbusier called for a viable alternative to suburban development which he feared. Suburbs even the lush Garden Cities promoted isolation and the waste of resources on private transportation. Le Corbusier was an especially stern critic of the American suburban explosion of the 1920s and 1950s. He called for French designers to avoid precisely this American dilemma. Mass transit, or better still, cities constructed for pedestrians fit Le Corbusier's model for <u>urbanisme</u> in France. That objective, however, contradicted the final major premise in his design theory: The call for open space and urban segregation by function. It is this last concept which has come to be identified most directly with Le Corbusier's urban design legacy. By separating towns and cities into residential, commercial, industrial and administrative quarters, like the old Garden City, and by advocating highrise construction he hoped to transform the urban environment into a more harmonious, efficient and pleasant place. Unfortunately the dimensions of the quarters in most of Le Corbusier's designs made pedestrian traffic impractical.

His urban designs used the planned environment to control many important aspects of social and cultural life. While Le Corbusier often eschewed direct comment on current political events and was reluctant to acknowledge the ideological characteristics of his designs theories, these elements were most certainly present in his own work. The post-war generation absorbed his urban models and their ideological principles. Physical land use design by its very nature is a form of regulation of private property by the State. Le Corbusier looked with great respect and a touch of jealousy at the powerful planners of the past and present. In one of his notebooks, he looked to the example of the despot Louis XIV who conceived immense projects and realized them by saying "We wish it," or "Such is our pleasure." Le Corbusier's rejection of old traditions of individual private property and his endorsement of authoritarian measures of regulation, of course, were the forces that had propelled him into projects in the 1930s for both Stalin's Russia and Mussolini's Italy. But in the post-war period of French history the compromise forming the basis of the Fourth Republic, itself legitimated a very weak form of this same philosophy.

Moreover, in the 1940s and 1950s, it appeared that this modern corporatist philosophy worked, if by that we mean society had achieved a very high degree of prosperity. The new urban environment took shape in the image of Le Corbusier. Keynesian theory also rested squarely upon the reduction of property rights and the increasing regulatory authority of the State. Like Keynesian economic theory, Le Corbusier's _urbanisme_ worked because a generation firmly believed it did and conformed their behavior and ideas to the philosophical assumptions of new doctrines. Rational beings accepted a rationalized urban environment because they collectively desired prosperity, modernity and urbanization over poverty and ruralness. The Keynesian scheme, like the Le Corbusier paradigm came partially unraveled during the late 1960s and early 1970s when doubt challenged the authoritarian model implicit in both systems.

The Revitalization of French Capitalism

During the Fourth Republic, French capitalism recovered from a decade of depression, and half a decade of war. Revitalization, however, did not come easily. Vital components of national fiscal policy such as town planning were eventually to become mired in the conflict between the centralized, sectoral development strategies of the CGP and local interests. Keynesian assumptions about the nature of economic growth attracted a corps of national planners from both the academic community and from wartime boards of the Resistance movement who believed that French national prosperity would be the direct result of the successful implementation of their modernization formula, what they called le Plan. During the 1950s, the conflict between the centralisers in Paris at the CGP and the provincial elites deepened. The new institutions of the Plan stimulated an intense wave of migration during these years, producing rapid, and highly selective urbanization across France. As migrants moved to find new jobs and new housing, the distribution of the electorate also changed in both the sending and the receiving districts. Significant voting drift accompanied the population movement explaining in part the erosion of support for the left wing political parties as well as the collapse of the Fourth Republic in 1958.

In 1945, France faced a choice between three methods of Reconstruction: The corporatist planning mechanisms of the late Vichy regime, the Marshall Plan backed by the moderates and Liberals who emerged from the Resistance, and the Stalinist central planning model supported by the French Communist Party.(1) Reconstruction policy addressed the relative backwardness of the French economy, which was blamed for the country's inability to defend itself against the German invasion in May 1940. Restoration of dignity to the national soul became the real goal of Reconstruction along with the renovation of the economy. Major urban industrial areas felt the crisis of backwardness most acutely. War-time decay was compounded by the flood of refugees. Between the Liberation of Paris on August 25, 1944 and the resignation of de Gaulle on January 20, 1946, the French created another new Republic, and more originally, fashioned a reconstruction and planning policy that carefully balanced these three ideologically distinct French approaches to economic management. The history of post-war planning has been that of a constant dynamic quarrel within the planning establishment, and within the larger political community over which type of guidance would be more prominent. The great shock to the system in 1968 would come from those who rejected all three forms of guidance, and the very notion of planned capitalism, planisme.

Post-war planners in France placed the emphasis in reconstruction strategies upon breaking the bottlenecks of slow growth from the early twentieth century. They identified the large agricultural sector, the poor state of energy production and the disorganization of communications and transportation as the critical blockages to modern economic growth in France. What the planners implicitly addressed in the first plans was the infrastructure of urbanization. National economic planning and concomitantly fiscal policy from the beginning rested upon national, or global, level urban planning. Decisions by the CGP in Paris set the parameters for French urban development, and approved local and regional plans.

The urban strategy in the Reconstruction period rested upon powerful decisions made in Paris for the entire nation, and upon serious contradictions. In the drive for rapid modernization, planners concentrated national resources on infrastructure not housing. Existing urban concentrations except the strategically vulnerable northeast and the Paris basin received the most reconstruction aid. These two exceptions, of course, already enjoyed highest levels of good quality infrastructure and housing both public and private. Planners also targeted rural, less unindustrialized areas for development, where the one-time gains from overcoming bottlenecks to growth would be very substantial. The amount of stimulation required to induce real economic growth was far more modest in regions like Brittany, or even the Rhône-Alpes than in the more wealthy Paris region. It did not escape the attention of Monnet and his close advisors at the CGP that the de-emphasized areas in the northeast and in the Paris basin coincided with the zones where the Communists and Socialists enjoyed especially strong electoral support. Those two regions grew slower during these years than the more conservative provinces. Retaining more of their active, and voting population in the provincial towns and cities benefited the moderate and rightist parties.

The urban strategy of the Monnet Plan became the core of the Second Plan, sometimes known as the Plan

Faure after the Radical minister Edgar Faure. This plan established an elaborate urban hierarchy to draw growth away from the older population magnets of Paris and the northeast. Beyond inducing of growth in the selected regions, this plan borrowed some techniques from Soviet urban planning. The Second Plan prohibited certain types of industrial development in Paris much as the Russians were doing in Moscow at the same time. For local and regional planners in the favored areas, rapid growth and centrally defined urbanization strategies came as a mixed blessing. For the first time, since at least the _révolution des maires_ under the early Third Republic, these communes and their needs received attention from national policy makers. Yet at the same time, local elites and planners lost a large degree of control over their own localities to the CGP in Paris with the rush to develop.

The history of urban policy making from the late 1940s through the fall of the Fourth Republic in 1958 can be characterized as a period of intense urban change within the ideological parameters established by the CGP in Paris. But on a deeper level, these years also produced a solid and well trained group of local planners throughout France, who looked increasingly towards a planning system in which they might exercise greater local and regional autonomy.

The Plans

Liberal, Keynesian planners around Monnet placed the Marshall Plan at the basic core of French planning policy with much of the theoretical concepts borrowed directly from the American New Deal. Like Myrdal and Keynes, Monnet and his close advisors preferred State stimulation of the economy through indirect intervention in the market place as employer of last resort. Their State purchased the last unsold goods in order to insure equilibrium in the market. And most importantly, these planners demanded that the State underwrite public works projects beyond the interest and capacities of private developers. In 1946, Monnet and his advisors wanted to see a vast extension of the administrative controls of the Liberal State to facilitate indirect but programmatic regulation of economy. Keynesian style economic management principles changed in France during the Monnet Plan (1947-52). As a consequence of the massive wave of nationalization under the pressure of the Communists and Socialists in the winter of 1944 and 1945, Monnet confronted some distinctly non-Keynesian management problems in the First Plan.(2) Nationalization of a broad range of fundamental industries from basic mining production to transport and communications produced a strong centrifugal drift of management power to the central Parisian planning apparatus, in spite of the fact that the first generation economic planners around Monnet rejected the soviet theory of highly centralized planning. Most stood in absolute horror of Stalinist notions of democratic centralism and a command economy. The fragile Tripartite Government failed to cope with this fundamental conflict between the Communist proponents of rapid nationalization with centralized management and the Liberals of the first Ministry of the National Economy who refused on ideological grounds to engage in long term management of vast sectors of the French economy. The adoption of the Monnet Plan for Reconstruction and Development placed reluctant Keynesian regulators in charge of nationalized firms. Crises of production soon broke out in the nationalized firms when the rank and file of the Communist trade unions reacted to the restoration of traditional labor management practices without even the illusion of workers' control over operations. Tripartism dissolved in March of 1947 when the Communist Party left the governing coalition to go into the opposition and to lead a series of strikes in the newly nationalized industries. Those sectors targeted for the most significant modernization programs under the Monnet Plan faced the most serious strikes and disruptions.(3)

The ancient French quarrel over the proper level of centralization was intimately bound up with the primary question of planning under the Fourth Republic. Nowhere was this more certain than in urban design. Vichy's promise of decentralized, corporatist planning apparatus had been genuinely popular at the local and provincial levels especially in areas like Brittany with a long history of struggle for autonomy.(4) Resistance forces in 1944 and 1945 swept through the communities of France, thoroughly disrupted in many places temporarily displaced the old local and regional elites upon whom much of Vichy's following had been built. Consequently, some of the most severe critics of centralization, and of the Stalinist program of the Communist Party on the most extreme right fell silent after the Liberation. Their absence in business and in town government allowed power to drift with the centrifugal force of the French left towards Paris. Only slowly in the 1950s the old local Vichy elite reemerged. It did so almost universally in the first instance in defense of local issues seemingly of mere parochial concern. In the 1950s, local opposition to centralist policies of the Fourth Republic gave many Vichyites an excuse to reenter political life in France.

In spite of strong disagreements over the purposes and execution of French economic policy, France achieved in the early post-war years a marvelous and new level of prosperity under the Monnet Plan and its successor the Second Plan.(5) But de issues at the base of the French planning system outlived the prosperity and brought France to the crisis of May 1968.(6) Does planning really work? Does it involve significant reductions of personal, social and civil liberties that are unacceptable to large segments of the New Left as well as the Old Right?(7) These philosophical issues also formed the essence of the social criticism of Le Corbusier's Modern Architecture Movement.

Monnet and the CGP

In the fall of 1945, General de Gaulle's Provisional Government turned the problems of immediate reconstruction and longer range planning over to the new Ministry for the National Economy under the direction of Mendès-France. From November 23, 1944 until its replacement by the CGP under Monnet in 1946, economic coordination slipped back into the pattern of the old Third Republic. Irreconcilable squabbles for jurisdiction within the bureaucracy resulted in a moribund economic policy reminscent of the pre-war Republic. This great administrative logjam was broken in part by the increasing pressure of the Americans through the Marshall Plan.

More conservative forces in the Finance Ministry crowded out the fledgling Ministry for the National Economy. Skepticism about the Radical and Third Republic ties of the Ministry for the National Economy permeated the broader financial community still clinging tenaciously to Walrasian ideas about balanced budgets and fiscal prudence. On the far left, the Ministry under Mendès-France faced serious challenge from the French Communist Party, emerging in 1944 from the long Resistance battle at the peak of its prestige and political influence. Radicals lost their political base in the countryside to the Communists and Socialists who swept the municipal elections April and May, 1945. The left parties returned in October to win a powerful majority in the Constituent Assembly elections.

The Communist Party demanded a sweeping program of nationalization in exchange for agreeing to the reestablishment of the Republic and for giving up its arms. The Communist vision of Stalinesque central planning relied heavily upon large nationalized units of production. The initial wave of State takeovers came during the winter of 1944-45 with the nationalization of the coal mines on December 14 and the seizure of Renault on January 16, 1945. More importantly the Assembly nationalized energy, transport and communications industries. State ownership of the airlines came on June 26, 1945. Gas and electricity followed on April 8 of the next year. The nationalization of banking during the December of 1945 confirmed the worst fears of the conservative financial community. Rising Communist power within the country clearly threatened their way of life. The Constituent Assembly elections of October 1945 gave the Communist Party the largest number of deputies on the left with 161 to the Socialist's 150.

Very early in the planning process, the CGP decided to treat most of the nationalized firms as traditional businesses operating in the marketplace under the same constraints of profitability and loss as any other firm. Only electricity and transportation came under special protection from the State. Urban planners in the local communities, therefore, dealt directly with the State in placing new factories or expanding old ones in the nationalized sector while still using traditional marketplace models like those created by Claude Pönsard.

Late in April 1946, the left block of Communists and Socialists in the Constituent Assembly succeeded in passing a draft of the constitution which effectively ratified their economic strategies including the nationalizations. On April 25, 1946, the nationalization of some insurances once again placed a large block of capital in public hands. But the tide began to turn against the leftist parties in early May when voters rejected the proposed constitution by a narrow margin. The second Constitutional Assembly met in June with the economic future of France still in doubt.

At the peak of Communist strength in France, Moscow allowed the long and often wistfully awaited moment of revolution slip away, perhaps forever. In the closing days of the war the head of the French Communist Party, Maurice Thorez returned from exile in Moscow to begin the task of dampening the fires of revolution in France in accordance with Stalin's Minimalist Strategy for the revival of the Western European Communist Parties. In 1944 and 1945, Stalin still held high hopes of receiving reconstruction aid from the United States. Stalin also recognized the logistical difficulties of supporting a sovietization of Western Europe when the Soviet Union had just suffered so much from the war. Hence, the French Communist Party followed the Minimalist Strategy and used their momentary political influence to nationalize a handful of critical sectors, to establish short-lived factory committees and to claim local government posts vacated by the Vichyites.(8) This Minimalist Strategy also appealed to the left wing of the old Socialist Party who favored nationalizations. Thus France emerged in the early post-war period with the largest nationalized sector of any Western style economy, with direct public ownership of slightly less than 15 percent of the large factories and businesses. These firms employed approximately 23 percent of the non-agricultural work force excluding the armed services.(9) Under these new economic conditions, the old debates on the proper configuration of socialism took on new meaning as dialogue over the actual management of real economic activities and not idle theoretical speculation.

Before the war, many of these nationalized industries had had an exceedingly poor record in attracting new capital for upgrading technology and improving marketing practices. As a group they were among the least productive and the least profitable in the entire French economy. Consistently poor management during the late Third Republic compounded problems in these industries. Depression and the Walrasian commitment to balanced State budgets slowed the growth of infrastructure.(10) For coal, electricity and gas, these structural blockages presented serious difficulties for the whole economy even before the Second World War. After the war, in several cases the nationalizations relieved the private sector of some of its worst credit risks. New capital from the Marshall Plan allowed these industries to purchase a whole new generation of technology. Productivity skyrocketed in many areas during the 1950s.

During 1945, Jean Monnet and a handful of advisors from the business world and academic community (Gaillard, Hirsch, Marjolin, Uri and Délouvier) met to lay out a Keynesian style of management as counter-proposal to the programs of the French Socialist and Communist Parties and Monnet focused the discussions on one key issue: The relative backwardness French economic structures in 1945. Of particular concern was the vast pool of underutilized labor in agriculture. Outmoded farming equipment and relatively small scale of production made conditions even worse. A full one-third of the labor force in 1945 worked agricultural production not including the large number of uncounted farmwives.(11)

Beyond the wastage of labor resources, Monnet's group also worried about the poor state of the transit and communications infrastructure which held back the growth of the whole economy. They examined the perennial French questions as well: The lagging birthrate, the vulnerability of the industrial northeast and Paris to invasion, the low rate of capital accumulation. By the end of 1945, these advisors and Monnet had pulled together a framework for the structural changes that would be encorporated in the Monnet Plan for the reconstruction and revitalization of the French economy.(12)

Like Lenin's policy of "governing the heights of the economy," under Monnet's Plan, the French State assumed the role of the most powerful entity in the market. Thus the State would act as guarantor for certain types of private loans, as well as being the purchaser of certain strategic goods and the employer of the last resort. These changes in State behavior were, in the first instance, the work of the handful of essentially private citizens in Monnet's personal entourage. The National Assembly endorsed their recommendations on December 21, 1945, when it created the CGP with Jean Monnet as Chief Commissaire.(13)

After the resignation of General de Gaulle on January 20, 1946, the Tripartite Government of Communists, Socialists and Moderates continued the nationalizations. But Monnet's successful efforts to attract healthy amounts of Marshall Plan dollars began to shift the balance of economic power in France into the hands of his planners who wanted to restore capitalism in a Keynesian form. The American reconstruction aid was, of course, specifically granted to France inorder to build a bulwark against Communism. During the period of vacillation and in-fighting within the coalition government for dominance over economic policy, Monnet at the CGP quickly established a firm but cool working relationship with the private business community. Increasingly alarmed by the growing number of nationalizations and the lack of a coherent direction in national economic policy, Monnet persuaded the financial community to made their peace with Keynesian ideas. As the government vacillated on economic policy, the CGP created an important role for itself by actually directing many aspects of fiscal policy. The CGP theories and policy proposals were developed in relative isolation from either the National Assembly or the Government, and with only wary approval from private financiers. Finally, on November 27, 1946, Monnet presented to the National Assembly a four point plan for the years from 1947 through 1950. It was approved virtually without dissent and without discussion. Monnet stood for rapid modernization, and on that point alone, there was consensus.

Monnet's Plan of 1946 promised full employment, a redistribution of the agricultural labor force, cheap electricity and improvements in transport and communication services. Monnet hoped to recover the 1938 level of production by early 1947, the level of 1929 by the following year and to exceed 1929 levels by 25 percent by the end of the plan in 1950. The distribution of investment credits in the first version of the Plan can be found in Chart One. Monnet targeted investment for two critical producer goods, steel and cement. Both materials were in especially short supply in 1944, and 1945, and still troublesome in 1946. By assigning high investment targets to construction materials, planners tried to ease the development of new factories, mass transit, roads, and housing. Under Pierre Massé Electricité de France (EDF) launched a massive French rural electrification program using special investment funds. These new energy resources boosted agricultural productivity. (Massé left EDF to become the head of the CGP in the 1960s.)

Of all the investment targets in the First Plan, only housing and urban infrastructure fell below anticipated levels by 1950. In large part, the failure of the Monnet Plan in these areas resulted from underlying political conflict between the moderate, Keynesian strategists around Monnet and the badly polarized local governments. While the Monnet Plan represented a careful amalgamation of generally accepted and very broad national economic goals linked to modernization no such consensus existed at the local level. France still lacked effective enabling legislation to govern land use. Local conservatives sought these new laws to protect their existing property rights from the encroachment of the central planning bureau. Ironically, left-wing towns wanted national help for town projects, such as new housing because local resources still remained in ex-Vichyite hands while Gaullist towns refused to cooperate with the CGP because it was the product of the left dominated national government. Monnet was reluctant to invest in the left towns and was frozen out of the conservative communities. Both local factions had found the critical gap in the French planning system: Land use regulation, <u>aménagement du territoire</u>.(14) Neither the national nor the local level had enough control to build over the objections of the other level of government. Housing and urban infrastructure represented nearly fifty percent of the projected investment credits of the Monnet Plan and the lack of effective enabling legislation for local land use made it the most underfulfilled portion of the entire plan.(15)

When Léon Blum formed his cabinet on December 12, 1946, France seemed stuck on a roller coaster of perilously high interest rates rapidly accelerating inflation coupled with unpredictable episodes of the choking off of credit. Ironically, of course, Blum also presided over the Popular Front Government of 1936, in the midst of depression, deflation and the rise of French fascism. While Blum acquiesced to the implementation Monnet Plan and set his economic agenda accordingly, he never abandoned his lingering fears about the authoritarian biases of the process of national economic planning.(16) France during the late 1940s reminded many observers of the last years of the

Third Republic. Vincent Auriol's election as President of the Republic followed Blum's resignation on January 16, 1947. Eduoard Herriot became President of the National Assembly on the twenty-first, and Paul Ramadier was selected as Premier. Yet it was all different from the 1930's because the Monnet Plan had created a regulatory process for economic policy which continued even when Governments fell. The CGP emerged under the new Republic as a regular feature of governance. Monnet's plan also had ushered in a subtle process of economic change which began to erode Socialist and Communist political influence. Monnet placed the substance of the old debates on economic policy beyond the immediate reach of the politicians in the Government and the Assembly. But as his urban policy showed the new process was far from apolitical.

The Politics of Planning in Towns

The Monnet Plan unleashed a tremendous wave of inflation with prices doubling between the end of 1946 and the end of 1947. By the spring of 1947 full employment had nearly been achieved though the real wages of the work force declined sharply. Chart Two shows the dramatic decline in real wages during the start-up phase of the Monnet Plan. Strikes broke out, beginning with the Renault works on April 25 and then moving throughout those specifically designated growth sectors which were key components of the Monnet Plan. Locomotive and wagon production stopped on June 2 and the national railway system faced a general strike five days later. Banks and credit institutions were struck on June 19. Coal miners went out on June 23 and indirectly reduced the production of electricity.

On August 1, the Communist led Confêderation gênêral du Travail (CGT) worked out an 11 percent general wage increase with the Comitê National du Patronat Français (CNPF) the recently formed employers' association. However, the Tripartite Government disallowed their agreement and the strikes continued in automobiles, steel production, Parisian mass transit and in the merchant marine. By November 23, a general strike gripped the country. Two non-Communist labor federations, the Force Ouvrière (FO) under Socialist Lêon Jouhaux and the Christian trade unions under Eugene Descamps opposed the strikes which brought these moderate trade union federations into direct

CHART 1

Investment Capital Under the Monnet Plan, 1947-50

Sector		Percentage
Energy		13.0%
Coal		2.5
Electricity		8.8
Other		1.7
Transport		11.1%
Rails		5.5
Other		5.6
Agriculture		15.8%
Steel and Cement		2.8%
Industry		12.6%
Housing		29.3%
	45.6%	
Urban Infrastructure		16.1%
Total		100%

Source: France. Conseil Economique, *Etudes et Travaux*, no. 7, Annexe, 29-30.

confrontation with the militant Communist CGT which led the strikes.(17) This bitter clash between the major French trade union federations fractured the organized labor movement at the precise moment when France was embarking upon a massive reorganization of many basic industries such as coal mining. The strikes in 1947 brought to an end Socialist and Communist cooperation.

Socialist Léon Blum attempted to form another ministry as the strikes escalated in the fall of 1947. He abandoned his efforts on November 28 after failing to resolve the crisis. Liberal Robert Schuman, Monnet's close associate, replaced Blum. Schuman relaxed the investment schedule of the Monnet Plan. In early December, the strike wave collapsed under the pressures of utter exhaustion and internal divisions. Schuman then offered a modest general wage increase as a means of finishing up the whole business. The general wage increase, of course, evaporated in the still heavy inflation. No change occurred in the real wages of the strikers--a fact that Schuman fully anticipated.

During the second year (1948) of the Monnet Plan, the same general <u>tableau</u> of events--inflation, strikes, general wage increases--threw French social and economic life into chaos once again. At the annual congress of October 11, 1948 Communist leader, Benoît Frachon, head of the CGT denounced the Marshall Plan as the source of the inflation.(18) He offered in contrast to the declining standard of living in the mining towns his vision of a Soviet France.(19) Frachon might have also blamed the Monnet Plan for stimulating the violently high inflation. Curiously enough, the coincidence of high inflation and targeted development zones escaped his notice.

After all, the Monnet Plan was just the national scale version of the Marshall Plan. But how could Frachon criticize the basis of the Monnet Plan with its almost Leninist strategy of "governing the heights of the economy"? Nationalization of the key industries in the targeted growth sectors had been the work of the Communists and Socialists in 1944 and 1945. Back in the fall of 1946, the Communist CGT enthusiastically welcomed the whole policy of full employment, cheap energy, better transport, and urban industrial development. The Communist Party and CGT in their famous Battle for Productivity of 1946 had helped restore both morale in the workplace and the general level of production. To reject such a popular goal seemed foolish and probably unpatriotic. Essentially the CGT and the rest of the left found themselves trapped with the Monnet style of economic management by 1947 and 1948. While Monnet's CGP was too Socialist for much of the traditional French business community, the same planning structure fell far short of the CGT agenda by the end of the decade. Chief economist and close advisor to the CGP, Alfred Sauvy hit the point squarely when he wrote "[Keynes] created the formula for the survival of capitalism." He might have added that the unlikely combination of Monnet, Thorez and Blum were the nurses that brought capitalism back to full health in the days after the Liberation.

The new Republic of the 1950s as an institution was far different than the old Third Republic, and the Fifth Republic of the 1960s intensified these new characteristics. Where the earliest of French Republican traditions had been based upon a relationship between the State and independently powerful individuals in the marketplace and society, the new Republic recognized a dramatic growth in the power of the State and a sharp reduction in the sphere of independent individual actions in the marketplace and in society. Keynesian economic theory was especially well suited to this new type of Republic since the reduction of individual autonomy of action in the marketplace easily meshed with Keynes' properly Positivist, and Freudian for that matter, assumptions about the regular characteristics of behavior by consumers, producers and investors.

In these years, the conservative political mainstream: Gaullism suffered from an internal contradiction. De Gaulle's personal following came those solid, middle level Frenchmen of the right. Extremist ginger-groups gave these mainstream Gaullists little peace. With the Poujade political movement in 1956, the rifts within the movement became even more serious. Poujade appealed to the small entrepreneur who had been left out of the Growth Miracle. As the capitalism of the family farms and the small shop gave way to agri-business and supermarkets, the Gaullist movement temporarily lost this segment of its constituency to special interest groups advocating a return to the old <u>mentalité</u> of the prosperous petty bourgeois. To some provincials, Le Corbusier's mechanical, modern and efficient approach to design and urban planning, seemed an affront to the basic values

CHART 2

Prices and Wages, 1946-1949

(1946 = 100)

	Wholesale Prices	Hourly Wages	Real Wage Rate
January 1946	100	100	100
January 1947	182	143	61
February 1948	320	239	- 20
January 1949	406	287	-139

Source: France. Ministère des Finances, *Inventaire de la Situation Financière* (1951), 144, 148.

of these neo-conservative ginger groups within Gaullism. Neo-conservative groups in this period tended towards a veneration of traditionalism which stressed the diversity of French provincial culture. Both Le Corbusier and Monnet spent much of their careers in attempting to purge that traditionalism from the French soul. Intervention by Parisian centraliser's was resisted with vigor, as were the impulses to standardize and rationalize land use in towns and small cities. Movements like the Poujadists, drew their candidates from the ancient local notables. These modestly wealthy civic leaders had strong parochial interests in the physical land use plans for their communities, since plans impacted directly upon the value and control of the only property that they possessed. It was from these groups that Le Corbusier's philosophy received the greatest resistance. Monnet's plan faced the same opposition in the provinces.

Local notables, who were the old elites of rural France, faced serious challenge from the Socialists and Communists during the reconstruction period. When the CGP initiated the rural to urban exodus it stripped away labor resources and pushed up wages in the countryside in the name of modernity. In some election districts migration, the changes distorted voting patterns for an entire decade. To these threatened elites urbanization and Le Corbusier's aesthetic principles for modern urban development were more than an insult to decency, they challenged to the actual survival of the old elite.

Housing Under the Fourth Republic

Two million housing units had been damaged or destroyed during the war. The pre-war housing deficit in 1946 stood at four to six million units. These shortages fell disproportionately in the rural areas and in the Paris region. Under the Monnet Plan, France tried to construct 200,000 new units with the majority of the homes targeted for the existing major urban zones. Many new units took the form of Le Corbusier's grandes ensembles in the suburbs of Paris. Their stark functional appearance reflected the scarcity of construction materials, the hurried nature of their placement and the frenetic pattern of labor mobility in the post-war period.(20)

Despite public housing programs, the vast majority of this new housing went to upper income, private purchasers who relied extensively on personal savings since mortgages remained virtually impossible to obtain until 1948.(21) Public housing under the new HLM program of 1948 attempted to stabilize the rental market by providing additional units in the middle income range. The law also froze some rents.(22) During this period private investors generally preferred to place their monies in the rapidly growing industries under the shelter of the Monnet Plan.

Le Corbusier's functional approach to architecture coincided with the needs of the narrow and aggressive economic growth plans that left little room for design frills. Yet the patterns of land use for the placement of the new residences and even public buildings in some ways still remained close to the practices of the Third Republic until the mid-1950s.(23) Land use planning only existed as an informal local consensus between civil administrators and local businessmen rarely carrying the weight of law. Industrial and residential site selection, however, was far from a random process. Under the first and second plans, the CGP selected new sites for development with little or no consultation at the local level. New construction in the short run from 1947 to 1954 was fostered in the existing developed zones in order to maximize the use of common infrastructure which was in extremely short supply. Those choices sometimes gave the illusion of a degree of local control since the actions reinforced the existing patterns of land use within the community.

The slow growth in urban infrastructure and in housing outside of the major cities reflected the low priority given to new urban development under the Monnet Plan. Another critical factor blocking development in many areas was the dramatic and temporary shift of local political power to the left as Resistance leaders displaced the local elites which had served the Vichy regime. The membership of town councils swung towards the left in the municipal elections of the spring of 1945 and only began to recede after 1952. Even in areas where the Gaullist Resistance dominated the local governments saw the wholesale disenfranchisement of large segments of the traditional local elite. These grassroots changes brought into decision making positions individuals who lacked previous experience in local administration, having served either in the opposition or in very subordinate capacities during much of the Third Republic. The local disruption temporarily destroyed the town level traditional elite consensus between civil administrators, businessmen and civic leaders over the specific goals for town development.(24)

Such basic questions of where to build the new road or the new sewer line seemingly mundane matters of simple engineering becamed intense political issues. For the Gaullist local leaders, the departure of de Gaulle from active political life in January of 1946 signaled the beginning of a retreat from national politics, and greater involvement in local government. As conservatives, the Gaullist political leaders appealed to the same constituency as the old local elite. Gaullists often appropriated the programme or traditional local agenda for development. During the following decade, this identification with the traditional development consensus proved to be extremely valuable in the survival and reemergence of Gaullism as a political force with firm local roots.(25)

This fundamental disruption of the local consensus and local government after the Second World War intensified the strongly vertical of decision making tendancies of the CGP. Keynesian macroeconomic theory, of course, strongly reinforced this trend toward strong national level oversight over local decision making bodies. In order to ensure an adequate flow of information to the central investment bodies in the government, the CGP needed regular, precise and standardized lower organs in the economy and in the State. The failure to achieve the complete organization of the economy on such a model was a primary cause of the shortfalls in the national plans of the Fourth Republic. Consequently, only 35 percent of the funds targeted for housing and urban development under the Monnet Plan were actually spent. Lengthy delays at the local level stymied many efforts to build housing.(26)

Planning After Monnet

Monnet left the CGP in 1950, to direct the European Coal and Steel Community, and was replaced by Etienne Hirsch as Chief Commissaire.(27) Hirsch turned the CGP in the following decade towards an agenda that went the next step beyond Reconstruction, to planning for new growth and increasing French competitiveness in the world market. Hirsch improved the French planning system by encouraging greater technical sophistication in the four year national economic forecasts that underpinned the plans. He also attempted to extend the standardization of planning towards the local level. During this next phase of economic planning, the CGP began drawing upon the wealth of statistical data generated by Alfred Sauvy at l'institut national de la statistique et des études économiques (INSEE) and l'institut national de la statistique des études démographiques (INSED). The two post-war censuses and a special industrial survey in the early 1950s yielded substantial and reliable information about patterns of urban growth and labor force change using more standardized measures of local conditions. Demographic studies with extensive modeling became widely used in CGP forecasting after 1952, and contributed significantly to the far greater precision in defining the goals of the Second Plan, known as the Plan Faure (1952-57). The Second Plan attempted to diffuse growth and development more fully throughout the French economy. A high priority was placed on limiting the growth of Paris in tandem with CGP's commitment to upgrading other regional urban centers.

Under the guidance of French urban economist Claude Ponsard, the CGP drew upon the new census data to create a sophisticated geographic hierarchy of urban uses in France. Planners and demographers designated a handful of major cities as poles-of- attraction.(28) Marseilles, Bordeaux, Grenoble, Le Havre and Lyons were to grow to counterbalance the centrifugal force of Paris, the primate city. The strategy certainly borrowed from Ebenezer Howard's classic Garden City design which promised a balance between competing urban zones. It also reflected the actual pattern of French migration in the period between the censuses of 1946 and 1954 where the shift away from agriculture brought millions to these same major cities.

The concept of slowing migration to the capital, however, failed. Planners had become better at measuring population shifts than at altering the actual movement of people. The shift in the active labor force in France by sector from before the First World War to 1954 can be seen in the third chart. The active population dropped after the Second World War. A large number of retirements of small proprietors, farmers on family farms and shopkeepers in small shops vanished during the post-war wave of consolidation. The relatively small size of the pool of job entrants during this period came from the very low French birthrate during the Depression and the war. Consequently, labor costs in the 1950s rose briefly as industries were forced to compete for the available manpower. Workers enjoyed much higher living standards in these years. Both the Socialist and Communist Parties lost electoral support among the working class. The intensely bitter Algerian War kept the size of the migrant work force small. All of these factors produced a moderate labor shortage. The Second Plan's agenda for deconcentration of industry to promote a broader national prosperity coincided with industry's own desire to entice more labor out of the poorly paid, underemployed agricultural sector.

Implementation of planning decisions became more difficult during the Second Plan. In the wake of the erosion of leftist support in the National Assembly open hostility broke out between the Communist and Socialist Parties which effectively precluded and joint policy proposals on the left. At the local level, ex-Vichyites began their comeback in the municipal elections of 1951, a process culminating in March 1952 with the Pinay government which lasted until December. An old line conservative and a late comer to the Resistance, Pinay restricted the growth of the money supply and tightened national bank credits in an attempt to hold back inflation in the rapidly expanding French economy. His policies echoed the cautious balanced budget approach of the late Third Republic that haunted French decision making through the Depression years. After breaking the inflation, Pinay turned the management of the economy over to the agencies that would implement the Second Plan.

From 1951 through 1957, national income in France rose by nearly 25 percent (20 percent in the still large agricultural sector, and 30 percent in industry). Income per capita increased by four percent each year. In contrast, the rate in the United States in the slump recession of the 1970s was only 0.8 percent. France created over 350,000 new jobs in industry, services and the government sector over the course of the Second Plan. Housing construction soared to unprecedented levels, with the actual construction of over 200,000 units per year. These new units were located primarily in the key regional cities which had been designated as poles-of-attraction to counterbalance the Paris region.

Planners targeted the new homes for all those persons pushed from the agricultural sector in to the industrial one. Marseilles, Bordeaux, Grenoble, La Havre, and Lyons received large allotments of public housing credits while the credits for the Paris region fell dramatically.(29)

The creation of provincial New Towns from wholly public funds crested by 1958. Communities like Mourenx at Lacq went up for the natural gas industry, Héronville-Saint-Clair for the autoworks at Caen, Bagnols-sur-Cèze for the atomic reactor at Marcoulé.(30) New Towns attracted the labor being forced out of the agricultural sector thus slowing the flood of migrants to Paris. Over the four-year cycle, the Plan supported these New Towns by pumping 6,700,000F into energy, transportation and housing. The Plan also reduced a variety of taxes for highly productive industries which chose to locate in provincial areas with poor records of job creation. Citroën, for an example, moved part of its operation into Brittany and Normandy. Renault and some of its subsidiaries followed as well. While the shift to the provinces meant escape from the high wage costs of Paris, the move still remained unattractive to a broad range of industrial groups. Paris was the optimum point in France for distribution within both the domestic and foreign markets. The research and development facilities of Paris could not be duplicated elsewhere. For a manufacturer with only one or two plants and a relatively small share of the domestic market, such a move was continued to be unthinkable. Only the very largest corporations like Citroën could take advantage of the lower labor costs and tax incentives.

In 1954 and 1955 the National Assembly enacted enabling legislation for urban planning. The decree on industrial development of September 14, 1954 established a broad range of financial incentives to employers to decentralize their operations away from Paris by specifying urban growth targets as poles-of-attraction. In December, 1955, another decree directly forbade the expansion of Parisian manufacturing and storage facilities beyond ten percent of existing capacity.(31)

The Assembly also altered parts of the planning process at CGP and the Ministry for Construction.

CHART 3
Active Population by Sector
(thousands)

	1906	1931	1946	1954
Agriculture	41.9%	31.0%	32.2%	26.7%
	8,240	6,250	6,200	5,124
Non-Agriculture	58.1%	69.0%	67.8%	73.3%
Proprietors	1,396	1,558	--	1,070
Independent	2,601	1,901	--	1,654
Wage Labor	7,415	10,449	9,882	11,304
(Unskilled)	(4,764)	(7,003)	--	(6,485)
Total	19,652	20,158	19,237	19,152

Source: Patrick Allard, Michel Beaud, _et al_, _Dictionnaire des Groupes industriels et finances en France_ (Paris: Seuil, 1978), p. 13.

Under the reforms, planning and construction were separated from each other. By the mid-1950s management not rapid modernization had become the primary goal for French planners in Paris. In 1954, the CGP was shifted to the Finance Ministry under Edgar Faure. This move intensified the support for elaborate econometric

modeling within the planning process as the extensive economic indicators collected for the Finance Ministry now came directly to the CGP as well.

A series of decrees on June 30 and October 18, 1955 accompanied the administrative reorganization. Four primary funds for economic management were established under the supervision of the Finance Ministry. These funds extended the scope of the older program les Fonds pour la Dévéloppement des Equipements Sociales (FDES) which drew directly on the capital reserves of the Banque de France and Treasury bills. These decrees created four new development funds: Fonds National de Modernisation et d'Equipement (FNME); Fonds National d'Aménagement du Territoire (FNAT); Fonds national de Productivité (FNP); and Fonds de Construction d'Equipement Rural et d'Expansion Economique (FCEREE). The Caisse des Dépôts et Consignations played a key role in coordinating these new public investment programs with private development. François Bloch-Lainé head of the Caisse led the movement to rationally coordinate both private and public investment capital under the guidance of the Plans.(32)

The Second Plan also addressed the site selection problems of housing and industry in an attempt to channel these investment funds in a balanced and orderly fashion throughout the country. A law of 1955 required departments and major cities to design land use plans for the placement of the new housing units in the precise areas where new job growth was being induced. Town planners drew up zones d'urbanisme prioritaire (ZUPs) which became the primary unit for local expansion.(33) These areas were defined by population density, housing, basic infrastructure needs and potential employment capacity. Each ZUP needed approval by the departmental prefect; and each large project using national funds still required approval from the Ministries of Construction and Finance. The central ministries pursued their oversight responsibilities very vigorously during the 1950s.(34)

By the mid-1950s local and regional leaders began demanding a system of planned growth which allowed a far greater degree of local control. Ironically, as in the nationalizations, it was the left deputies who sponsored the enabling legislation for greater regional autonomy in planning. The greater regional and local autonomy simply tightened the controls of the restored old town elites across France. From this greater regional autonomy for leaders of the local business community, the local consensus on the right flourished and came to firmly underpin the Gaullist regime. In the decree of June 30, 1955, only the very largest projects, such as New Towns and large apartment complexes in the Parisian suburbs, still required central approval while small projects could be initiated at the local level.

External Influences on Planning

The Schuman Plan also played a role in the growth miracle of the 1950s. The National Assembly ratified the Schuman Plan on December 13, 1952, the day after approving the Second Plan. In 1950 Monnet and Schuman left domestic planning and began an extended analysis of the entire question of the economic renovation of Europe. The Schuman Plan identified the areas in the European market where France faced the most favorable market conditions. The plan called for growth in the traditional French products--wines, food stuffs, *objets d'art*. But, new fields also were stressed: Consumer durables, automobiles, high technology.(35) To an extent during the Second Plan development goals in the domestic economy became tied to those fields where the planners felt that the French had a clear competitive advantage within the European community. With Monnet and Schuman at the helm of the Europe-wide planning process, the CGP held an important vantage point in long-range policy making. The regions with targeted industries received development aid and those with less favored industries saw their funding sources reduced as French planning became more sophisticated in its assessment of the total European market. Under the influence of the Schuman Plan, regional development during the Second Plan came to be focused on the improvement of the general infrastructure in the Moselle valley, the reorganization of urban land uses in the Bas-Rhône and Languedoc region and the industrial development of the departments in the southwest. Older developed areas such as the coal mining and steel producing region of the Nord-Pas-de-Calais received less attention from planners. According to Schuman and Monnet, it had become cheaper to import finished German steel than to produce steel in France. Their cosmopolitan approach to economic planning disturbed the chauvinistic segment of French society which still keenly felt the wartime losses. In the late 1950s, de Gaulle appealed to that deep nationalistic current, which was an early indication of his own ideological distance from Monnet's planning tradition.

All this tremendous expansion, the Growth Miracle of the 1950s rested upon an increasingly fragile political structure. The left wing forces that had given the early Fourth Republic definition continued to decline while the Gaullists became increasingly disenchanted with the Fourth Republic. The number of left voters and deputies fell from a high point by the Liberation period of nearly fifty percent of the electorate to barely a third during the first elections of the Fifth Republic as seen on Chart Four. The two periods of the most dramatic decline in leftist electoral fortunes coincided with the most intensive years of the Monnet Plan from 1947 to 1950 and the Second Plan from its effective implementation in 1956 through abandonment eighteen months later. The election of former Vichyite René Coty, on December 23, 1953, as President of the Republic confirmed the shift to the right. A couple of weeks later on January 12, another conservative, André Le Troquer replaced Edouard Herriot, the veteran statesman, as president of the National Assembly. On October 10, 1954, the Congress of the Socialist Party instructed its deputies that they should refuse to join the Radical ministries, first that under Mendès-France and then that of Edgar Faure. In this more conservative political atmosphere that the Second Plan had been approved by a divided Assembly in May of 1955, with most major areas of ideological dispute deferred to the CGP for resolution.(36) The Assembly chose not to debate the Plan in detail and that reflected the weaknesses and uncertainties of the party groupings during the last years of the Republic.

The Third Plan went to the National Assembly on March 15, 1958. But a few weeks later the crisis of May 13 brought down the Fourth Republic.(37) During the late spring of 1958, the Algerian war reached its breaking point. Military leaders had become frustrated and angered by their inability to defeat the vast popular guerrilla movement in 1956 and 1957. The generals in North Africa vented their frustrations on the Governments in Paris. On May 9, 1958, word came that the Algerian national liberation movement had executed three French prisoners. General Salan, the top ranking French general in Algeria, on the same day sent back to his superiors in Paris an ominously worded telegram that seemed to threaten the overthrow of the Republic at the hands of the generals in Algeria. Over the next few days a variety of political and popular figures approached General de Gaulle asking him to rally to the support of the Republic. On May 23 committees of _salut public_, like those that had welcomed Napoléon I back from Elba, sprang up in the southwest and near Lyons (a target for rapid growth during the Second Plan). The next day a committee of _salut public_ in Ajacco proclaimed Corsica independent. Many politicians in Paris took the news as the first signal for a general revolt by the military against the civilian government in Paris.

De Gaulle stepped into this crisis on May 27. He accepted extraordinary powers from the Assembly to protect the Government from a potential military revolt. Only the Socialist deputies dissented. Even some of the Socialists broke ranks a few days later when de Gaulle sought approval for his new Government from the Assembly. The Socialists split 42 for de Gaulle and 49 against in the vote of June 1. By then the potential military insurrection had evaporated and French authority had been firmly reestablished in Corsica. Indeed, the settlement of the crisis had been so swift that many observers were left questioning exactly which general had really planned the coup, Salan or de Gaulle.

Conclusion

In this supercharged political atmosphere, the Third Plan's overly precise and graduated investment projections did not correspond with the violently wide swings in the money market and in trade, as the economy in 1958 and 1959 reacted to the major shifts in political power as de Gaulle settled into office. In spite of political upheaval economic expansion continued. It simply began to occur in the wrong places according to the Third Plan. Even with all the turmoil in the political arena, national income raced

CHART 4
Post-War Elections in France

Date	Deputies Elected		Percentage of Total Vote			Percentage of Abstentions
	Communists	Socialists	Communists	Socialists	C + S	
October 1945	161	150	26%	23%	49%	25%
June 1946	153	129	25%	21%	46%	22%
November 1946	183	105	28%	17%	45%	28%
June 1951	101	107	26%	14%	40%	25%
January 1956	150	99	25%	15%	40%	21%
November 1958	10	40	18%	15%	33%	32%

Source: Richard Hamilton, *Affluence and the French Worker in the Fourth Republic*, (Princeton: Princeton University Press, 1967), 22.

ahead at the very respectable rate of three to four percent per capita during the late 1950s. De Gaulle began his presidency in prosperity and new found political stability.

CHAPTER FOUR

The Gaullist Minuet (1958-1968)

Gaullist France has defied narrow historical judgement, but historians of the early Fifth Republic generally agree that the regime was built upon a powerful internal contradiction. De Gaulle appealed to the neo-conservative national elite because the General offered political stability, higher international prestige and the protection of domestic economic interests. The new President placed the powerful centralizing institutions that had emerged under the former Republic in the hands of administrators faithful to French capitalism. At the same time, his electoral coalition stood squarely upon the local *notables*, those well-born and successful local elites throughout the provinces. The two constituencies, the neo-conservative national cadre and the local *notables* held certain values in common, but their primary economic interests were diametrically opposed. Perhaps the most dramatic contest between the factions within the governing coalition came during the Fifth National Plan. That policy was cut to narrow Keynesian specifications. The Keynesian formula for prosperity fit very well with the Gaullist drive towards a powerful State apparatus, that at the same time could claim to stand upon a scientific understanding marketplace behavior.

By early Fifth Republic, Le Corbusier finally received the acclaim that had eluded him for so much of his career. A full generation of French urban planners, architects, engineers and civil servants had grown up with Le Corbusier's models. They made design decisions using his artistic and theoretical framework, much in the same way that the economists in the CGP and at the Finance Ministry based economic policies on Keynesian assumptions. The previous decade of real growth and broadening prosperity gave planners the opportunity actually to build new towns, to redesign industrial suburbs and to renew city slums.

Under the Fourth Republic, the Construction Ministry built _grandes ensembles_ and new towns with dispatch and with highly centralized decision making structures. By the Gaullist period, a backlash against central planning structures was felt in Paris. Deconcentration of planning for physical land use became one of the most controversial issues within the Gaullist movement during the early Fifth Republic. _Urbanistes_ (planners) trained in Le Corbusier's image overwhelmingly rejected all moves to resuscitate municipal Taylorism. Planners feared the parochial attitudes of the local _notables_ and the constraints of local budgets. It meant rolling back the entire Movement for Modern Architecture and rebuking Le Corbusier himself. In the early Fifth Republic the neo-conservative centralizers and the local _notables_ fought each other for dominance in the Gaullist movement over the issues of urban and economic development policy.

Le Corbusier's own work was modest during the last decade of his life. It consisted mainly of lecturing and clarifying his earlier design principles. These final influences will be examined in detail in the following chapter, which analyzes the breakdown of the Gaullist historical moment during the late 1960s. The stark message of Le Corbusier's New Brutalism sketches in a sense fore-shadowed the Gaullist crisis of 1968. The May riots in Paris brought the early Fifth Republic to a close, ending the illusions of collaboration between the two key factions in the Gaullist coalition. Neo-conservative national elites saw their interests temporarily eclipsed by the local _notables_ who claimed more autonomy for regional and local decisions. The debates of 1968 took on a stark character, and many observers feared that the Fifth Republic would not survive the criticism.

New Directions in Urbanization Policy

President Charles de Gaulle reorganized French political structures under the new Constitution of 1958, with a far stronger central focus in policy making. But this political centralization was carefully balanced by a more rigorous and active local and regional Gaullist elite. In exchange for their political support the provincial leaders demanded a deconcentration and streamlining of town planning procedures. In a sense, national economic and town planning, <u>planisme</u> and <u>urbanisme</u> were recast by the Gaullist regime in an even more properly Keynesian framework than actually had been the case under the late Fourth Republic. Instead of Soviet-style, aggressive nationalizations and large public projects, the State favored the indirect regulation of essentially private investment decisions. Keynes had advocated precisely that less intrusive formula in the 1930s. When Keynes' wartime aide, Jean Monnet welcomed the General to office in 1958, he offered full support for de Gaulle's attempt to "stabilize" France and to redefine economic policies.(1)

In the late 1950s and early 1960s, the Gaullist Fifth Republic drastically reorientated urban policies, and began strengthening the powers of the local and regional elites. The Government favored private development instead of public development, drastically reducing the historic commitment to New Towns, Garden Cities. This transition in urban policy making came in stages because of strong opposition from neo-conservative centralists within governing circles.

The first step came when the Ministry of Construction assumed many of the urban oversight tasks of the CGP during the failure of the Third Plan, which had been directed by the centralist Chief Commissaire Etienne Hirsch. In 1960 and 1961, the the Interim Plan replaced the regular plan. After the 1962 legislative elections which placed a firm Gaullist majority in charge of economic policy making in the National Assembly, the Ministry of Construction was forced to relax some central controls over urban planning. The growing tendency to favor local and regional Gaullist special interests in town planning emerged as an important political issue by 1962. Hirsch left the CGP, but the provincial Gaullists failed to replace him with one of their own. Another committed centralist, Pierre Massé became the new head of the CGP. Under Massé, the CGP fought to recover the planning authority which had slipped away to the regions.

Valéry Giscard d'Estaing became Finance Minister just as Massé joined the CGP. While determined neo-conservative centralists like Massé and Giscard retained nominal control over urban and economic development, their positions constantly were undercut by the intense factional rivalries within the governing coalition.

At the same time, sociologists and economists from a wide variety of ideological viewpoints began to critique the successes and failures of urbanisme in the post-war period. Some analysts regarded planned change as a modern means of behavior modification on a mass scale. Like critique of the Radicals of the late Third Republic, to this new generation of critics these controls seemed to threaten individual autonomy in society and in the marketplace. Their debates foreshadowed the ideological dimensions of the crisis of May 1968. In the short run, however, the anti-planiste arguments bolstered the hand of the provincials against the centralists within the Gaullist coalition.

The planning formulas of the new Republic placed great emphasis upon clarifying and expediting funding decisions through the central ministerial chains of command. Regional and departmental prefectures took charge of implementation. For the largest of the nationalized industries, like Renault or EDF, central ministerial intrusions into production questions virtually ceased. The new approach swung heavily towards indicative planning. State control increasingly rested upon the central monopoly in the information services: INSEE and INED, and on the budget constraints of the Finance Ministry. Consequently, the educational apparatus of the CGP expanded. The administration and social science sections of the Grandes Ecoles grew. In 1963, central oversight for urban planning was shifted once again, going from the Ministry of Construction to the CGP which was housed in the Finance Ministry. The change signaled the recognition of the fiscal significance of the large scale investment decisions by the central government and the smaller projects of towns and departments. Such development decisions accounted for a very large component of total public expenditures. Coordination of the magnitudes and timing of such investment decisions was of course central to the French style Keynesian management. The old configuration of the CGP in one ministry and the urban development bureaux in another had hampered efforts to balance the economy during the early Fifth Republic.

The Fifth National Economic Plan (1965-1970) represented by far the most synthetic statement of the new approach to planning. It became the immediate focal point for the anti-planiste rebellion in May 1968.(2) The Fifth Plan was conceived and drawn, of course, from 1962 to 1964, precisely when the change in planning policy was the center of debate.

The period from 1958 to 1968 saw a powerful diffusion of real economic growth and development in the provinces: The goal of the Second and Third Plans. Real economic growth, improved living standards and a popular perception of prosperity the electoral fortunes of the French left. Yet the growing conservative voting block in the National Assembly and in the local town councils found itself increasingly uncomfortable with the development strategies of the central Gaullist government. As anonymous large corporations swallowed up the small entrepreneurs, part of the identity of provincial Gaullist voters evaporated along with the small shops and farms. The reaction by the surviving provincials finally pushed the Gaullist centralists from office after the 1965 presidential election.

In 1965, François Mitterrand, with the blessings of Jean Monnet, unsuccessfully challenged Charles de Gaulle for the presidency of the Republic. Mitterrand supported a restoration of the centralism of the late Fourth Republic. De Gaulle to the dismay of some who had welcomed him in 1958 swung closer to the provincial faction in his coalition. While the debate in 1965 focused upon the critical ideological issues separating the _planistes_ of the Fourth Republican left and the new Fifth Republic right, it did not anticipate the dimensions of the gap between the _planistes_ and _anti-planistes_ that marked the 1968 crisis. Hirsch and Monnet broke with de Gaulle in 1965. De Gaulle's support of regional special interests on the issue of membership in the Common Market alienated both of the former chiefs of the CGP.(3)

Le Corbusier drowned at the resort Cap-Martin in 1965 also leaving his ideas to an uncertain future. Centralist and provincial interests within planning for towns and the French economy became more politically important after 1965.

Supple Planning for a Mature Economy

Hirsch directed the last plan of the Fourth Republic: The Third Four Year Plan of 1956-60. His technically sophisticated plan rested heavily upon complex and rather optimistic econometric forecasting of employment and real growth. Hirsch pledged the projected growth in tax revenues under this proposed bubble of prosperity to cover an extensive public works effort by the Ministry of Construction, a proposal with more than a casual similarity to the Haussman episode of the Second Empire. Twelve free standing, comprehensive New Towns, housing nearly 2,500,000 residents all with heavy State subsidies, left the drawing boards for implementation over a short four year plan cycle. Hirsch and the CGP hoped to use the new housing and urban infrastructure to retain labor in the countryside, and slow the migration to Paris.(4)

The Third Plan allocated public works funds through the Construction Ministry using a model of distribution which had been produced under the direction of Claude Pönsard, the urban economist, and Alfred Sauvy, the economic historian.(5) As key advisors to the Third Plan, Pönsard and Sauvy persuaded the CGP to make its decisions on the creation of infrastructure and housing based upon a carefully defined hierarchy of urbanization. This hierarchy of cities placed Paris, dubiously known as the primate city, at the top of the scale, with eight other major urban areas designated as poles-of- attraction, each having enough growth potential to eventually balance the attraction of the capital for labor and business. The remaining cities in France fell along a scale that extended down to <u>cantons</u> of a mere 2000 persons at the bottom parameter of urbanization. In this urban hierarchy, the demarcations often failed to follow traditional provincial boundaries, much to the dismay of the regionalist factions in national politics. In Brittany, for instance, the new system assigned the ancient provincial capital of Nantes to the adjoining region of the Pays de la Loire. While the hierarchy of urbanization broke down into a series of sub-national networks, following the logic of von Thunën's rings (as they had been modernized by Törg Palander and Bertil Ohlin), these clusters did not resemble older historical entities in many cases. The key to the system was a primary allocation of urban space and function on the simple basis of contemporary population densities.(6) In its most simplistic form, the Third Plan attempted to guide the allocation of new public works and economic growth on the basis of the population distribution. This basis for the allocation of State development aids became an important factor in the competition between cities and regions during the late 1950s and early 1960s, which indirectly fueled older provincial rivalries. After the mid-1950s, rural regions, smaller cities and towns became very concerned about their levels of outward migration which put the region or urban zones at a serious disadvantage in the competition for funds from the State.

The second objective of the Third Plan intended to complete the work of Monnet Plan by transfering even more labor from agriculture into the more modern industrial and service sectors. These changes in the rural employment picture widened the gap between the growing urban zones and the declining countryside. In turn, this employment strategy placed agricultural regions at a disadvantage in competitions for government aid. Alfred Sauvy envisioned the Third Plan as the chief vehicle for a one time reduction in the size of the rural work force which would thrust France into a Second Industrial Revolution, thereby guaranteeing prosperity for the next generation.(7) He argued that modern industrial expansion, with a leap into new technologies, could only take place when large amounts of labor were transferred to the industrial sector, temporarily producing an abundant pool of cheap labor that in turn would induce business to invest large amounts in new plants and equipment. If it was to remain cheap and attractive to business, this massive transfer of labor must be held outside of the Paris region with its notoriously high wages and strong trade unions.(8) Hence the development of industrial and service sites in other major cities was critical to holding labor in the relatively lower cost matrix of the provinces.

The French never really had a chance to discover whether this system of governing State investment on the basis of population density worked since de Gaulle abandoned the Third Plan in 1959. The Third Plan fell far short of its targets in almost every category. The process of redefining planning policy under the new Fifth Republic began as soon as Hirsch left the CGP.(9) Important changes both in fiscal policy and in urban development followed his departure. Monetary stabilization and stimulating job growth in the private sector formed the core of the Interim Plan for 1960 and 1961. A less heralded third policy permitted Paris to resume unfettered suburban growth.

Under the early Fifth Republic, the State and the planning process slipped into the hands of a group within the governing elite that fully appreciated

Keynes' dictum that direct State control over production, nationalization, was unnecessary for the successful management of the marketplace and capitalism. A key architect of the new policy Valéry Giscard d'Estaing, helped transform in French planning strategies during the early 1960s when France took up supple planning. With great insight the Finance Minister Giscard pointed out that "public expenditure, which represents 40 percent of national production, and covers all fields of activity, taxes on income and expenditure of individuals and companies, and stimulating action on their investments, are powerful weapons in society's fight to gain control of its own development." Giscard defined this role of the State by analogy to the human body, where the State "must let the mechanisms of the market regulate the basic workings of the economy, which it can then correct and complete. In this way the conscious mind picks up and guides spontaneous movements."(10)

The legislative elections of 1962 and the Fourth Economic Plan for 1962 to 1965 provided the vehicles for recasting planning philosophy along more properly Keynesian lines. In a moment of great embarassment, the Socialists failed to find candidates to stand for election in many districts. Incumbent Socialist deputies often rejected the party label. Even moderate regionalist candidates swung towards the Gaullist coalition, seeking multiple endorsements. The French Communist Party fielded candidates in most districts but did extremely poorly, obtaining less than 20 percent of the vote and fewer than 15 percent of the seats in the Chamber of Deputies.(11) A large block of voters abstained from the election to oppose the seemingly authoritarian features of the new Gaullist Constitution.

These elections in 1962 refocused the attention of the French political system on its regional diversity. The Gaullist coalition attempted to consolidate its grassroots under the General by identifying with regional civic and business elites, each striving to maximize the economic well-being of their regions, at the expense of every other region and sometimes with France as a whole. This competitive and decentralist model indirectly buttressed the powers of the local and regional elites which held great real economic power over the jobs and well-being of the vast majority of the French work force. Even as late as 1972, small businesses with fewer than 200 workers employed 36 percent of the labor force as seen in Chart One. Roadway renovations, for instance, were of vital significance to small businesses who depended completely on local traffic. These small and medium sized businesses had to worry about the specific impact of every modest decision for the configuration of the urban environment in their particular town. State tax incentives and public investment policies also loomed very large in the calculations of these highly vulnerable local businesses.

The Fourth Plan in some ways began to deconcentrate the structure of planning decision making to the regional level, giving these regional leaders in the business community a glimpse at dynamic control over their immediate economic environment.(12) But these changes were an illusion to a great extent, since the next Fifth National Economic Plan swept away hundreds of these small businesses in a massive wave of mergers.

Gaullist economic planners increasingly turned towards regional level schemes for the implementation of planning policies during the 1960s. Where the planning decisions of the Fourth Republic and especially in the Second and Third Plans had been implemented from the central CGP and the ministries, the Fourth Plan on the contrary went into effect under the decrees of March 14, 1964 for regional and departmental reform. As during the Vichy years, regional prefects drew up new master plans for the assignment of land uses and for major public works projects. The decree of December 4, 1964 completed the regional decision making framework, by charging regional chambers of commerce and industry with the duty and privilege of advising the regional prefects on the most important local projects and on the most effective means of implementation.

These decrees by Premier Georges Pompidou established a Commission de Dévelopment Économique Régional (CODER) for each of the twenty French regions.(13) The new regional development corporations formed the core of the new approach to French planning under the Gaullist regime. Each regional prefect or his designee chaired the development corporation which reported directly to the CGP on the regional level implementation of the national economic policies. Regional prefects carefully selected the membership of the CODER from technical experts on their own staff and among the faculties of local universities, prominent businessmen, trade union representatives and local civic leaders. CODER members met frequently in general sessions to propose and discuss local projects which might satisfy the objectives of the national plan. Regional prefects either approved or disapproved of the proposals but did not initiate them. An approved project could receive the State funds from categorial aid packages under the direct control of the regional prefect. If the available State funds were insufficient to complete the given local project, as they invariably were, the regional prefect could either solicit more funds from local businesses or from the State by requesting a special act of the National Assembly. In either case, the regional prefect's effectiveness in completing local projects rested most critically upon his ability to win the active and enthusiastic support from the local business community in the planning process, and the equally strong support of the regional political leaders who played the key role in maneuvering a special funding request through the National Assembly. Regional prefects rotated among the regions like their department level counterparts. The practice of rotating provincial officials developed during the Napoleonic period, when it was introduced as a method of binding these administrators to the national regime and as a means of discouraging local favoritism. In the 1960s, rotation undermined the effectiveness of the whole notion of deconcentration under the CODER decrees of 1964.

The exceptions came in regions with strong traditions of provincial autonomy, like Brittany. The CODER provided a tangible reward to the well organized local Gaullists for their support of Gaullist candidates. In Brittany, local leaders had generated their own coherent development strategy well before the creation of either CODER or the regional prefects. It had been precisely these same regional and local elites that had criticized and deserted the Third and Fourth Republics over the issue of excessive centralization of administrative controls. Some of these same local leaders had played the same role under the Vichy regime's development corporation in Brittany. While the planning and administrative structures of France were effectively deconcentrated with the creation of CODER in 1964, the new system can scarcely be characterized as more democratic, since the process remained closed to the vast majority of the French.

CHART 1
The Structure of Industry by Number of Workers

Fifth Plan 1965-70

	1962		1972	
	Employees	Firms	Employees	Firms
Size:				
+1000	27	0.1%	29	1%
500-999	13	1.0	14	2
200-499	18	6.0	20	8
100-199	13	9.0	13	11
50-99	11	14.0	10	18
20-49	12	34.0	10	57
10-19	5	35.0	3	23
ALL	100%	100.0%	100%	100%

Source: Chantel Lepêtre, La Concentration des établissements industriels français en 1962 et 1972 (Paris: INSEE, 1976), series E, no. 43, 14.

Yet the success of CODER in winning the support of local elites played a major part in the survival of the Fifth Republic and the Gaullist regime in 1968.

France reached an important plateau before the Fifth Plan in the modernization of housing, in transport, in urban infrastructure and in basic job skills. While these improvements in the French condition varied a great deal across regions and by social groups the quality of French life in general stood among the best in Western Europe. Some serious blockages to further growth, however, loomed in the near future in precisely these same areas of intense modernization. During the Fourth Republic, housing starts had failed to keep pace with housing needs in Paris which led to sharp increases in housing costs for many Parisians. Shanty towns sprung up in the suburbs for those Parisians forced out of the housing market. By the end of the 1960s, rents in Paris by a very general measure stood about 17 times above the level of 1948, with the largest increases coming during the late 1950s and early 1960s when the controls on Parisian growth ended. In a survey of household consumption in 1963 and 1964, in preparation for the Fifth Plan, INSEE determined that Parisians as a group spent a far larger portion of their incomes on housing than other Frenchmen, as indicated on Chart Two. Half of the average household budget in Paris went to rent or mortgage payments. That severely reduced the remaining disposable income in Paris as well as the ability of households to save. Despite the onerous housing costs of the capital, there was also great wealth in the city. Parisians owned ten times more automobiles than other Frenchmen.

In November of 1964, l'Institut National des Etudes Démographiques (INED) estimated that at least 200 _grandes ensembles_ of 1000 or more units had been built with nearly half located in the Paris region. Fifteen of the major housing projects can be found on Chart Three. At least 60,000 units came into use each year during most of the post-war period, housing upwards of 2,000,000 residents by the mid-1960s. The _grandes ensembles_ offered a relatively generous average of 3.3 rooms per household when the typical French household only had 2.67 rooms. However, the public housing in the _grandes ensembles_ had 4.10 persons per household or 1.25 per room which far exceeded the French average of 3.12 persons per household with 1.01

per room. Effectively, the public housing projects placed more residents into less space and into fewer rooms per person than did traditional housing.

Housing costs formed a major obstacle to the expansion domestic consumption throughout the country. As in the 1930s, the social distribution of disposable income in France during the early 1960s did not permit the lower middle class and workers to purchase cars and major consumer durables like televisions in large quantities.(14) One major goal of the Fifth Plan was to widen the domestic market by altering the distribution of income. Using data from the survey of household income, planners saw a clear trade-off between housing costs and car ownership in France, on the eve of the Fifth Plan which can be found in Chart Four. Urban planning to reduce housing costs became a critical component the new plan. Private housing projects, especially in the capital received enthusiastic support as the regime aimed for higher levels of home building under the new plan for the late 1960s.

Industrial Consolidation and Urban Change

The Finance Ministry's vision for overcoming these economic bottlenecks formed the core of the investment strategy of the Fifth Plan. Giscard became the Minister for Finance and Economic Affairs in January 1962. During the next year, he launched a rigorous stabilization plan which remained in place through 1966. Inflation leveled off, causing a severe economic slow down in 1964 and 1965. The economic distress placed the reelection of President de Gaulle in some jeopardy when he faced François Mitterrand and the united left in the presidential election of 1965. Giscard's monetary policies met with an internal wave of Poujadism in the Gaullist movement. In 1966, de Gaulle formed a new government, but declined to reappoint Giscard to the Finance Ministry. Instead, de Gaulle offered a consolation prize: The Public Works Ministry. Giscard angrily rejected the post. Giscard and his Independent Republicans broke with the mainstream of the Gaullist coalition in the mid-1960s. They formed their own separate political party in preparation for the National Assembly elections in 1967. The Independent Republicans demanded *dirigisme*, directed economic policies in the hands of a neo-conservative national elite in their platform, while

CHART 2
Distribution of Household Incomes: 1963-64

	Paris	Excluding Paris
FOOD	29.4%	56.3%
HOUSING	50.6	31.0
ENERGY	8.3	11.5
AUTOMOBILE	11.2	1.2

Source: France. Enquête sur les Budgets familiaux 1963-64 (Paris: INSEE, 1964), 306-307.

CHART 3

NEW TOWNS AND MAJOR GRANDS ENSEMBLES

(1950-1960, population over 5,000 persons)

1. Mourenx-le-Neuf
2. Aubervilliers
3. Bagnols-sur-Cèze
4. Saint-Etienne
5. Saint-Dizier-le-Neuf
6. Montbéliard
7. Strasbourg
8. Lyon
9. Sarcelles
10. Vitry-sur-Seine
11. Stains
12. Saint-Denis
13. Pierrefitte
14. Poissy
15. Massy-Antony

the Gaullist majority carefully waffled the issue in hopes of holding their constituency among local _notables_ while not rebuking the national elite.

As Finance Minister Giscard fostered growth in the private sector among the largest corporations. From 1963 through 1966, Giscard waged a concerted struggle to control the rate of inflation, which was running at about eight percent in the early 1960s.(15) Stabilization of the franc enhanced French products on the world market, leading to a highly favorable trade balance by 1965. In addition, the stable domestic monetary conditions and growing international market restored confidence in French industries at home. However, since tight money was at the base of the plan to reduce inflation, it was only the very large, independent corporations who were able to take advantage of this highly favorable business climate. In the tight money market small businesses lacked access to enough capital to keep pace with the changes in technology. Many small businesses suffered irreparable losses under Giscard's tight money policies.

This induced monetary contraction produced a strong wave of consolidation of French industries, beginning in early 1964 and accelerating under the aegis of the Fifth Plan. Under the law of July 12, 1965, the initiator of a merger received a sizable tax break. Take-overs dominated the business community for the next several years. These tax incentives were revoked in 1967 but the consolidation movement continued under its own momentum.(16) In 1967, the CGP's preliminary report on the Fifth Plan indicated that "the progress of the mergers conforms increasingly to the recommendation of the public authorities in the matter of reorganizing industrial structures."(17) The goal of breaking through technological bottlenecks by increasing the size of individual corporations was being met and exceeded by the mid-point in the plan cycle.

Planners at the CGP placed a high priority on the restructuring of industry to reduce the number of inefficient producers in any given field of production. Large firms especially in the growth industries and in foreign sales bought out small businesses in order to close down small shops. The large firm acquired control of a greater share of the market for a particular product through the merger. Generally, the

CHART 4

EXPENDITURE OF HOUSEHOLD INCOME 1963-64

	Food	Housing	Energy	Automobiles
Farmers	47.0%	40.1%	9.5%	3.4%
Farm workers	59.9	28.8	10.8	6.5
Major executives	45.2	5.0	1.0	48.8
Artisans	32.2	--	1.2	66.6
Minor executives	47.0	14.8	2.4	35.8
Liberal professions	10.5	41.5	24.3	23.7
Technicians and managers	13.7	68.5	16.3	1.5
Salaried employees	23.2	67.3	6.8	2.7
Foremen	13.2	56.3	22.2	8.3
Skilled workers	32.4	41.9	24.5	1.2
Unskilled workers	57.9	14.0	16.2	11.9
Domestics	91.4	5.9	9.9	--
Military	53.6	36.1	9.9	0.4
Other employed	31.0	55.4	11.6	2.0
Retired and unemployed	32.9	14.5	51.7	0.9
Average	34.5%	40.3%	19.6%	5.6%

Source: France. Institut national de la Statistique et des Etudes Economique. Enquête sur les Budgets Familiaux 1963-64 (Paris: Documentation française, 1964), p. 117.

larger corporations already possessed superior technology, more abundant sources of cheap labor and better supplies of raw materials. In such cases the smaller firm was either shut down or reduced to producing a few specialized components for the larger enterprises. The dramatic growth in large businesses can be seen in Chart Five for France as a whole. In 1962 only 0.1 percent of the firms in France employed more than 1,000 workers and by 1972 the number of these very large firms had doubled. Large firms gained new employees faster than small firms lost workers, suggesting that new recruits to the work force flocked to the consolidated industries.

The rate of merger and of wealth consolidation during this period exceeded all previous waves of concentration in modern French history, consolidation rates by economic sector can be found on the sixth chart. Concentration was the strongest in the areas of manufacturing, transportation and communications, and the very poorly defined service trades. The jump in concentration of enterprises with small work forces of between 20 and 49 workers reflected the massive merger wave in the service trades.

Employees of the smaller firms suffered high levels of unemployment because their skills were often obsolete within the higher technological level of the consolidated corporation. Since many French employees obtained their housing from their employers, the mergers forced large numbers of workers out of their homes. To remedy to this problem, the Fifth Plan called for the creation of large amounts of public HLM housing and privately sponsored housing. With the dual offer of employment and new housing, the large consolidated firms hoped to induce labor to migrate to newer and more productive plants. In this way, the plan attempted to channel labor migration into what Alfred Sauvy had called a rational human geography.(18) With the exception of the flow to Paris, the migration followed industry to regions with the newest plants and the lowest wage levels.(19)

The new regional pattern of industrial consolidation transformed many parts of France. Brittany underwent the most dramatic amount of consolidation while region of the Nord experienced the least amount. In the 1960s, the old industrial northeast saw the first signs of the decay that eventually came to dominate French textiles and metals two decades later. Foreign textile manufacturers, for instance, began securing an important share of the domestic market as early as 1965 by taking advantage of the rise of new synthetic fabrics. The vast array of synthetic textiles required major changes in the manufacturing process, but the French firms failed to switch over to the newer technology in time to protect their position in the domestic market. Both natural textiles and metal working were labor intensive industries. During the 1960s, the more automated and hence less labor intensive electronics and small motors industries grew at a faster pace than the older basic industries in the northeastern departments.

Unlike the older industries such as steel, the newer light industries did not need to be located near the sites of raw materials which were heavy and expensive to ship. Gaullist policies for regional development during the mid-1960s fostered industrial expansion in the regions of the south, center and west. These policies resulted in a net loss of jobs in the older industrial northeast by the end of that generation. Under this new regional policy, industrial consolidation and renovation also fell primarily in those regions with relatively low wage rates: The areas outside the northeast. With the exception of Paris which held a special position in the competition for new plants and new jobs, the Gaullist industrial policies shifted economic activities towards a new geographic distribution in France, as can be seen in the statistical appendix.

Beyond the Paris region, employers provided housing for nearly a quarter of all French households by 1968.(20) Company subsidies for housing development gave the post-war growth industries a great deal of flexibility in their site selections. Industries requiring relatively large work forces such as automobiles often chose new sites in regions like Brittany with poor living standards and housing conditions. Low living standards permitted employers to pay less in wages. Despite the intensive private and public building programs for housing, supplies failed to keep up with demand in many regions. The vacancy rate in rural areas had been rising during the previous decade as young workers fled to the urban jobs, but under the regional development plans of the 1960s vacancies declined as workers remained in smaller towns. In the Bourgogne region, for example, three major growth industries--electronics, chemicals and automobiles--aggressively expanded their operations. Jobs in the Bourgogne region grew at an astonishing 25 percent per year when the national rate was merely 15 percent. At the same time housing vacancies fell below the level of 1954. Comparable figures can be found for other regions in the statistical appendix.

The magnitude of the merger wave during the Fifth Plan was only one aspect of the broader policy of upgrading and rationalizing the leaders in French industry. Many specific objectives of the Plan for increasing the world market share for French industry rested firmly upon the merger strategy. In the 1960s, the expansion of the network of energy production (electricity, gas and coal); the staking out the French claim in the market for consumer durables (automobiles, refrigerators and washing machines); and the movement into the market for high technology and light electronics, all played crucial roles in planned development. The largest and most powerful corporations which emerged from the consolidation wave of the 1960s were precisely those industries identified for intensive expansion by the National Plan of 1965 (see the statistical appendix).

These giants of the French economy included a handful of businesses in the public sector, ranging from rails and utilities to automobile production. By the late 1960s these public enterprises employed 34 percent of the work force. In contrast, during the same period the supposedly more socialized Sweden employed a mere ten percent of the national work force in the public sector. Despite the Gaullist ideological disapproval of nationalized businesses, these firms led the drive towards consolidation and modernization under the Fifth Plan. During the 1960s, the French public corporations were highly successful from the phenomenal profitability of Renault to the great growth in electric production at EDF.

In the private sector, major consumer durable firms such as Peugeot, Michelin, Thomson-Brandt led the market. Their growth spurred expansion in firms in the basic industries like de Wendel and Empain-Schneider by the end of the Fifth Plan (see the appendix for details). Among the early leaders in the high technology market during the 1960s, Thomson-Brandt and CGE recorded the highest returns on their capital investment. Amidst all this growth, however, certain problems remained. Productivity in the financial

CHART 5
Intensification of Industrial Structures, 1962-1972
(1962 = 100)

	Change in Number of Employees	Change in Number of Firms
Size of Work force:		
1000	200	100
500-999	100	111
200-499	200	222
100-199	0	222
50-99	0	444
20-49	-200	333
10-19	-200	-1333

Source: Chantal Lepêtre, La Concentration des établissements industriels français en 1962 et 1972 (Paris: INSEE, 1976), séries E, No. 43, 14.

CHART 6

ECONOMIC CONCENTRATION AND WEALTH CONSOLIDATION IN POST WAR FRANCE

(1950-1970)

Sector	Percentage of firms with one act of concentration	Percentage of firms with more than one merger	Increase in Capital Concentration	
			Percent	Current France
Agriculture; fishing; mining	1.83%	5.52%	0.81%	175,014,210
Energy; gas; oil	1.29	1.94	0.38	82,475,106
Manufacturing	51.40	36.71	44.30	9,525,591,715
Commerce	3.57	5.37	0.99	213,825,090
Transport; communications	12.12	11.19	8.90	1,915,211,622
Services	27.81	31.94	43.83	9,425,467,018
Diverse	1.95	7.31	0.76	164,521,085
TOTAL	99.99%	99.99%	99.99%	21,502,105,846

Source: France. Commissariat général du Plan, *Concentration et Politique des structures industrielles* (Paris: INSEE, 1974), 44-45.

sector as in the conglomerate Suez remained low in contrast to industrial productivity. The notably lower level of productivity of the Suez corporation had considerable consequences for the urban management programs of the CGP and local planners in Paris. To recapture productivity subsidiaries of Suez turned to real estate development and to bidding for major public works projects.

As an old colonial enterprise, the Suez Company built the Suez Canal in Egypt in 1858. In concert with British investors, Suez proceeded to reap the full rewards of its control over Egyptian mineral and commercial wealth much as the railroads exploited the American West at the same time. Nearly a century later, the reformist regime of Nassar nationalized the Suez holdings. The Anglo-French invasion of 1956 failed to restore French control over the Suez holdings in Egypt. The Suez Company placed the blame for the failure of the invasion and their losses upon the inept colonial policies of the Fourth Republic, which undermined the Republic's standing in the larger financial community. After de Gaulle came to power, Jacques-Georges Picot, the general manager of Suez, arranged a settlement of the Suez claim with the Egyptian government in 1959.(21) The Suez consortium received nearly 322 million francs and the freedom to turn its full attention to the company's extensive operations in France, Britain and South America.

The Suez corporation drew a valuable management lesson from the Egyptian debacle. Adopting the rule of the triple play as a development strategy, Suez placed one portion of the capital holdings in banking and insurance; a second portion in industry, commerce and construction; and the third portion in highly diversified stocks and bonds.(22) Under this new investment strategy, Suez achieved a very high degree of vertical integration of its interests by focusing the firm's great financial powers upon a few carefully selected projects. Two subdivisions, one in public works and La Hénin in the private sector housing formed the foundation Suez operations in the area of town development.(23) Suez entered the most dynamic urban construction markets, by concentrating their efforts in Paris, Lille, Bonnières, Colombes, Saint Nazaire, Saint Brevin, Caen and Lyon.(24) Suez directly benefited from the Fifth Plan which relaxed the old limitation on growth and development in the capital.

Competition from foreign corporations, especially in the prized field of high technology, forced French corporations like Suez to become adroit masters of the domestic French market. During the early days of the Fifth Republic, American corporations claimed a near monopoly in some fields of high technology, such as computers, radar and communications. Through the careful structuring of foreign corporate charters under the Gaullist plans, French industry began to shift the balance by introducing the American technology into French operations but retaining important management controls over actual production.(25) Under the Fifth Plan in 1966, the major French corporations in the electronics and computer industries joined together in an attempt to exert leadership in this new sector by creating a domestic rival in *la Compagnie Internationale pour l'Informatique* (CII). The success of this strategy of absorbing foreign technology then reconquering the domestic market came in 1973 when CII took over Honeywell-Bull with the American firm ending up with the minority share of the management.

Despite Gaullist policies which produced nearly full employment and a growing standard of living in the 1960s, France remained plagued by sharp social divisions. Indeed, it can be effectively argued that the prospering economy of the 1960s made the limitations of class even more difficult to bear. The growth policies of the Fifth Republic did not include an emphasis on upward mobility for either the lower middle or working classes, even while promising higher standards of living for many in French society, except for foreign workers.

During the first decade of the Fifth Republic, up through 1968, in many ways class conflict and the stress of great social divisions took on non-traditional forms of expression. Instead of the large scale mass movements of the turn of the century, a diffuse type of working class resistance sprang into existence. Some key leaders of the Republic like Giscard even speculated about the obsolescence of social classes and the class struggle.(26) The working class new towns and *grandes ensembles* reflected the depths of the alienation of these communities from the planning system and the philosophical principles which created them. Juvenile delinquency at Sarcelles outside of Paris was five times higher than in traditional working class quarters of the city proper during the 1960s.(27) Much of the youthful crime in Sarcelles in these years consisted of random vandalism against the housing complex itself, with all those thousands of monotonously identical household cells, each reflecting Le Corbusier's standardized man. Violence against residents at Sarcelles sprang from racial tension among youth gangs. The great public housing complexes had been consciously designed for youthful populations in the 1940s and 1950s as an alternative to the squalid Parisian slums for large families with low incomes. During the 1960s the crisis of juvenile crime was a symptom of the remaining frustrations in the new suburban ghettos.

The widely reported studies by urban sociologist Paul-Henri Chombart de Lauwe during the mid-1960s focused upon the deep alienation and isolation of the traditional homemaker in a _grand ensemble_.(28) In these complexes the physical environment of the home has been reduced to three or possibly four small rooms, often at great distances from shopping, recreational activities and potential part-time employment. Such a home environment lacked the physical freedom of the rural peasant house with the open accessible landscape, or the urban activities of a city apartment that stood on a busy street. As a consequence of the Fifth Plan's strong emphasis on geographic mobility, the network of family, friends and neighbors has been continually disrupted further restricting the social contacts of the traditional homemaker. Studies of the women in _grandes ensembles_ by both the State and the popular press during the 1960s revealed a high incidence of alcoholism, chronic depression and divorce among women in these planned communities.

Other serious problems of the public housing projects received considerable public scrutiny during the mid-1960s. Maintenance and repairs were criticized for poor quality and for being slow. Few public services existed for the special needs of the elderly, the infants, the handicapped, and in some _grandes ensembles_ for everyone else as well. Mass transit connections remained underdeveloped. The glaring popular criticism reduced the attractiveness of public housing for many households. In the investigation by urban critics Gilles Ebriq and Pierre Barjac at the end of the 1960s, they found that 1.2 million (11 percent) of the 11 million public units went unoccupied because of the uninhabitable condition of the unit or public reluctance to rent.(29) At the same time an examination of the housing conditions of immigrant labor by urban economist Bernard Granotier estimated that at least 100,000 persons lived in shanty-towns, with another 500,000 residing in barracks and other dwellings far below the standards of the most dismal HLM complex.(30) Public housing programs in the 1960s still failed to provide minimally adequate shelter for a large portion of the working population in France.

The record of housing and living conditions during the 1960s for the immigrant labor force was a sober indication of the consequences of planned capitalism for those who were left without bargaining power in the planning process. Where the French worker may have seen his chance for upward mobility stifled during the 1960s and his household threatened by new social pressures, the circumstances of most immigrants were far worse. Immigrant labor played a critical role in the strategy of increasing the total mobility of the French labor force under the Fifth Plan and in the rational redistribution of labor skills and of the active population across the country. The high turnover rate of immigrant labor allowed French industry to keep a large portion of their payrolls at the lowest wage level which kept total wage cost down and often freed the industries from paying pensions. Construction, metal working, mining and agriculture employed large numbers of migrants. Approximately two million foreign nationals lived in France during the early 1960s, with 60 percent of these immigrants working in the paid labor force. In effect, this large group, eight percent of the total male labor force constituted a bottom parameter in both wage rates and in living conditions. The common immigrant practice of sending 30 to 60 percent of their earnings back to families in their native country left the foreign worker with a standard of living far below that of the Frenchmen earning a minimum wage.(31)

Giscard's tight money policies of 1963, wage restraints and the practice of hiring migrant labor combined in the mid-1960s to produce high levels of real economic growth with relatively mild inflation rates. The gap between the migrant's wages and his low general standard of living during the period may in part explain why the French economy escaped a severe inflationary spiral of rising wages and rising prices during those years. While wages rose for many French workers, the total wage bill to employers remained stable, since it was kept down by the low immigrant wages. The combination of low wage costs and low living standards restrained increases in prices. In effect, the immigrants paid the heavy price for French prosperity during these years. The high geographic mobility of the immigrant households effectively excluded them from the benefits of the HLM program. Even though the housing program had been opened to foreign households on a non-discriminatory basis in 1959, the high turnover rate meant that these households constantly lost their standing on waiting-lists for the HLM units which were kept by each commune. Of the two million migrants only 2,200 households had managed to secure HLM units by 1967. The overwhelming majority, perhaps 65 to 70 percent of the migrant workers in France accepted substandard housing conditions in the oldest urban slums.

Algerians and other Africans suffered the worst living conditions. According to Granotier, "the blacks live in the least tolerable conditions. They are packed like sardines (sometimes four to a bed), in cellars with ceilings too low for standing; they live in the back of shops, in alley-ways, in attics and in farm sheds. The beds are pushed together, clothing hung on the walls, and even then little free space remains in these quarters. The ventilation is inadequate, and without heat winter colds are a peril to all. The dampness of the cellars penetrates both the inhabitants and their belongings. Rats are as common as the fleas. And for these inhuman conditions a bed goes for 30 to 35 francs (a week) or more."(32)

Against this stark picture of the continuing housing crisis in France, especially in Paris during the 1960s, the record of real growth in housing can be missed. After all, amidst the record of poverty, overcrowding and tacky construction, Ebriq's study also found that the CGP's policy for private sector, usually middle class housing had been warmly received.(33) The spurt of new construction in the early 1960s--primarily private middle income housing--actually restrained price increases in that portion of the market by expanding the housing supply in the French capital. The CGP succeeded by the late 1960s in freeing-up a greater portion of household income for the purchase of durable goods like automobiles and refrigerators. Great conglomerates like Suez with its La Hénin subsidiary entered the construction and real estate field with special attention to Paris during this period. In France, the number of owner occupied units grew between 1962 and 1968 by the highest rate in Western Europe and America. Ebriq and Barjac estimated that the value of property in Paris increased by as much as 50 percent per year during the late 1950s and early 1960s, even with the restraint of a rapidly expanding in housing stock.

In 1967, France was full of contradictions. Rapid growth still left a fifth of the households in the capital in desperately inadequate housing conditions. In comparison with the last years of the previous two Republics, political stability had finally been achieved. But beneath this surface of relative political calm, important fissures lay below the surface. The troubled alliance of the Socialists and Communists in the mid-1960s had fallen into disrepair. For their part, the Communists still clung to the old Stalinist leadership, symbolized by Maurice Thorez. That liability proved costly when Soviet tanks rolled into Prague during the following summer to bring down the Dubchek regime. Mitterrand's poor showing against de Gaulle in 1965 left the Socialists with confusion and bitter intra-party feuds. The Gaullist movement also suffered from dissension.

In 1967, Giscard's Independent Republicans decided to stand on their own as an electoral party, distinct from the Gaullist coalition. In the 1967 elections to the National Assembly, the followers of Giscard fought other Gaullists in a bitter struggle for power at the grassroots level. A year later, in the midst of revolt bordering on revolution, the Independent Republicans supported the Government out of loyalty to the Fifth Republic, but their support for the de Gaulle was tepid at best. Giscard denounced the Gaullist position on the regionalism in the referendum of spring 1969. Humbled by vote on the referendum, de Gaulle resigned infavor of Georges Pompidou. The new President rehabilitated Giscard by returning him to the Finance Ministry. The next presidential primary pitted Pompidou against the regionalists in of the Gaullist coalition as led by Chaban-Delmas and Michael Debré. Giscard's _dirigiste tendance_ was restored to the center of policy making with the victory of Pompidou in the general election.

Conclusion

France under the Gaullist governments of the 1960s achieved a high level of economic growth within the frameworks of the National Plans. The Gaullist political movement as a coalition of many special and often contradictory interests had some difficulty claiming the accolades of success. Dissenters like Giscard pushed Gaullism towards more conservative and technocratic policies, while the regional elites demanded a more deconcentrated approach to economic control. Despite these powerful contradictions, the minuet continued, resulting in the Fifth National Plan. These policies for the last half of the decade of the 1960s were the clearest statement of planning theory and practice that France has produced during the post-war era. As a critical political statement of Gaullist policy, the Fifth Plan also represented the composite of compromises upon which the coalition stood. That political movement, that plan's philosophy were precisely what the rebels of 1968 sought to rip to shreds.

CHAPTER FIVE

Planning for the New Brutalism (1945-1965)

While Le Corbusier spent the last decade of his life perfecting the architectural style that he called the New Brutalism, at the Commissariat Général du Plan planners laid the foundations for the Fifth National Plan. In 1968, critics of the Plan and especially the opponents of its urban strategy saw far too much Nietzsche in both propositions. These *anti-planistes* doubted the wisdom of a society managed by Supermen.

The Fifth Plan, 1965-1969

The Fifth Plan has been widely recognized as the quintessential statement of the Gaullist method of controlling national economic growth. It was that and far more. This plan rested upon the fundamental concept of class collaboration the explicit as philosophical foundation to managed capitalism. But this Gaullist corporatist system received only halting support from French trade unions, whose leadership feared antagonizing younger radical members in the rank and file. As a form of corporate governance, Gaullist planning in the mid-1960s was only partially successful.

Nowhere did corporate theories and practical realities clash more openly than in the work of the CGP's subcommittee for urban management the *Groupe des Structures urbaine de la Commissariat de l'Équipement Urbaine*.(1) This national level urban planning commission included representation from the financial community, developers, academics, State agencies and labor. Louis Leroy, who succeeded Bloch-Lainé at the *Caisse des Dépôts et Consignations* presided over the deliberations. His fellow executive from the Caisse, Salliard presented the final report of the group's recommendations in March 1965. The Communist, Socialist and Christian Democratic trade unions all had representatives on the urban commission. Among the labor representatives, the Communist Confédération générale du Travail (CGT) delegate found himself least comfortable on a planning board designed expressly for the purpose of fine-tuning the capitalist mode of production. Indeed, the CGT representative objected to many formulations in the final report and eventually refused to endorse its recommendations. For instance, the urban management commission of the Plan strongly endorsed the private development of New Towns and housing projects (les grandes ensembles).(2) The CGT repudiated this part of the Plan for urban management on the grounds that it gave to private interests responsibilities and prerogatives that should belong to the public. In keeping with the position of Mitterrand, the Socialist Force Ouvrière trade union representative also vehemently opposed the privatization of town planning.

The Christian Democratic trade unions Confédération Française Démocratique du Travail (CFDT) found the corporatist town management practices in the Fifth Plan to be more compatible with their traditional ideas for organizing the economy. The Gaullist Fifth Plan coincided with a critical moment of ideological adjustment in the Christian Democratic trade union movement, as new leaders began breaking with the old vision of French Catholicism and corporatism. Alone among the labor associations in France, the CFDT was founded on an openly corporatist model of labor relations. Until 1947, the first article in the federation's governing document stated that "the federation finds the inspiration for its activities in the social doctrine as defined in the Rerum Novarum encyclical."(3) During the Vichy years, the CFDT under the leadership of Joseph Zirnheld signed the Manifesto of the Twelve in November of 1940 which called for a French version of Mussolini's Labor Charter. The Manifesto stated that the labor organizations under the Pétain regime would take an anti-capitalist formation and the "capitalist regime will be superceded by a regime where the economy is directed to serve the whole community."(4) As early as August 25, 1940, Zirnheld, had written to Pétain that "the words 'Corporatism', 'organization by profession' and also 'work, family, country' are not foreign to Christian syndicalists."(5) It was only late in the war, in June of 1943 when the Pétain regime was already faultering that the CFDT repudiated the French Charter of Labor.

War time collaboration gave the old leadership of the CFDT considerable insight into the post-war planning practices. Their early post-war leaders were among the most candid analysts of much of post-war planning. The CFDT denounced the centralist planning of the Fourth Republic and ideologies on which it rested. Georges Levard, who succeeded Zirnheld, wrote the tract *Les Chances et Périls du syndicalisme chrétien* in 1955, where he strongly argued for a return to the war time practices of class collaboration and for the legitimacy of corporatism. On November 6, 1964, the old *Confédération française des travailleurs chrétiens* (CFTC) changed its name to the CFDT in an attempt to appease a growing dissident movement in the rank and file. Thus these unions made the transition to the new Gaullist style of corporatism, that sought an identity outside of the Vichy past. Levard's successor, Eugene Descamps assured his unions that "nothing was changed except the name."(6) During the Fourth Republic the CFDT had viewed national economic planning under the direction of center-left governments with considerable skepticism, but under the Fifth Republic plunged energetically into the work of sub-committees of the CGP. Descamps recognized the continuity of Vichy practices under the Fifth Plan which he described in the official union history. In 1964, he insisted that "today it is clear that for the unforeseen future, the Plan and nothing else will rationalize those activities which allow the dominant model of civilization to develop."(7)

Gaullist planners at the CGP created the sub-committee on urban development of the Fifth Plan precisely to rationalize economic activities of this sort within the scope of planned capitalism. The urban subcommittee established as a priority the creation of twelve million new units of housing between 1965 and 1985.(8) They retained the urbanization hierarchy of the Third Plan but made voluntary the participation of municipal governments in non-market allocations of industry, housing and infrastructure. The new Plan liberated the city of Paris from most restraints on employment and residential growth, though funding failed close the wide gap in urban services that had appeared during the past eight years of restricted expansion. In the authorizing decrees, new public housing required a corresponding commitment from the private sector to create new jobs at the site with the local town planners functioning as intermediaries. The local planners solicited a suitable employer with a capital development subsidy from CODER and then arranged for the appropriate authorizations of new public HLMs or other subsidized housing projects. If public housing proved difficult to secure, town planners could appeal to the regional prefect who in turn attempted to obtain a special State grant or funding from the private sector within the region.

The sub-committee rejected free standing New Towns in favor of satellite cities that integrated the community into existing conurbations. In reality, these new communities often became bedroom suburbs. A special section of the sub-committee under sociologist Chombart de Lauwe suggested new minimum guidelines for providing an adequate mix of employment opportunity, infrastructure, commercial services and recreational facilities, in addition to housing. The urban commission mandated in the report that each satellite city of 100,000 have an autonomous employment base for sixty percent of the active population, and that the town provide ninety percent of its own needs for shopping and recreation.(9)

As indicated in Chart One, five new towns sprang up in the Paris region under the Fifth Plan. In each satellite city, private employers helped develop the town plan in conjunction with their own needs for urban services such as roads and utilities. Some of the new communities in the Parisian suburbs actually began development under the earlier policy of free standing public New Towns, but they came to completion under the new guidelines with the active participation of the private sector. Totally public New Towns, of course, belonged to the Fourth Republic's style of planning which saw the State as direct manipulator of employment, housing and transport in the act of creating a new community. In August of 1961, Paul Délouvier became the head of the planning district for Paris, and directed development during the period when urban policy underwent this important shift. At the Finance Ministry in 1962, Giscard strongly opposed Délouvier's original proposals with their heavy State subsidies. Giscard led a movement in the Finance Ministry for stronger fiscal control over all urban development.

During the early 1960s the publicly financed New Towns came under increasingly severe attack from such conservative journals as La France catholique, Spécial, Correspondance économique and l'Homme nouveau. At the same time, the left trade unions denounced the private New Towns charging that they represented unacceptable limits on the autonomy of workers by linking employment and residence. Private New Towns looked like old company towns to the left critics. As the political debate became more polarized in 1962, the construction projects in already authorized new communities slowed down. Giscard broke the stalemate by taking greater direct control over the Parisian New Towns under the decree of February 14, 1963 which shifted urban management from the Ministry of Construction to the CGP which was directly responsible to the Finance Ministry. At the same time, the CGP established as a primary policy that housing should be built at sites with existing unused capacity for roads, sewers and other infrastructure. The new policy aimed at consolidating suburban growth and limiting future growth to existing metropolitan areas.

Prime Minister Georges Pompidou strongly supported Giscard's position in a letter to Délouvier on April 4, 1966. Pompidou denounced the failure of the earlier New Town strategy by citing the example of "suburbanites who live in _grandes ensembles_ of Trappes or the small houses of Saint Genéviève des Bois, ignore the New Town, and continue to make long trips to go to work, to shop and to spend their leisure time."(10) Under the Fifth Plan town development planning turned to private developers to remedy these problems of isolation and misallocation.

Délouvier resigned in January 1969, after the Finance Ministry's position had been consolidated in the aftermath of May 1968. On April 16, 1969 two decrees followed which effectively terminated the legal authority of departmental and city planners in Paris to initiate New Town projects. The Conseil d'Administration now reserved those initiatives to the public sector; and the private sector was left largely to private real estate developers, like the Suez Company's Hénin Society.(11)

Housing Patterns and Domestic Consumption

During the Fourth Republic, the failure of housing starts to keep pace with housing needs in Paris created sharp increases in housing costs for those Parisians who could still meet them, and mushrooming shanty towns for those Parisians forced out of the housing market.

CHART 1

Five New Towns in the Paris Region: The Employment Base

Cergy-Pontoise	Ivry	Marne-la-Vallée	Melun-Senart	Saint Quentin-en-Yvelines
Johnson France	Presses univ-ersitaires de France	ORTF	Fiat	Fiat-Unic
SAF	Biscuits Belin	Rowntree-Mackintosh	Russenberger	Pennaroya
Lorilleux-Lefranc	Pikarone	William Saurin	Imprimerie Victor Michel	Le Nickel
Knoll Internatl	Fulmen		Berger SA	UFAP
Gillet	Knickers		Société Général	LMT
Feau, Tollens	Société Souple Tube			Tailor
Ericsson	Société Durieu			Prola
SAGEM	Centre de Tri des PTT			La Seineurie
Préfecture et les Services fiscaux publics	AOIP			Bachi
3M France	Carrefour-mater-cal téléphonique			
EDF	Richard le Droff			Honeywell

CHART 1 continued

Cergy-Pontoise	Ivry	Saint-Quentin-en-Yvelines
Allocations familliales	General Electric Plastique	Banque industrialle et commerciale de la région ouest de Paris
Ordinal	Services fiscaux régional	Direction régionale des Télé-communications
Maison de l'habitat	Mackenzie Hill	Schwartz-Haumont
	Silic	
	Centre de Recherche Honeywell Bull	
	SNECMA	
	Société Général	
	FFF-SACI	
	SIFRAM	

Source: Préfecture de la Région parisienne, *Cinq Villes nouvelles en Région parisienne* (Editions MAPE, Paris: 1974).

By the end of the 1960s, rents in Paris on a very broad level stood about seventeen times above the level of 1948 with the largest increases coming in the late 1950s and early 1960s. In a survey of household consumption in 1963 and 1964 INSEE, the national statistical bureau determined that Parisians as a group spent a far larger portion of their incomes on housing than other Frenchmen.(12) Indeed, the large housing commitment severely reduced the remaining disposable income for the purchase of consumer goods or for saving, thereby holding back the entire economy.

While the housing drain on household incomes was less severe outside of Paris, it constituted a major block to the expanding domestic consumption throughout the country. For example, the household consumption survey of 1963 and 1964 revealed that middle and lower middle income groups obtained larger and more modern housing units than the average French worker by committing an extremely large share of their incomes to housing. This housing preference left fewer funds in the household for the purchase of an automobile or other major consumer durable goods. The same study found that unskilled workers as a group were more likely to accept less attractive but cheaper housing in order to be able to purchase an automobile.(13) The Fifth Plan's housing policy targeted as a major objective lowering the cost of housing for the lower middle classes and working class in order to stimulate general domestic consumption.(14) Expanding automobile ownership, of course, ran diametrically against the urban theory of Le Corbusier who rejected the commuter suburb.

During the Fifth Plan, the CGP responded on three levels to the housing shortage in the Paris region by relaxing the restrictions in Paris, by encouraging regional level decision making, and by revising the HLM program in 1966 to be more attractive to the developers of lower middle class housing.(15) Gaullist planners during the mid-1960s targeted the lower middle class for special attention. Their loyalty at election time to the Gaullist political movement provided stability to the whole Republic, especially during years of crisis like 1968. The new HLM program reduced the term of the mortgage from 45 to 40 years, increased the permissible interest charge from one percent to 2.6 percent and reduced the initial down payment from 15 percent to five percent.(16) It was hoped that these more attractive financing terms would draw more private capital investment and greater interest from developers. Caisse underwrote the new financial arrangements by securing the loans directly against the French State.(17)

Housing construction nearly achieved the Plan's projected goal of 250,000 to 400,000 new units per year. HLM backed one-third of the new homes, under the Fifth Plan. The new housing policy introduced a subtle but major change into the French national housing market. Public corporations like the Caisse and the private developers effectively exercised managerial control over the property. Housing starts began to fluctuate along with the general construction market. In 1967 and 1969, a slow down in housing starts appeared to jeopardize the CGP's goal for the total number of new units under the Fifth Plan. So the State stepped into the housing market with special block grants to the regions suffering the greatest short fall. It was a classic application of Giscard's Keynesian formula where "an advanced society . . . must let the mechanisms of the market regulate the basic workings of the economy, which it can then correct and complete. In this way the conscious mind picks up and guides spontaneous movements."(18)

Because the seven New Towns in the Paris region built before 1960 lacked any significant private employment base, the planners of the satellite cities under private development considered the older communities failures. Funds for the early New Towns fell dramatically even though the populations in these communities grew. By 1968, the property values of the older communities had declined so far that some units had simply been abandoned by their owners.

In early 1968, the CGP issued a progress report on the private satellite towns and the accomplishments of the Fifth Plan in urban zones. The report reemphasized the importance of the policy shift which insisted that "urban growth and industrial growth in large measure must be a pair," and declared that "more and more urban management has taken up a positive attitude towards the collaboration of the State with private industry. This collaboration at its root reflects the commonality of the factors which influence urban and industrial site selection."(19) The CGP proclaimed the new policy a stunning success.

Where was Le Corbusier?

During the early years of the Fifth Republic and the last decade of his life, Le Corbusier divided his time between lecturing to *urbanistes* and constructing a series of minor projects. The Unités d'Habitation at Nantes, Berlin and Briey-en-Forêt followed the earlier work at Marseilles. In design, they represented nothing new. Unlike his designs from the early twentieth century, these projects were generally well received in the proposed communities. Le Corbusier's reputation as a modernizer and an innovator finally had found an appreciative audience. This subtle change in the career of Le Corbusier coincided, of course with a significant change in the personnel of urban planning throughout France. By 1960, a generation of urban planners (*urbanistes*) had taken positions of authority in the municipal and state agencies for urban land use planning, and they had been trained to view Le Corbusier's work as the norm of modern architecture and urban design. These new planners, also, stood one generation away from the fierce ideological clashes that had deadlocked the Third Republic.

Like Keynesian economic managers, the French *urbanistes* trained in Le Corbusier's theories, firmly believed in their mission to remake the urban environment in a more rational fashion. At the same time that Le Corbusier's theory came to dominate French urban development a certain stagnation settled into these designs. No longer did Le Corbusier and his students have to defend themselves against law suits charging them with visual vandalism of the French landscape. Physical planning had become routine and seemingly uncontroversial. Lewis Mumford, the English historian and long time critic of Le Corbusier's work called this new urban environment "sterile." Three years after Le Corbusier's death the urban activists of May 1968 went further, condemning the "new" *urbanisme* as alienating and authoritarian.

Le Corbusier personally supervised the construction of his last major project, the monastery, La Tourette between 1957 and 1960. The monastery reflected the earliest and most consistent principles of Le Corbusier's urban and architectural theory. La Tourette contained one hundred cells with relentlessly linear features while the facade resembled the late medieval monastery of Ema which the architect had admired in his youth. La Tourette has also been called the "heavy church" for its massive, solid qualities. Le Corbusier gave this style of architecture the unfortunate name, the New Brutalism. He devoted the last period of his life to this final phase of the Modern Architecture Movement. For someone of his generation, born into the serene fin du siècle then shoved into the furnaces of the two world wars, the idea of an Age of Brutalism came very easily. Le Corbusier's critics quickly to pointed out the parallel in the architect's new style and Oswald Spengler's new barbarians. Le Corbusier never escaped the memory of his flirtation with fascism.

Conclusion

It was the brutalism of the rational economic man, and the system which had created him that drew the anger of students and young workers in the spring of 1968. Many institutions in French life came under close scrutiny and criticism during the May events in Paris, but the most graphic and best articulated target of the protest was certainly Le Corbusier's urbanisme. At the same time, the new urban France was the symbol of the successes of the growth miracle of the post-war period, of the hard fought reforms of the early sewer Socialists, of the artistic integrity of Le Corbusier's planning, of corporatist Gaullist strategies and, of course, the symbol of everything wrong with the system. Urbanisme was elitist, authoritarian, sterile, alienating and dehumanizing to those who rejected the very fundamental positivist premises on which the planning process stood.

CHAPTER SIX

May (1968)

> Le Corbusier wrote in 1925 "If the 'Voisin' plan is studied, there can be seen to the west and south west the great openings made by Louis XIV, Louis XV, and Napoleon: the Invalides, the Tuileries, the Place de la Concorde, the Champ de Mars and The Etoile. These works are a signal example of Creation, of that spirit which is able to dominate and compel the mob." (The City To-morrow (London, 1947), 282-3, originally Urbanisme (Paris, 1925)).

Student protests against the American war in Vietnam and over domestic French issues peaked in the late Spring of 1968. Unrest began on the Nanterre campus of the University of Paris at the end of March. Standing in an isolated Parisian suburb this spartan campus bore the heavy hand of Le Corbusier's brutalist architecture as well as being plagued by poor construction. Ceilings leaked, plumbing worked fitfully and the commutes to Paris were very long. By May 3 the message of the New Left activists at Nanterre reached the Sorbonne in the heart of Paris. Several days of street fighting left casualties among both students and police. Universities throughout the country responded to the outbreak of violence in Paris by closing down.

On May 13, the spontaneous strikes spread beyond the students to young workers at the Renault auto works in the Parisian suburb of Billancourt. Auto-gestion, as it was called, challenged everything that was established in the system, including the leaders of the great left-wing trade unions. The May Movement owed its history to anarchism of the most romantic sort. The powerful Communist trade union attempted to curb the wild cat strike at Renault, without success. In the following week, strikes broke out all over France. After the initial failure of the Communist and Socialist trade unions to suppress the walk out, the unions reluctantly joined in the labor stoppages. The strike wave forced President Charles de Gaulle to abruptly end his State visit to Romania and return to France on May 20. He confirmed the loyalty of his army commanders and proceeded to liquidate the crisis. De Gaulle's solution was twofold. He dismissed the Assembly, calling for new elections, ineffect asking for a referendum on the Fifth Republic. Then de Gaulle appealed to his political supporters to march with him down the Champs Elysées in affirmation of the Republic. Over half a million Gaullists turned out on a few hours notice. The election of late June 1968 gave de Gaulle a solid majority, by greatly reducing the size of the Communist and Socialist delegations in the Assembly. Most New Leftists rejected the electoral process altogether, so their impact was not directly felt in the election of the new Chamber.

May 1968, however, was far more than a student riot that got a bit out of control. It was a moment when France considered the quality of modern life and contemporary institutions, and validated what existed. Across France, the Fifth National Economic Plan (1966 to 1970) consolidated the philosophical and structural changes in French planning that came with the Fifth Republic. With the institutions of the CGP in place, even the rebellion of May 1968, and the subsequent departure of de Gaulle the following year did not seriously disrupt the cycle of growth. May 1968, however, did focus French attention on the implications for political institutions and civil liberties of *planisme*, its sophisticated system of State economic and social planning. Political discussion returned to the violent sting of the great debates of the Third Republic in the 1880s and the crisis years of the 1930s.

Crisis on the Left, Continuity on the Right

In the 1960s, France found herself with an aging French Communist Party that had long since jettisoned the rhetoric and the practice of revolution for a militant trade unionism within the legal limitations set by French style supple planning.(1) The other major left party, the Socialists, now led by moderate Resistance leader, François Mitterrand, called for more humanism and less bureaucracy in economic management. They conveniently forgot their past as important architects of highly centralized planning under the last Republic. The May events brought into focus a social and cultural crisis within French society that had been brewing since the end of the Second World War. Student rebels in Paris, and by young workers across the country identified alienation as the symbol of the great failure of the Modern New France. At the base of the ideological disaffection with the Fifth Republic was the diminished role of individuals in society, the economy and the political life of France, under more collectivist forms of governance like planning. Moreover, the critics charged that planning merely replicated the intense divisions of class in a new form. May offered a powerful critique of the implicit social controls in urban planning. Rebels rejected of the Positivist assumptions behind Marxism and behind the Liberal worlds of Howard and Taylor. At the same time, the critics of _urbanisme_ could not reject the result of rational urban development which had meant a markedly higher standard of living for most Frenchmen.

On the eve of the crisis, the Socialist Party took a new name the _Fédération de la gauche démocratique et socialiste_ (FGDS) but continued the old Reformist tradition of Paul Brousse.(2) Moderates and Liberals found the economic future brighter. Many secured admission for their sons, and now even some daughters to the prestigious civil administration schools and the universities; or found them places in large corporations.(3) But the old dreams of taking over the family business and becoming a new de Wendel had vanished.(4) Gaullists still faced internal dissension between the technocratic centralists and the broad mass of small businessmen, but the ranks of the Poujadists had diminished greatly.(5)

In 1968 the challenge to national economic management came from an entirely unexpected direction: The New Left of the baby-boom generation. The sharpest criticism came from precisely those young adults who had benefited most directly during the 1950s and 1960s from the spectacular improvement in the French standard of living, including the first generation of broad based, mass university level education. The May Movement challenged the foundation of both the managed, supple, capitalist system and almost as vehemently it did the doctrines of the traditional left.[6] Students, intellectuals and young workers denounced the glaring inequities in French society. Students sympathized with the conditions of poorly housed immigrant workers which contrasted sharply with the affluence of the middle level bureaucrats in the Parisian suburbs. The alienating, stale world of the bureaucracy and especially financial institutions was reviled as being particularly demeaning to the human spirit. It was as if the Parisian students in the spring of 1968 had looked closely at Le Corbusier's Plan Voisin de Paris, at his skyscrapers and the ants below, and recognized themselves. According to New Left critics, great government public housing projects in the Parisian suburbs, the grandes ensembles led to intrusive remedies by social service agencies on the one hand, and, on the other hand, to juvenile delinquency, alcoholism and suicide.(7) Finally, the cost of rapid industrialization in environmental terms was beginning to be calculated by 1968. The theme of social pollution as if society were drowning in its own filth recalled the image of decay found in Céline's descriptions of the 1920s.(8)

By 1968 France had created a modern economy with the classic characteristics of advanced economic development. The agricultural work force had been reduced to 14.8 percent with many of the actual field laborers being foreign migrant workers from North Africa and the Middle East. While agriculture was still a greater portion of total GNP than in rival European economies, like Germany, it was smaller than Spain, and consistent with the overall economic strategy of France within the world market. Agricultural products, the oldest of French staples--wine and food stuffs--provided important foreign exchange currency which in turn permitted France to acquire sophisticated new technologies from the United States.

In keeping with the Gaullist foreign policy strategy of fostering independent European positions on strategic and economic issues, French industry under the Fifth Plan internalized and redeveloped the borrowed technologies especially in the fields of telecommunications, mass transit, office machines and automobiles.(9) Often this strategy for expanding domestic research and development led to the creation of new plants with research sections, to the rapid adoption of the newer technologies in actual production lines and to an expansion in the technical study fields at the university level. An indication of the success of the internalization of research and development can be seen in the decline in the number of unskilled workers in the active population, in Chart One.

French migration patterns also changed in the mid-1960s.(10) While the strong centrifugal pull of Paris remained pervasive in the economy, the attraction of provincial jobs and better housing conditions in the rural areas grew. During the mid 1960s, France generated nearly 175,000 new jobs per year, which reduced the unemployment rate of the active population by about one percent. Several factors, however, clouded the popular perception of employment conditions. Administrative and middle management jobs grew only by 0.6 percent in 1967 and stagnated completely the following year, precisely when the new French educational system, inaugurated by Christain Fouchet in 1962, began graduating its first class from the vastly expanded university system. Not only were there fewer jobs for this group but many more women graduates. The number of women with the credentials to seek work in the middle income, middle skill range almost doubled in the 1960s. As it turns out, however, women workers in the unskilled range were somewhat less likely to be in the work force during their twenties, than had been the case with their grandmothers during the Depression.(11) The real expansion in income for the working class yielded more family time for households than had been possible in previous generations. Finally, the Algerian and Turkish foreign workers had established their niche in the economy, and effectively competed with native born French in the lower skill categories.(12) The foreign student also appeared at the French universities in far larger numbers than ever before, and while not directly seeking scarce middle class jobs in France, the foreign students increased the competion in the classroom.

By 1968, most French housing, even in the rural areas, had running water, electricity and the communal amenities of recreation, transport and cultural services. The great exceptions to the broad improvement in the standard of living were in the southwest, and in parts the Paris region. In the southwest, the Midi Pyrénées, and Aquitaine still suffered from a lack of industrial jobs and from poor transportation connections with the remainder of France. As for Paris, the picturesque housing conditions created by a thousand years of chaotic growth played such a vital role in the tourist trade that many groups actively opposed any efforts at urban renewal. The attempts to rehabilitate the Halles and the Marais districts produced new housing units at extraordinary prices, which drove the original residents into distant suburbs.(13) In 1967 and 1968, alone the cost of housing went up by 12 percent in Paris. Despite these exceptions, overall housing conditions improved dramatically in France during the Fifth Republic, as shown in Chart Two.

The brief slow down in job growth in 1967 and 1968 coincided with an increase in Parisian housing costs, that hit students especially hard. Many found the promise of first generation upward mobility snatched away, and turned to the streets to signal their disappointment and frustration. The May rebellion obscured much of what was solid, prosperous and Gaullist about France in the late 1960s. The Gaullist coalition had been slowly and successfully consolidating its political base in the heavily Catholic regions such as Brittany and the Pays de la Loire, in the less developed southwest, on the industrial borders from the Nord to Alsace to Savoy. In these areas the Gaullist deputies successfully edged out their rivals on both the left and the right. The Gaullist vote grew as indicated in Chart Three peaking in the year of the spring crisis.

Rapid population growth in these Gaullist leaning regions favored a continuing expansion of the Gaullist electorate. These targeted regions also stood near the bottom of the scale in the regional distribution of wages, as shown in Chart Four but they experienced a very strong rate of job growth during the 1960s, especially in the larger modernizing industries--automobiles, telecommunications, chemicals and transport equipment. For instance, Brittany had the lowest regional average wage in industry yet experienced the second greatest growth in jobs in France. In contrast, the left leaning Paris region lost jobs while wages stood about 25 percent above the national average and 40 percent above breton wages.

Column One of Chart Four indicates the regional growth in jobs in France. When these patterns were regressed against such indicators of modernization as the presence of growth industry, better housing (including owner occupied units as a measure of household prosperity), investment levels and population growth, much of the decline in the electoral fortunes of the left parties can be explained as indicated in the statistical appendix. Quite significantly, income seems to have been redistributed during the period of planned growth towards those French who were geographically mobile making the transition from farming to urban occupations and coming to live in areas that were far more conservative in 1968 than they had been in 1946. This happened especially in the older industrial areas from the Nord to Alsace to Savoy.(14)

The decade before 1968 produced real changes in life styles and consumption patterns that few in France wished to give up. In consumer goods the French had 2.8 cars for every car a decade earlier, 4.8 televisions, 2.5 refrigerators and 3.8 washing machines. Real wages grew between 1962 and 1967 by an average of 3.6 percent per year. Overall the decade of growth gave France the second greatest increase in GNP per capita in the European Economic Community. The protests in 1968 came precisely at the point that the "French Dream" seemed to be slipping out of the reach of the lower middle and young working class.

Where did these conditions of the marketplace and the ballot box leave the French left in 1968? While the Socialist Party under Mitterrand participated in the planning process it favored a position of stronger central control over private interests. The Socialist Party advocated a fuller integration into the European market.(15) The Communist Party under Marchais faced internal troubles over the relationship of the French party to the Soviet party and the troublesome problem of Stalinism.(16) While the Communist Party nominally clung to the old centralist planning strategies of the Stalinist Five Year Plans of the 1930s, that position was under attack by several factions within the Party. Neither Party's position appeared to be especially appealing to the French electorate in the mid-1960s. In the March 1967 both parties failed to present a credible challenge to the Gaullists. The Communist Party scored only 22.4 percent, against 37.7 percent for the Gaullists. The Socialist Party trailed the Communists with only 18.7 percent of the vote. In the legislative elections a loose collection of centrist and conservative candidates including Giscard's Independent Republicans received 13.4 percent which indirectly helped the Gaullists. From these election results in 1967, few observers would have guessed that the Fifth Republic was in any danger of being

Chart 1
Unskilled Workers in the Active Population

1906	64
1931	67
1946	NA
1954	57
1962	53
1968	50
1975	41

Source: Patrick Allard, Michel Allard, et al, *Dictionnaire des Groupes industriels et finances en France* (Paris: Seuil, 1978), 13. *TEF: Tableaux de l'Economie Française* (Paris: INSEE, 1981), 33.

overturned by angry mobs in the streets of Paris. May of the following year took the country by surprise.

Neither of the old left parties anticipated the flood of criticism which was aimed in May at the problems of pollution and town level participatory democracy. Both issues crystalized a broad range of New Left criticism of the qualitative problems inherent in the French model of capitalist *planification*. The problems of industrial pollution were especially acute in the area of Savoy with its fragile mountain valley environments, in the old industrial zones of the northeast and the heavily populated Paris region.

The development of the electric industry from the 1940s to the early 1960s in Savoy was typical of the disputes that were at the heart of the argument between environmentalists and *planistes* in 1968.(17) Electric production in the Maurienne and Tarentaise valleys began during Vichy in 1941 when the rural farming area had less a quarter million residents. Industrial development went hand in hand with the creation of model communities in the late 1940s to house the industrial work force. In the 1950s an aluminum factory had been set up at Uzel, and subsidiary operations followed. During the spiral of prosperity in the 1950s and 1960s, much of the regional work force shifted into the modernizing sectors of the economy. Instead of leaving the valleys to seek better jobs and housing, young peasants of Savoy remained at home and multiplied. Soon the population overwhelmed natural resources of the valleys. By the mid-1960s the air and water pollution had become so significant that some tourist guides warned visitors to avoid the area. In 1968, the environmentalists in Savoy roundly denounced the materialist values of the *planistes*, who had designed working environments with little regard for natural resource limitations, like clean air. The degradation of the quality of the natural environment seemed to confirm the sense of arrogance in man's ability to plan over the earth's natural ability to regenerate life. Yet the environmentalists in Savoy and throughout France failed to refute satisfactorily the counter-arguments of the *planistes* that the guided growth of the post war period had produced a marked improvement in the material standard of living. French voters in 1968 showed sensitivity to the arguments of the environmentalists in the primary round, but

Chart 2

Housing Conditions 1962 - 1973
(in percentages)

	Proportion Owner Occupied			Proportion Overcrowded			Average Number Persons per Unit		
Years:	1962	68	73	62	68	73	62	68	73
Region:									
Paris	30	33	35	46	40	30	2.7	2.7	2.7
Champagne	43	44	46	32	26	20	3.1	3.2	3.1
Picardie	46	48	52	29	25	20	3.3	3.3	3.2
Haute Normandie	35	38	41	36	29	20	3.2	3.2	3.0
Centre	48	49	53	39	31	18	3.1	3.0	2.9
Basse Normandie	40	43	44	39	32	21	3.3	3.2	3.1
Bourgogne	46	47	49	35	30	19	3.0	3.0	2.8
Nord	40	43	45	26	22	16	3.3	3.3	3.2
Lorraine	38	40	42	31	24	14	3.4	3.3	3.1
Alsace	46	45	48	23	18	12	3.3	3.2	3.1
Franche-Comté	44	45	47	30	24	15	3.2	3.2	3.1
Pays de la Loire	48	51	55	46	37	23	3.3	3.3	3.1
Bretagne	51	55	58	54	42	28	3.3	3.2	3.0
Poitou-Charentes	53	55	59	39	31	20	3.3	3.2	3.0
Aquitaine	47	48	52	33	26	16	3.3	3.2	3.0
Midi Pyrénées	54	54	54	37	28	16	3.3	3.2	3.0
Limousin	53	54	55	37	29	18	3.1	3.0	2.7
Rhône-Alpes	38	40	41	41	33	21	3.1	3.1	3.0
Auvergne	49	49	51	38	31	21	3.1	3.0	2.9
Languedoc	48	49	50	35	27	17	3.1	3.0	2.9
Provence/Corse/ Côtes d'Azur	38	39	42	42	34	26	3.0	2.9	2.8
FRANCE	41	43	46	39	32	22	3.1	3.1	3.0
(excluding Paris)	44	46	48	37	29	20	3.2	3.2	3.0

Chart 3

Votes for Gaullist Deputies in Primary Elections

	Percentage
1958	20.4
1962	31.9
1967	37.7
1968	43.6

Source: Anthony Hartley, *Gaullism: The rise and fall of a political movement* (New York: Outerbridge & Dienstfrey, 1971), 271.

Chart 4

A Comparison of the Rates of Job Creation and Wage Levels by Region

Regions	I 1960-1970* Rate of Job Creation	II Distribution of wages (French average = 100)
Basse Normandie	49.3%	82
Bretagne	37.6	76
Poitou-Charentes	37.6	80
Centre	35.0	83
Pays de la Loire	34.0	85
Haute Normandie	29.5	95
Auvergne	27.7	88
Picardie	26.0	91
Bourgogne	25.6	85
Franche-Comté	18.5	96
Aquitaine	14.6	91
Midi Pyrénées	14.2	90
Champagne	12.7	85
Languedoc	12.6	90
Limousin	12.3	78
Alsace	10.7	92
Rhône-Alpes	8.9	96
Provence-Corse-Côtes d'Azur	8.0	105
Lorraine	3.5	94
Nord	2.6	91
Paris	-3.1	126
AVERAGE	30.0%	100

Sources: Michel Hannoun et Philippe Temple, *Les implantations industrielles et l'emploi régional en France* (Paris: INSEE, 1976), séries E, no. 40, 13. (I)

V. Briquel, *Les comptes régionaux des branches industrielles en 1970* (Paris: INSEE, 1975), séries R, no. 21, 29. (II)

*Enterprises with more than one hundred employees.

confirmed the position of the *planistes* in the final tally.

Participatory democracy at the level of town governance has never had a clear place in French history. The conservative town elite coming right out of the pre-modern tradition of village elders, and the more recent Socialist town elite coming out of the Millerand years of the Third Republic, have shared perhaps only one thing in common, the exclusive class character of their rule. While the modern French Socialists left long championed the devolution of power to the economically disenfranchised, they generally believed in transferring power to the benignly bureaucratic State which wielded its authority in the name of the workers. For them, the strong, Socialist run State would contain the excessive powers of the employers. Neither left party advocated anything resembling direct democracy. The Communist Party for its part remained wedded to the old Leninist line of democratic centralism, which made participatory democracy either fanciful or downright heretical. Thus opposition to State intrusion or State incompetence in the managing of local communities, in the late 1960s had no logical home on the left, and perhaps none on the right.

Participatory democracy became the rallying cry in May 1968 of the *Groupes d'action municipale* (GAMs).(18) The urban reform movement criticized the lack of direct community control over the physical and social development. Ironically, in a majority of cases these groups developed from the neighborhood councils that had been voluntarily established by SCIC (*la Société Centrale Immobilière de la Caisse des Dépôts et Consignations*) in 1966 to advise private developers on the fine tuning of residential designs to meet the needs of particular communities. Operating on lending principles similar to the American Federal Housing Administration of the New Deal era, the SCIC provided long term mortgage funds for the construction of approved local projects, such as housing, sewers, public works. In the mid 1950s, under the leadership of François Bloch-Lainé, the *Caisse* had backed a wide number of local development corporations to upgrade local infrastructure.(19)

In 1967, SCIC and SCET (*la Société Centrale pour l'Equipement du Territoire*) underwent a massive reorganizations to make housing and other urban development projects more attractive to private developers. Under the new guidelines, the opportunities for local planners to change the designs of private developers were markedly reduced. Residents of the planned communities found the promise of collaboration in the whole process snatched away. A final blow to the independent actions of SCET was delivered in the fall of 1968 when de Gaulle tapped *Caisse* funds inorder to bolster the franc in the foreign exchange markets. De Gaulle's action effectively shut down many domestic urban projects.(20) For the GAM movement the growth in private control over urban development after 1966 became a symbol of the anti-consumer biases of French supple planning. Local concerns from mundane matters of inadequately installed plumbing to analysis of the moral dilemmas of the American war in Viet Nam came to be framed within the GAM critique of *urbanisme*.

At the core of the disputes over environment and the popular role in local governance was a fundamental cleavage in French society over the implications of *planification* for civil and personal liberties.(21) A solid constituency in both the old left movements and in the Liberal Keynesian movement believed that the intervention of the State of in the marketplace created material well-being. Their arguments rested upon properly determinist positions on the interrelationship of the economic environment and the general welfare of the society. French Keynesians and Proudhonian Socialists would certainly have been at home in the Second Empire as well as in the Fifth Republic. The coercive aspects of a social system which molds individual and group behavior to fit the planners' expectations for behavior came under fire in 1968. Norms of social behavior were generated by the French technical elite, who clearly imposed arbitrary and decidedly anti-democratic values upon society. For example, when the town planner improved the major transit artery between the small suburb and the city of Paris, he did so to anticipate an increase in commuting to and from the capital: The actions of thousands of commuters. The road improvements, however, reduced the commercial activity in the suburb as local merchants failed to effectively compete with the Parisian department stores. These changes in the suburb can benefit or destroy a particular individual or segment of the community, and they represent a process governing society that for all practical purposes is closed to popular oversight. The rationale for making planning technocratic in the first place was precisely to isolate decision making from the undue influence of the most seriously impacted parts of society and to allow plans to be generated in a manner that maximizes total social welfare--in the eyes of the planner at any rate.

The message of Le Corbusier in 1950, "to measure, to standardize and to allocate" established the fundamentally anti-democratic hierarchy for much of post-war town design.(22) But the problem facing France in 1968 was not that easily resolved by simple decentralization. Since the question of the devolution of central planning and town planning power remained locked in the long struggle between the old left and the right for control over local government. To simply hand town planning decisions over to a New England style town meeting in France was unthinkable for the Socialists and Communists. Indeed, some of that most vocal supporters of deconcentration of planning power in 1968 came not from the New Left but from the old Vichyite right, and from the local elites who were wedded to the Gaullist coalition.

In the June 1968 elections to the National Assembly, regional _notables_ delivered the biggest electoral victory of the Gaullist coalition since the founding of the Fifth Republic. The Gaullists received a clear majority of 292 out of 485 deputies, with the Communist Party dropping from 73 to a mere 33, with the Socialists declining from 116 to 57. Leftist support remained strong only in the center of France, in the Paris region, and to the south in the Midi-Pyrénées. All three of these regions had been major targets for urban renewal during the Fifth Plan, and the Centre region for rural industrialization as well as urban development. The debate over _planisme_ in these regions served as the focal point of the legislative campaign, with the Gaullist candidates supporting a further deconcentration of planning power to the local communities and the left parties clinging to the old centralist formula of the Fourth Republic. In these regions the electorate soundly rejected the Gaullist candidates. In the border regions of the west and the east, the results went in the opposite direction as the Gaullists did especially well in those areas that were rapidly improving under strong local initiative, such as in Brittany and the Rhône-Alpes.

In the urban reforms of September 9, 1968, de Gaulle warmly endorsed the model of regional deconcentration of planning. He declared that:

> It is on the participation of those organizations which are interested in regional development, that we intend to base the new order that will ensure the existence of France. Among the key aspects of this order has been the creation of regional jurisdictions, the appointment of regional prefects, the institution of CODER and of development corporations. We must now broaden the efforts at decentralization and give the regional prefects adequate means of administrative control. It is necessary to give the prefect a regional council of representatives from diverse economic, social and academic backgrounds. This council must know about all the projects concerning maintenance and development in the region, and especially about those items in the Plan. It must also allocate the resources of the State, by special tax levies in the regions and by loans.(23)

Many of these reforms paralleled the designs of Vichy and clearly rewarded the loyal Gaullist regional elite for their overwhelming support in the critical spring elections. The proposal continued the trend in French planning under the Fifth National Plan which emphasized the contributions of the private business and civic sector in effective implementation of *planisme*. In effect, the historic, or traditional Gaullists moved very quickly in 1968 to co-opt the issue of deconcentration from the New Left, which was left naked in the wind, without a platform or voters.

Conclusion

The crisis of May left the Socialist and Communist Parties deeply divided. The New Left bitterly criticized the Socialist Party for supporting a definition of planning that made the concept of Socialism a pale imitation of the old capitalist system, which appeared to exchange alienation from the

Chart 5

Left Votes for Deputies in 1968
(in percentages)

Region	Communist Party	Socialist Party	Total
Basse Normandie	9	10	19
Bretagne	19	13	32
Poitou-Charentes	15	19	34
Centre	20	19	39
Pays de la Loire	8	18	26
Haute Normandie	26	17	43
Auvergne	17	22	39
Picardie	23	16	43
Bourgogne	16	25	41
Franche-Comté	12	23	35
Aquitaine	16	22	38
Midi-Pyrénées	14	30	44
Champagne	19	19	38
Languedoc	22	20	42
Limousin	19	29	48
Alsace	7	9	16
Rhône-Alpes	16	17	33
Provence/Corse/Côtes d'Azur	18	16	34
Lorraine	13	18	31
Nord	23	21	44
Paris	27	16	43

bureaucratic manager for alienation from the old *patron*. The sharpest criticism was reserved, however, for the French Communist Party, still faithful to Stalinism. In the following four years, the Socialists and Communists made concessions to the position of the New Left, by picking up the issue of *planification démocratique*, but in neither case going so far as to reject the existing portions of their party programs that were diametrically opposed to the formulation.

A more viable explanation for the resurgence of support for Socialist and Communist candidates in the 1973 legislative races can be found in the radical slowing down of the national migration rate at the end of the Fifth Plan. The OPEC crisis of 1973 further reduced economic activity and internal migration fell off once again. The poles-of attraction strategy for an urban hierarchy of development, including labor force growth and development during the 1950s and 1960s had been successfully channelling workers to the major eight urban zones. This migration had largely been at the expense of the medium and smaller regional cities, where in some cases the migration of upwardly mobile workers reduced the size of the left electorate in the short run. With the slowing growth rate in the 1970s, the left, and especially the Socialists rebounded to important victories in 1978 and to take the presidency from the Gaullists in 1981. Planned migration goals for labor during the 1960s under the Fourth and Fifth Plans contributed to the decline of the left votes through the process of climbing the urban hierarchy. Planned labor goals were not met in the 1970s under the weight of external shocks from the world market for petroleum and the rapid inflation of the late 1970s, and the old electoral geography of 1945 and 1946 began to reemerge in France.

CHAPTER SEVEN

An Assessment of the Quality of Urban Life (1968-1950

In his analysis of *urbanisme*, Dreyfus has presented much of the case for the New Left of 1968, and in some ways for the earlier protest of the humanist theorists of the old Third Republic. In its simplest form, this humanist argument denies that it is possible to end alienation by the creation of rational harmonies in the Positivist sense. Those rational harmonies yield only the false socialisms of Stalinist Russia and fascist Germany.

These charges were rebutted in France by the traditional left parties and by the Giscardians in the 1970s. Giscard and his neo-conservatives countered with a functionalist analysis, based on Keynesianism, which attempted to present itself within the French tradition of Republican civil liberties, yet at the same time was properly rational and Postivist in the best nineteenth century sense of the terms. In the political debates after 1968, assessments of the quality of life for urban France were posed in precisely these terms. The New Left evaluated urban change by the qualitative impact on social life, while the new conservatives measured urban life in terms of economic prosperity. For their part, the traditional French left parties found themselves uncomfortably close to the judgments of the new conservatives.

The Humanist Critique of Urbanisme

In his own words, the problem raised by Dreyfus and the New Left after 1968 was "demystify in the first place *urbanisme*, which is *rationalité* in essence, and a living *ideology*."(1) In essence, he rejected the whole of the Positivist experience in culture, society and the economy. Like Foucault, Althusser and Marcuse, Dreyfus argued that the code word *urbanisme* simply masked the most relentless and repressive homogenizing forces in modern life.(2) He attributed these forces to the exploitative nature of capitalism and the technocratic State. The virtue that Le Corbusier saw in "the right angle of *la droite* attests to the scope of [state] power and its grandeur," alienated and frightened Dreyfus.(3)

This humanist, even romantic, collectivist vision certainly went back in French thought at least as far as the Conspiracy of the Equals by Babeuf in 1796. During the Great Revolution, that early anarcho-communist insurrection called property itself into question. In theory at least Babeuf in theory at least, appealed to the most benighted in Paris, those even poorer than Jacques Roux's Enragé. With the attack on property, certainly a prerequisite for a capitalist economy in virtually any form, Babeuf immediately separated himself from Saint Simon, Comte and even Proudhon, with their more powerful, and more materialist theories of rational management of property. While the humanist vision in socialist thought did not entirely disappear with Babeuf's execution in 1797, the capitalist and socialist rationalist theorists did their best to eradicate it during the following century.

Curiously enough, this socialist-humanist tradition reappeared in the writings of many late nineteenth century Russian anarchists such as Petr Kropotkin. It was through the writings of Prince Kropotkin that this French humanist tradition came to the attention of Ebenezer Howard. The original edition of Garden City in 1898 owed a great deal of its vision to Kropotkin's *Kleb i volia* and *Fields, Factories and Workshops*.(4) Kropotkin's utopian scheme for the organization of the ideal commune certainly contained many features as old as Plato's Republic, and was far more reasonable, if not rational, than Fourier's phalansteries with their third sex. Kropotkin, however, formulated his utopian scheme in the context of a bitter quarrel with his Russian Marxist rivals Plekhanov and Lenin with their relentless scientific determinism. Kropotkin's utopian vision found an unexpected sympathetic audience in Fabian circles and among early urban reformers such as Howard. For his part, Howard tried to make the argument that his urban plan represented a practical implementation of socialist humanism. Howard walked between the two position by arguing that rational development also could be humanistic. The elimination of waste, that great bogey of industrial capitalism, meant more abundance which eventually would push Howard's England to a new plateau of material well-being where competition and conflict would be meaningless, petty and obsolete.(5)

In England, the philanthropic capitalists who built the first model town promptly exorcised any glimmerings of socialist-humanism in the original Garden City proposal. Among capitalists and Socialists in the late nineteenth century, the powerful determinist faith left little room for humanist ideas in business or in party programs. Yet it is significant that the few humanistic flourishes of the original Garden City proposal were so effectively and completely purged from early urban plans in both England and the rest of Europe. These ideas contained the germs of heresy. While planning goals can be framed in the language of socialist-humanism, as Howard did to some extent in 1898, that is far from a necessary element of the formula. Urban design can function quite well in the hands of committed rationalizers. The New Left of 1968 insisted that the early humanist proposals were doomed because the idea of private property was retained.(6) Property and humanism can not coexist according to the new humanists.

What is town planning but the arrangement of property in space, to maximize its utility, and hence, its value? Given this primary assumption, it is not in the least incongruous to find Keynes in his General Theory of 1936 advancing a new home mortgaging scheme, relying fully on his "multiplier," and to find George Marchais in the annual party report of 1978 bitterly denouncing the inequalities of modern French capitalism which gives more color televisions per capita to the bourgeoisie than to the working class: Hearth, home and color TV, the calling cards of the new Positivists.(7)

In the face of such concrete, salient appeals to common well-being as well as individual self-interest, the neo-Marxists like Foucault and Marcuse, and the New Left environmentalists could only pose a more ephemeral demand to improve the quality of French urban society. The improvements in the quality of life sought by the humanists included the reduction in alienation of the individual from the complexity of society itself, less emphasis on materialist values and more attention to spiritual and emotional fulfillment, but at the same time more social harmony and integration.(8) These concerns led the New Left to champion causes such as the civil and human rights struggles of the foreign workers in France who suffered from some of the most abominable living conditions in Western Europe and from racism including that at the hands of the Communist trade unions. This humanistic movement of the late 1960s eventually produced substantial changes in the quality of life afforded to some segments of French society such as foreign workers. For examples these temporary residents became eligible for regular HLM housing subsidies, they gained entrance into French higher education, they became entitled to welfare subsidies and were given voting privileges in some municipal elections.

But the essence of this humanist critique should not be missed. The New Left and especially the neo-Marxists offered France a moralist argument that condemned the sins of Positivism and scientific socialism: The faith of Marx himself. By unhinging their critique from rationalism as it had been defined in the late nineteenth century in favor of humanist concepts, these new theorists like Dreyfus failed to comprehend some of the most profound changes occurring in their own society. Generally unequipped to understand the complex econometric forecasts that underpinned the planning policies of the post-war period, the New Left critics underestimated the formidable power of these policy instruments to shape and manipulate vast areas of French life from the distribution of employment and living standards to the geographic balance of the electorate. It is not surprising that the politicians of the traditional left parties quickly turned away from the weak theories offered in 1968. While there were attempts to co-opt some portions of the student New Left movement and a related experiment with Euro-Communism in 1973 and 1974 (Communism with a humanistic face), these minor currents faded quickly under the onslaught of the faithful <u>dirigistes</u> at the helm of both the Government and the opposition. The new right regimes of Pompidou and Giscard, and eventually the left Governments under Mitterrand promised a sober return to the properly rationalist and centralist urban policies.

Some Definitions of the Quality of Life in Urban France

Given the vast gulf that separates the humanist and rationalist approaches to the nature of society and for urban culture within that society, it is impossible to offer a single list of criteria by which French urban life can be evaluated in the 1970s. At the CGP in 1970, René Fraisse offered a paradigm for analyzing the quality of urban life from what he identified as the three basic tendencies in contemporary French political thought.(9) Fraisse has provided a useful starting point in his report which was prepared for the CGP in the wake of the May events. The CGP used the Fraisse model in an attempt to sort out the traditions within French *urbanisme* as it had developed across the twentieth century. Fraisse identified three major problems facing French urban planners: The lack of public infrastructure, imbalances in urban growth, and *la mentalité* which looked back to a happy pastoral, rural past.(10) Fraisse identified three sets of solutions to urban problems: "*Naturalism*," "*culturalisme*," and "*progressive-fonctionnaliste* can be found in Figure One." Not surprisingly, he favored the latter approach to urban policy making while viewing the other tendencies as serious impediments to modernization.

Fraisse defined Naturalism as a stern individualism that rejected the centralization of governance. In its place, families held society together in a relatively depoliticized framework where social stratification arose primarily from differences in wealth. Interestingly enough, naturalists according to Fraisse were relatively indifferent to public ownership of some lands, if at the same time private property is maintained as a cornerstone of the economic system. The naturalists held an optimistic view of society as generally being prosperous. In keeping with the devotion to family structures, this *tendance* showed a strong preference for single family homes in a suburban, or even semi-rural setting, with a well developed road system.

Culturalists, in contrast, found self-expression through participation in the commune or city where life is collective and participation encouraged. A well integrated economic structure for urban life was important for culturalists. This group believed that neighborhoods within urban areas needed separate identities, but the function of urban policy must be to

FIGURE ONE

THREE MODELS OF URBAN THEORY

	Naturalism	Culturalism	Progressive-Functionalism
Ideology	Individualism. Rejection of tradition return to natural conditions Age of Gold/Post Industrial.	Urban society is the place to create culture of interest to each citizen.	Promotion of techical progress, and collective values. Belief in rationalism.
Cociology	Rejection of centralism, cells, single family households, depoliticized. Stratification by wealth (except if land is public). within Against	Self Organization of neighborhood with symbolic and practical unity. Strong communal life. Strong partici-pation.	Specialization of roles. Bureau-cratic control. Variety of social categories
Economy	Free enterprise. Private property No problem with low incomes: society is supposed to be rich.	Integration of costs/benefits within plans. Against specula-tion. Each Neighborhood self-sufficient.	Town is the total productive complex. Separate factories and residences. Each neighborhood has has a function in city.
Urban Life	Integrate with rural.	Simplify towns.	Rationalize.
Land Ownership	Continue.	Diverse opinions	Discontinue.
Housing	Many single family houses.	Variety of collective style.	Collective.
Communications	Strong freeway system.	New intra-town roads.	Replace neighbor-hood roads with thoroughfares.

Source: France. CGP. Plan et Prospectives (Paris, 1970), essai par R. Fraisse, 17-18.

serve the interests of the community as a whole by not allowing any one segment to dominate. Housing should be restricted to collective dwellings within an urban environment that fosters a high level of communication inside the city. While this position does not completely deny the existence of private property, it would be largely obsolete in this framework.

Functionalist-progressivism places full faith in the promotion of progress through rationalization and collective values. Roles in society are assumed to be highly specialized and bureaucratic coordination is a vital social function of government. Residences and workplaces are separated into distinct quarters in a city. Function defines space with housing being highly collective and private ownership being discontinued as too cumbersome to regulate. Streets with person names should give way to thoroughfares with route numbers.

Writing for the Center for Urban Research in 1970, René Magan stated the problem in a slightly different way when he distinguished four stages of urbanization as indicated in Figure Two.(11) The lowest level, Stage Zero is spontaneous urban growth, or the absence of _urbanisme_. Stage One is Liberal regulation of urban development. Stage Two is highly interventionist Liberal direction of urbanization. Finally, Stage Three is totally controlled urban centers. Magan attributed _bidonvilles_ such as those housing foreign workers in the Paris region to _urbanisation spontanée_ and at the opposite extreme the total centralization of urban planning decisions which "is secretly the dream of every urban planner." Magan went on to point out the "the most advanced level of urban planning is only practical either in a socialist or centralized authoritarian economy. But is also present in an industrial or mining company town where power is completely in the hands of capitalists who own the land, control the buildings and control the employment."(11) Both Fraisse and Magan developed salient typologies for the key elements in contemporary French urban policy debates without mentioning social class. They represented the attempt by the new conservative technocrats to create a new framework that escaped the divisions that brought down the previous Republics and were the focus for debate in 1968.

In the 1974 presidential campaign between the Gaullist incumbent Georges Pompidou and François Mitterrand the joint candidate of the left parties, the quality of life issue figured prominently in the debate. Yet neither candidate was willing to propose changes outside of the general framework identified by the existing planning traditions, as identified by Fraisse or Magan. Pompidou tried to co-opt the issue by replacing the old Ministry of Urbanisme with the new Ministry of Environment and the Quality of Life. Neither side in the debates succeeded in satisfying the humanists who generally refused to vote in that election.

The key problem with the quality of life issue was one of definition. Humanists and rationalists lacked a common general premise against which French urban life could be evaluated. No real agreement was possible since the humanists rejected the notion of normative criteria for evaluating social and even physical conditions, and most rationalists could not conceive of society without normative categories.(13) Essentially, the quality of life issue in the presidential debate of 1974 came down to a question of whether the glass was half empty or half full for the rationalists like Pompidou and Mitterrand, while the humanists thought all along that it should be a tea cup. For example, the Presidential candidates argued over the relative success of the intense housing modernization programs of the post-war period. In 1945, only one household in ten had indoor plumbing but by 1972 that number had jumped six-fold. Yet the deviation from the norm was significant: Forty percent of the need for indoor plumbing went unmet.(14)

Those norms rarely interested the humanist critics. They sought changes in the patterns of social class and racial integration in housing instead of accounting for easily measured and count physical changes in housing quality. The new questions, however, raised the issue of subjective conditions in decision making. What about the situation where Group A wants more social integration of rich and poor, of foreign and native-born within the same housing complex, but Group B, the wealthy and native born prefers to remain separate? Does integration mean improving the quality of life for Group A while diminishing it for Group B?(15)

Concern for the quality of life among humanists was, of course, no less real because it involves subjective and contradictory criteria, that apriori defy normative evaluation. But because the humanist

FIGURE TWO
Four Types of Urbanisme, and Urbanization

Type 0	Spontaneous urbanization -- the absence of all planning
Type 1	Regulated urbanization -- purely Liberal planning
Type 2	Directed urbanization -- Liberal interventionist planning
Type 3	Dictated urbanization -- comprehensive planning

Source: René Magan _et al_, _Conception et instruments de la Planification urbaine_ (Paris: CRU, 1973), 6.

approach rested essentially on a marriage between radical individualism and collectivist consensus it provided little that could be used to understand the contributions and failures of normative planning for the growth of French urban culture.

Neo-Conservative Urban Criteria

The record of French urbanization can be evaluated using the rationalist criteria for controlled urban change. Assuming for the moment that economies to some extent behave the way we believe they do and that Keynesian Frenchmen think of themselves as consumers who follow in aggregate the savings, investment and consumption functions laid out in the General Theory, urban life can be seen as part of economic development.

Under these conditions, an important critierion for urbanization, for example, has been the development of employment and housing in the same geographic site. In the period from 1948 to 1968, France has been especially successful in meeting this goal for urban planning. In the 1960s, the geographic coincidence of job growth and housing expansion was particularly strong. The early Third Republic also was dominated by a *dirigiste* urbanization and housing policy firmly in the hands of a modernizing elite: Grandfathers and grandsons of l'Ecole des Mines generally. They wrote the first public housing legislation and built the first company towns to unite employment and residence in one site. The gap between saw urban policy and the late Third Republic floundering as France lost faith with the old rules of Classical Economics. As the consensus among businessmen and politicians waned housing and employment became less coordinated in site selections. These patterns indicated that the highly monopolized marketplace before First World War decade succeeded in optimizing site selection for housing and employment. As Pareto and Walras observed in their models for late nineteenth century market behavior, Planning in the hands of Monnet and his CGP also optimized site selection. As René Magan pointed out in the CGP report of 1970, a common link existed between the late nineteenth century company town and the *ville nouvelle* of the 1960s. He might have added that Howard's Garden City was the conduit.(16)

A second rationalist criterion for successful urbanization was the clarification and regularization

of institutions. Here only part of the criterion has been successfully met. National level administrative controls across the post-war period shifted oversight in urban development towards the Ministry of Finance and the CGP. But the strong decentralization movement pulled considerable decision making power away from the national elites at the CGP in Paris by buttressing authorities at the regional and local levels.(17) The mixed signals stymied development across France.
The strongly dirigiste faction came to be identified with Pomipdou and Giscard, and their regionalist opponents with the historic Gaullists such as Jacques Chaban-Delmas and Jacques Chirac. It was no accident that Giscard's Independent Republicans came overwhelmingly from towns too small to be effectively modernized at the local level where growth in employment, housing, schools, and new roads required external intervention. The deputies and ministers of the historic Gaullist mainstream, generally, came from large cities which generated some of their own urban improvements.(18)

Finally, there has been the idea which Giscard advanced in his pre-election tract French Democracy (1975) that planning has somehow rendered the "holy war" between the classes obsolete.(19) Giscard's premise, that the clearly understood and common body of knowledge about the means by which the economy could be technically manipulated under Keynesian formulas, effectively ended the perils of poverty that had driven generations of Frenchmen to protest and revolution.(20) That was the old corporatist promise of the end of class struggle in new code words.

Old Left Urban Criteria

To see the half empty glass, from the perspective of the French left parties, several additional rationalist criteria are needed to define the quality of urban life. In general, the left has accepted the first two premises already identified by the neo-right. Communists, however, have taken extreme exception to some of the more classically Keynesian features of urban policy-making after 1964, and to the policies of Pompidou and Giscard in the 1970s. Under the leadership of Pierre Massé from 1963 to 1966, the CGP increasingly turned to contract planning, where private developers in contractual relationship with the French State design and build everything from public works to housing to plants and equipment at the nationalized factories. Like Giscard, Massé intended French planning to be an aide to the private sector, to enhance the prosperity of the business community. As in the title of Massé's famous little book, *La Plan ou l'anti-hasard?* (1965), planning meant risk avoidance for industry that indirectly helped insure general prosperity.(21) From the Socialist and Communist perspective, Massé's risk avoidance at the national electric company meant public profits through low wage rates. The left wanted to govern industry through planning inorder redistribute power among the French social classes.

The Socialist demand for a strong policy of public controls land and industry of course, went back to the early public service ethic which had been raised by Henri Sellier and his colleagues in the better government leagues.(22) For the most part, the French courts struck down municipal socialist legislation in the 1930s which had relied on the public service doctrine that had little basis in French law. While the origins of the public service idea went back to Saint Simon's Council of Newton and Proudhon's Peoples' Bank, the notion was as current as the Common Program of 1972 which denounced contract planning infavor of great public controls. As early as the preliminary discussions of the *urbanisme* section of the Fifth National Plan in 1964, the Communist led *Confédération Général du Travail*, rejected the whole concept of privatization of planning and actually withdrew from the work of the sub-commission of the Plan over this issue.(23) The balance of class power in planning was important to the traditional left.

Socialists and Communists also believed that an important criteria in evaluating planning was how well the policies redistributed wealth and income.(24) For instance, the HLM program enabled some lower income working class individuals to buy property. Even greater access to housing credits was demanded in Socialist and Communist programs during the 1970s. For most of the Fourth Republic and until 1964 under the Fifth Republic, the housing system in France clearly contained many elements intended to redistribute wealth in the form of residential property. Only under the privatization program of the late 1960s, and after the housing reform of 1977, did housing priorities begin to shift away from the use of housing policy as a means to redistribute property ownership in French society.

The clearest and most comprehensive statement of contemporary Socialist concern about urbanisme can be found in the Plan intérimaire for 1982-1983, by Michel Rocard, Ministère du Plan et l'Aménagement du Territoire early in Mitterrand's presidency. Rocard cast the Socialist programme in the language of the quality of life issue. He called for a humanist reform to ameliorate working life, improve common social bonds and better the daily life of everyone, but used properly rationalists tools to achieve these goals. Rocard demand more New Towns.(25)

Alluding specifically to the public service tradition of the 1930s, Rocard argued for more support for mass transit, in both urban and rural areas, for park and ride lots, and upgraded stations throughout the system, in place of facilities that served the individual in the private automobile.(26) Continuing the commitment to the poles-of-attraction theory of the 1950s, Rocard's proposal called for rapid rails between Lyons, Marseilles and Paris, which he carefully referred to as the "région de Ile de France," not to disquiet the decentralist camp. He also raised the issue of the relationship between the quasi-judicial regulatory boards for HLM credit, for example, and the rights of the individual as a consumer a resident or an city dweller. Consistent with the Socialist preference for collectivist solutions, he insisted that individual redress be left to the regular courts and that progressive regulatory decisions should safeguarded against undue special interests.

In presenting the Socialist position on recreation in urban settings, Rocard borrowed language from the Positivists of the last century when he wrote "the conquest of leisure time is one of the great challenges at the end of this century."(27) The potential frustrations of free-time worried the Socialists, just like they had bothered Taylor at the turn of the last century. Rocard's plan proposed flexible hours for public services in communities, overtime pay, a fifth week of paid vacation and more collective cultural activities. In part, these suggestions reflected an acute sense of the small dimensions of living space in modern urban households, the lack of common meeting places outside of the workplace and physical isolation of suburban life.

As for New Towns, Rocard suggested reforming the law of July 10, 1970, which tipped the balance in development towards central collaboration with private industry, by-passing local authorities. Interestingly enough, the criticism was not leveled against the potentials for speculation in the system or the violation of the redistributive idea, but merely the great operational inefficiency of the program. Rocard also encouraged New Town planners to take fuller advantage of energy saving technologies when designing model communities.

The fact that Rocard and his Plan intérimaire fell on hard times early in the Mitterrand presidency and both were abandoned, should not undercut the value of his statement. This plan was what Mitterrand would have done, if he could have done it. The scheme for urbanism contained all the critical features of twentieth century Socialist thought on urban change. Socialist ideas also coincided with important elements in the Radical political tradition. It was not by accident that Pompidou had called Mitterrand the Edouard Herriot of the Fifth Republic.

There lies the secret of the success of French planning and especially urban planning, its roots go back to the broad consensus of the mainstream of the Radical movement which evolved out of the révolution des maires in the late nineteenth century much like the Progressive movement in the United States at the turn of the century. A broad consensus still remains between neo-rightists old leftists and some Radicals on the governance of localities, according to predictable norms of demographic, social and economic behavior under physical planning.(28) To be sure each faction prefers its own ideological formulation but at the base, they all share a rational, functionalist belief that seeks to maximize material well-being, minimize waste and to broadly develop the whole of the nation over the specific enhancement of any special region or individual.

The Balance Sheet: Housing, Infrastructure

Using these rationalist criteria, a balance sheet of French urbanization policy can be constructed to evaluate the urban planning system in two of the most critical areas: Housing and infrastructure. By the early 1970s, housing conditions in France had improved greatly over the conditions at the end of the Second World War. Yet socio-economic segregation remained a pervasive in French social life. Benoît-Levy's dream of separate hamlets for workers, artisans and men of letters had been realized. As Chart One indicates, units without modern plumbing have been designated by the French housing census bureau as "uncomfortable" and these units are disproportionately found in the rural areas and in working class quarters. Middle class Frenchmen, in contrast, generally live in housing at the level of comfort of any Western European society except for Sweden.

The underlying dynamic which produces this severe segregation by social and economic classes is the great inequalities in the distribution of income in France. As Rocard pointed out in his interim plan, France has the greatest skewing of earned income in Western Europe.(29) The degree of comfort in housing units, as shown in Chart Two, is directly related to the ability of the residents to pay for housing in the private market. Over half a century of public housing programs in France has not eroded the power of the private market to segregate residences by income and social class. The HLM program, with its modifications, actually has reinforced the skewing of the distribution of modern housing. In 1973 the bottom thirty six percent of the households, those earning less than 20,000F per year, owned only seven percent of the HLM units and eleven percent of the units financed by the Crédit Foncier. This bottom third of French society rented 24 percent of the available HLM units. The broad range from lower civil servants to very skilled workers to the true middle class, making from 20,000F to 60,000F, constituted a slight majority of the households in France in 1973: Fifty five percent. This middle group owned 84 percent of the HLM units and 72 percent of the Crédit Foncier homes, while also renting over 70 percent of the HLM rental units. Loucheur had succeeded in giving the French middle class affordable housing. The tiny wealthy elite rarely needed public assistance in securing housing. Nearly eight percent of wealthy households had homes that lacked modern plumbing and other conveniences. These residence were usually the old family chateau of the eighteenth century or earlier.

Even though these figures indicate a badly skewed distribution of housing by socio-economic group or in French fighting words class, the overall development of property ownership in the twentieth century has been far more complex. At the turn of the century, most

Frenchmen lived in rural areas, where home ownership often reached 60 or 70 percent of the individual farmsteads, and up to 50 percent of the village homes.

These dwellings, to be sure made up that bulk of the national housing stock which lacked the most rudimentary elements of comfort, and these homes were very poorly served by the public infrastructure of France. Yet property is status in French society. Propertied peasants and villagers possessed more than land. They held the *mentalité* that Monnet sought to exorcise from French culture. At the same time, home ownership was extremely rare in large cities like Paris and in the industrial or mining towns of the northeast, where as few as ten percent of units were owner occupied. Early twentieth century demographers saw the traditional home ownership patterns as a serious obstacle to expansion of the population. Peasants were presumed to limit family size inorder to pass on an undivided farmstead. Urban dwellers kept families small of out fear of incurring higher rents in larger quarters.

After the Second World War, the massive shift away from farming and rural life, could have simply replicated these conditions in the larger cities and the emptier countryside. But following the initial decline in the number of owner occupied units in the late 1940s, the number of such units began to rise dramatically as a portion of the total number of households in urban areas. The former French peasants and villagers successfully transferred their life style of home ownership into the urban realm where housing costs and housing quality were much higher, and where their housing demand fueled a need for more public infrastructure. This demand for private housing and the willingness of the migrants to devote unusually large sums of savings to the ownership of property pushed the forecasts of housing demand in the early national plans well beyond their upper limits. Malinvaud's summary of forecasts and outcomes for the four major plans of the post-war period, in Chart Three, shows the critical role played by household fixed capital formation in the underestimation of each plan. In each forecast this category was the only one substantially incorrect.

A close inspection of the CGP planning models for household fixed capital formation from 1952 through 1964 reveals a failure even to recognize and include

Chart 1

Housing Comfort According to Socio-Economic Status, 1973

Socio-economic Status, Head of Household	Degree of Comfort	
	Lacking Modernization	Modern Comforts
Farmers	64.6%	35.4%
Farm Laborers	60.0	40.0
Business Owners	20.1	79.9
Professionals/Executives	4.4	95.6
Middle Management	11.3	88.7
Skilled Workers	25.0	75.0
Manual Workers	31.7	68.3
Services	44.2	55.8
Other Active Workers	18.0	82.0
Retired	58.1	41.9
Average	39.0	61.0

(Lacking modern comfort has been defined as a unit either without water, on with water alone without WC.)

Source: France. CGP. _Rapport du Comité de l'Habitat: Préparation du 7e Plan_ (Paris: Documentation française, 1976), 19.

Chart 2

Income, Home Ownership and Housing Comfort, 1973

Annual Income	Lacking Modernization	Modern Comforts
<10,000F	74.7%	25.3%
10,000-15,000F	62.1	37.9
15,000-20,000F	49.2	50.8
20,000-30,000F	35.5	64.5
30,000-40,000F	26.0	74.0
40,000-60,000F	17.8	82.2
60,000-80,000F	11.7	88.3
>80,000F	7.6	92.4
Average	35.0%	65.0%
Mean Income/Year	20,320F	37,130F

	Purchased with HLM Financing	Purchased with Crédit Foncier Financing
<10,000F	0.2%	2.2%
10,000-20,000F	6.9	8.8
20,000-30,000F	25.4	20.7
30,000-40,000F	29.0	23.3
40,000-60,000F	29.2	27.6
>60,000F	9.7	17.4
Mean Income/Year	38,740F	42,600F

Source: France. CGP. *Rapport du Comité de l'Habitat: Préparation du 7e Plan* (Paris: Documentation française, 1976), 19.

home ownership as a variable. As indicated on the fourth chart, despite the wide polarization of housing and housing credits in France, home ownership jumped by 4.6 percent between 1962 and 1968, and another 5.3 percent from 1968 to 1973. Chart Five has broken down housing by method of finance and by region. The rapidly urbanizing areas like Brittany and the Rhône Alpes had high levels of both public housing subsidies and privately financed dwellings. Slow growth areas such as the old industrial northeast, in contrast, maintained the company towns and other early forms of corporate control as a relatively large segment of the total housing stock. In these regions, the old practices discouraged home ownership by individuals.

The underestimates of housing need in the four major post-war plans, resulted in major distortions in the timing of the rate of growth for residential infrastructure. On the whole, however, infrastructure designed for industry was developed in the desired proportions. Part of the explanation for the widely different experiences in residential areas (the ZUPs) and in the industrial parks (the ZIUPs), was the structure of the forecasting models used in policy making. In the Second and Third Plans, residential infrastructure was treated as a constraint. Planners used that assumed limit to deflate the indicators of housing demand. They believed that as roads became too crowded and schools were filled beyond capacity home buyers would drop out of the market. This approach to modeling failed for several reasons. These migrants were not discouraged by the inadequate public services in the rapidly urbanizing areas, and the reasons are not difficult to find. Urban migrants left behind even less adequate and more antiquated infrastructure in the tiny towns and villages of rural France. Urban life was a radically different life-style for these first generation city dwellers, and comparative judgments were difficult to make without the reference points that accumulate over a family life cycle. Finally, the plans even those inadequate ones for residential infrastructure did promise improvement in the measurable foreseeable future. Inconveniences and inadequacies could be viewed as temporary. And the only viable alternative for many migrants was returning to the countryside, where conditions were worse.

In contrast to the urban residential growth forecasts industrial planning carefully integrated dynamic infrastructure variables within the basic

Chart 3

Regional Housing Indicators

Region	Percentage of Units Owner-Occupied		
	1962	1968	1973
Paris	29.7%	32.5%	35.3%
Champagne	42.7	43.5	46.2
Picardie	45.6	47.8	51.7
Haute Normandie	35.4	38.2	40.8
Centre	47.5	49.0	52.6
Basse Normandie	40.3	42.6	44.3
Bourgogne	46.1	47.1	48.5
Nord	40.1	43.2	44.7
Lorraine	38.2	40.4	42.0
Alsace	45.6	45.4	47.9
Franche Comté	44.1	45.3	46.5
Pays de la Loire	48.1	51.0	54.9
Bretagne	51.4	55.3	57.8
Poitou Charente	53.0	54.9	58.9
Aquitaine	46.9	48.4	51.5
Midi Pyrénées	53.7	53.8	54.1
Limousine	53.3	53.8	55.4
Rhône Alpes	38.0	39.6	41.3
Avergne	48.9	49.3	50.7
Languedoc	47.7	48.7	49.9
Provence-Côtes d'Azur-Corse	37.9	39.1	42.2
France	41.3	43.2	45.5
France excluding Paris	44.4	46.1	48.3

Source: F. Marchand, Les collections de l'INSEE, Séries R. (1975), 26.

Chart 4

Forecasts and Outcomes, 1952-1970

	1952-57 Second Plan		1957-61 Third Plan		1959-65 Fourth Plan		1965-70 Fifth Plan	
	F	O	F	O	F	O	F	O
GDP	124	130	120	116	138	140	132	133
Consumption:								
Households	na	134	119	114	135	138	129	129
Government	na	129	104	105	129	144	136	118
TOTAL:	122	133	na	na	135	138	129	128
Fixed Capital:								
Firms	na	150	120	119	147	152	136	150
Households	na	139	92	102	134	176	110	131
Government	na	143	127	129	185	176	164	142
TOTAL:	124	147	115	117	149	161	134	145

Source: J.J. Carré, P. Dubois & E. Malinvaud, French Economic Growth (Stanford: Stanford University Press, 1975), 463.

Chart 5

Division of Housing Status by Region
(1973)

	I	II	III	IV	V	VI
Paris	19.2%	9.5%	6.6%	16.4%	36.3%	12.0%
Champagne	30.2	12.3	3.7	17.3	24.0	12.5
Picardie	32.3	10.4	9.0	11.8	22.2	14.3
Haute Normandie	25.3	9.2	6.2	18.6	30.2	10.5
Centre	34.9	12.4	5.3	11.3	25.1	11.0
Basse Normandie	28.7	9.6	6.0	12.1	26.3	17.3
Bourgogne	33.2	9.5	5.8	9.7	26.0	15.8
Nord	27.1	11.8	5.8	10.5	26.3	18.5
Lorraine	26.9	10.4	4.7	10.9	32.0	15.1
Alsace	32.0	9.9	6.0	10.2	29.4	12.5
Franche Comté	26.9	14.8	4.7	14.0	26.6	13.0
Pays de la Loire	32.6	14.9	7.4	8.5	21.3	15.3
Bretagne	34.6	17.2	6.0	6.7	22.3	13.2
Poitou Charente	39.3	12.2	7.4	6.6	20.6	13.9
Aquitaine	34.5	11.7	5.3	6.9	28.7	12.9
Midi Pyrénées	35.9	12.8	5.4	6.8	25.2	13.9
Limousin	41.1	9.8	4.5	7.3	22.8	14.5
Rhône Alpes	22.6	13.5	5.2	12.1	32.6	14.0
Avergne	37.0	9.5	4.2	6.1	28.4	14.8
Languedoc	33.3	11.0	5.5	7.5	25.3	17.4
Provence-Côtes -d'Azur-Corse	25.4	10.1	6.7	7.9	36.9	13.0
France	28.1	11.4	6.0	11.3	29.4	13.8
(excluding Paris)	30.5	11.9	5.8	9.9	27.6	14.3

I - Owner occupied, inherited.
II - Owner occupied, HLM or Crédit Foncier financing.
III - Owner occupied, private financing.
IV - Rented, HLM aides.
V - Rented, private.
VI - Other, including farm laborer lodging, employer furnished housing.

Source: F. Marchand, Les collections de l'INSEE Séries R. (1975), 29.

forecasting models. Communications, transportion and energy delivery formed the key elements in the industrial forecasts. The key difference between the models for two sectors was that household projections were driven off course by greater than predicted demographic changes and by homeownership demands, while industrial growth remained close to the projections.

To some extent, France abandoned this highly successful industrial policy of the 1950s and 1960s after the OPEC crisis of 1973. The great jump in energy costs sucked large sums of capital out of France, as in most of Western Europe, for a period of 18 months which should have coincided with the high point in the cycle of the Sixth Plan. Instead, the plan was wrecked. Unemployment began to mount. With the unusual extraction of capital from the economy as France struggled to pay for its oil, the State found itself unable to borrow at favorable rates inorder to initiate a classic stimulation policy with public works. Under these new conditions of very high interest rates, it cost the State more to create public jobs in construction and in the GEN (les Grandes entreprises nationales), than the State could hope to recover in revenues. It was cheaper just to pay unemployment compensation. Thus, the charm of Keynesian economic theory ran into its first serious crisis of confidence in post-war France.

This new strategy of abandoning public works stimulation policy in the wake of the OPEC crisis had profound implications for French urbanization policy. The Eighth Plan for 1979 to 1985, which Giscard wrote and Mitterrand dropped, used the DMS model (Modèle dynamique multisectoriel).(30) Under DMS planning the active industries including some of the GEN, only purchased the amount of new construction actually needed to expand their particular operations and maintain profitability. Public works felt a similar constraint. This parsimonious approach to construction and public works meant that these old reliable mechanisms of post-war fiscal policy would no longer be used for employment stimulation. The new industrial infrastructure policy relied on cost effective contract planning in its clearest form.(31) The Eighth Plan delineated this new employment policy for France.(32) The Eighth Plan argued that France needed more skilled workers with high technology training, and should correspondingly reduce the number of unskilled manual workers like those found in the construction trades. It was better for France to have highly trained workers and produce goods that the Third World could not duplicate. By implication this new formula meant that it was more efficient to pay the least skillful workers not to work, if they could not be trained for work at a rate consistent with their marginal product. Mitterrand and Rocard's plan denounced the Eighth Plan as creating a permanent underclass of unemployables in France.

Conclusion

The quality of French urban life has improved dramatically during the two decades of planned urbanization even with all the false starts and contradictory policies. More French have come to share in the benefits of urban culture and society. Yet certain long standing forces in French history, such as the peasant's desire to own property, have confounded growth schedules at the CGP. Planners neither forecast that preference, nor were able to recast it in a policy direction that they preferred. Planning faced concrete limitation.

Whether the changes have produced satisfaction with the quality of life for the individual in French society depends in large part on that Frenchman's alignment along the ideological spectrum from humanism to rationalism. The rationalists of the New Right and the Old Left would have us believe in the long run value of the post-war mechanisms for improving the quality of urban life. The humanists doubt that the quality of life can be improved with *urbanisme*.

CONCLUSION

In modern France, urban planning has developed in a complex ideological and political framework with a carefully delineated social contract for the administration of urban social and economic life.(1) Le Corbusier played a major role in formulating this political philosophy and in creating the language of physical land use planning. His system of ideas championed modernity which he defined as rationalization and standardization. Modern society was destined to live in his *grandes ensembles* that reflected the studied and purposeful regularity of the monastery at Ema. To Le Corbusier and his students, urban planning meant banishing the archaic melange of housing and the twisted streets of the pre-modern European city. Moreover, Le Corbusier saw this renovation of the urban environment as essential to renewal of the French spirit which had been overwhelmed by the tremendous loss of life in the First World War. Thus Le Corbusier's *urbanisme* went far beyond the sketches of an artist. It was an appeal for a new social contract in modern France. Implementation of his philosophy guided the rebuilding of urban France after the Second World War. French urban planning was both an art form and a social theory.(2)

Like Le Corbusier's own work, *urbanisme* developed during two distinct phases. The period of theoretical development and experimentation under the late Third Republic was followed by intense and widespread implementation after the Second World War. During both periods, *urbanisme* and Le Corbusier faced sharp criticism. To his critics in the 1920s, his modern architecture seemed sterile and anonymous. These arguments reemerged in the May 1968 protests. Yet the magnitude of the transition over half a century should not be missed. Where *urbanisme* had been a novelty during the inter-war years, in by the 1960s it formed a critical component of the modern French state. In the 1920s, the criticism of *urbanisme* came from the political forces in power and was directed against a theoretical movement of only minor significance at that time. By 1968, popular opposition to urbanisme directly challenged the State's decision making authority. In the 1950s, France adopted a highly ordered and precisely structured social and economic philosophy with urban planning being one of its most obvious manifestations. That new social contract survived the protests of the late 1960s intact.

As we have seen, urbanisme and Le Corbusier's urban designs originated in the Postivist social scientific theories of the late nineteenth century. During that orderly and optimistic period in European intellectual history, society placed great value on man's rational ability to structure his universe, whether the immediate task be in the marketplace, the laboratory or the towns. Garden City was one of the more elaborate examples of this intellectual movement. In reality, the Garden City Idea gave proper philosophical form to a concept already used in the company town. Ebenezer Howard's achievement was to place a generalized version of the company town within a broad framework for urbanization that went far beyond the needs of a single employer. Howard's ideas stimulated a movement of land use reform by placing the single utopian community within a broad social scientific theory. In France, Le Corbusier completed Howard's work.

Garden City to its critics contained many of the corporatist features of the older company towns. Corporatism also began its revival during the late nineteenth century with Leo XIII's encyclical Rerum Novarum of 1891. Corporatism demanded the end of Marxist class struggle and the return to the tranquil economic and social behaviors of the mediaeval guilds. After the First World War, corporatism's promise of stability, order and predictability held wide appeal. Le Corbusier's urbanization strategy rested squarely on corporatism.

Le Corbusier's new buildings for old cities were monumental like the majestic mediaeval cathedral holding a diverse congregation with a common bond. Both types of buildings housed an amalgamation of activities and persons, which denied the individual his separate identity. Individual ownership of an entire building became an oddity in Le Corbusier's urban world. Indeed the notion of private ownership by the modestly prosperous bourgeois who had been the backbone of the Third Republic was swept away with the decrepit old buildings of the nineteenth century city. Apartment cubicles replaced the family foyer. The legacy and an inheritance that had bound generations together, the family home disappeared. Like the cathedral builders Le Corbusier wanted to build his monumental businesses and residences at the heart of old cities like Paris. But many of his plans at least during his own lifetime failed to win approval from investors who perhaps too clearly understood that his architectural designs were intended as the deathnell to their own historic age. The monumental Unités d'Habitation went up in great isolation at the edges of the major cities. Le Corbusier never forgave the critics of his urban philosophy. He had seen his new city structures as eliminating the need for automobiles by revitalizing worn out big city neighborhoods thereby returning cities to the central prominence in cultural and social life that they had enjoyed before suburbanization. Central cities and central State authority played a prominent role in Le Corbusier's plans for urban France.

Le Corbusier firmly believed that the relationships between these monumental structures and their uses a rational set of problems which could resolved by fully understanding the scientific laws governing social behaviors such as commuting and shopping. The key to successful planning rested in measuring and accurately predicting human behavior patterns. This concept of human behavior left very few issues to be decided by legislatures.

Neither Ebenezer Howard's model nor Le Corbusier's grand designs left room for the old decision making processes associated with Liberalism nor for chaotic freedoms of nineteenth century urban life. Urbanisme was an intensely corporatist phenomenon from the beginning.(3) In mediaeval corporations the most skilled guild masters made the critical decisions from their experience and expertise in guild affairs. In the same way, Le Corbusier's plans specified elite controlled decisions. He believed that urban land use decisions were best left in the hands of urban planners preferably with little or no interference from legislative assemblies. Indeed, he saw such Liberal-style decisions becoming obsolete in the twentieth century. The correct and verified understanding of the patterns of human behavior, Le Corbusier argued, yielded social laws like Newton's great physical law of gravity that were beyond the scope of any legislature to alter. Urban reformers like Maxime Leroy and Henri Sellier gave these ideas political significance before the Second World War.

Le Corbusier taught planners that their first task was to measure existing behavior and when necessary modify it to be in greater harmony with the optimum patterns of human behavior: The governing social laws. Modification came through adjusting physical conditions in the urban environment. For example, if mass transit was a desirable norm for daily commuting, which Le Corbusier firmly believed, then residential densities must be great enough in an urban zone to support such a form of transportation. It followed that single-family homes in suburbs should be discouraged and urban high rises fostered.

Le Corbusier's second concern, as an artist, was with the aesthetic integrity of urban design. He instructed urban planners to look for the pure forms which he ascribed to the modern development of standardized industrial production. As a painter, Le Corbusier had been attracted to cubism. He preferred manufactured forms over organic shapes. Le Corbusier firmly believed that artistic creation was a solitary project. The unique vision of an artist might require the aid of fellow artists and engineers to implement, but the conception necessarily was the act of a single individual. This model for the artistic unity of urban landscapes left no room for popular oversight.

As the artist's medium, urban design, intruded on far more complex social and political relationships than oil and canvas. The plans for an urban environment usually involved property owned by several different parties often with differing interests. In order to give full artistic freedom to the urban planner, Le Corbusier advocated the nationalization of land. He argued that reducing private ownership rights would permit planners to design the urban environment for the common well-being of society and in a manner consistent with their own artistic visions. Like Newton's great corporate council as described by Saint Simon, artists and poets reigned over the mere men of commerce and industry in Le Corbusier's urban decision making model.

Urban planning's experimental phase, the era of municipal Taylorism ended with the collapse of the

Third Republic in 1940. Large scale urban planning came into being during the two post war republics. Post-war French economic planning has been aptly described by Stephen Cohen as operating under the great corporatist cathedral of the Plan.(4) Clearly, urban planning was one of the most corporatist elements within the entire economic planning system.

During this period of widespread urban land use planning, critical decisions by were made for the whole society with little legislative control. Economists such as Claude Pönsard and Alfred Sauvy successfully urged a policy redistributing the national population around poles-of-attraction. Growth limits for Paris and the targeted regional cities came from State agencies, not the National Assembly. While the Second National Plan was ratified by the National Assembly, the administrators of the Commissariat Général du Plan wrote it.

Under the late Fourth Republic and early Fifth Republic, the National Assembly created a wide variety of autonomous development corporations to handle local and regional growth. Legislative powers devolved to administrative agencies in these actions. National urban development goals within the framework of national economic planning fed through an elaborate array of CODERs, ZUPs, ZACs, and SCETs. Corporatist ideas supported the strategy of deconcentrating administrative controls within urban planning. Ironically, the deconcentration of urban planning decisions came exactly at the same point that the tight fiscal controls of the Fifth Plan choked off investment in France, which in turn doomed many local plans.

Dissension over the quality of French life crept into public debate during the last years of Le Corbusier, partially foreshadowing the 1968 crisis. Certainly, the Keynesian idea, and perhaps the myth of the State's ability to successfully govern the economy and avoid grave crises of disequilibrium came under question in the late 1960s. To the extent that Keynes' corporatist vision provided the whole underpinning for the urban planning system as well as for economic planning, the climate of doubt put the entire governing process in jeopardy.

It is noteworthy that the demystification of Western style planning began at the same time that Le Corbusier's generation began to fade from public life.

The young enthusiasts of the Taylor method, of cubism, and of *urbanisme* were in their seventies and eighties by the time of the May rebellion.

After Le Corbusier, and after the crisis of 1968, France like much of Western Europe emerged with a broader set of alternatives for urban development than had been available during the "growth miracle" days of the 1950s. The limits of rational state power seemed to have been reached. Humanists advocated participatory democracy and a further deconcentration of decision making power to municipalities, while urbanistes in the tradition of Le Corbusier still remained loyal to central controls.(5) These contradictions often stymied development throughout the country in the late 1970s. Doubt produced choice, which led to polarization and stalemate.

Whether the humanist or rationalist model is more satisfactory, and indeed which model works best, still remains an open question. External pressures and misfortunes have plagued the French economy during the 1970s and 1980s, making it virtually impossible to predict the longevity of Le Corbusier's strategy for urban development.(6) The best measures we have seem fully contradictory. The quality of housing for most French citizens has improved dramatically since 1946, yet it has done so largely under the aegis of private property. Home ownership has grown in virtually every region of the country. Thus the quality of life in housing goals of municipal Taylorism, of Henri Sellier, Georges Benoît-Lévy and Le Corbusier in the 1920s have been achieved through means that they themselves certainly would have rejected.

ENDNOTES

CHAPTER ONE

1
The point at issue is whether urban growth comes about as a result of population growth, which stimulates the demand for new housing, under all financial conditions, or whether the rate of interest charged on mortgage capital, for instance, might limit either new construction, or population growth. A Keynesian formulation of the problem would place great emphasis on the short term rates and conditions for lending capital for housing, while on the contrary, the position of Chaunu places more weight on the long run pressure of population growth. After the Second World French housing policy was buffeted between these two approaches to analyzing the basis of equilibrium in the housing market, but neither position fully dominated policy making. While Michel Lescure has gone a long way in providing an excellent data rich picture of the terms of lending in the housing market in his study of 1982, even he can not directly measure the relationships in the housing demand function between interest rates and population change. The chaotic state of early French statistical records on housing effectively probably will preclude any direct quantitative analysis of this question, beyond the Paris region.

See:
Pierre Chaunu, in Le Bâtiment Maisons rurales et urbaines dans la France traditionnelle v.1 (Paris: Mouton, 1971), 21.

Abel Chatelain, Les migrants temporaires en France de 1800 à 1914: Histoire économique et sociale des migrants temporaires des champagnes françaises au XIX et au début du XX siècle, 2 vols. (Lille): Université de Lille III, 1977).

Michel Lescure, Les Banques, l'Etat et le marché immobilier en France à l'époque contemporaine, 1820-1940 (Paris: l'Ecole des Hautes Etudes en Sciences Sociales, 1982), 360-482.

2
Jean Bastié, La Croissance de la banlieue parisienne (Paris: Presses Universitaires de France, 1964), 264-66.

Pierre Barde, Les Communes et la question de l'habitation (Paris: Sirey, 1932). 1-25.

Jean Cazenavette, Extension des villes et lotissements: Projects régionaux d'urbanisme (Paris, 1936).

3
Jacques Dreyfus, L' Urbanisme comme idéologie de la rationalité: le refus de l'ordre de la difference (Paris: CREDOC, 1974), 2 vols. i-iii.

Borrowing heavily from the ideas of Jacques Lacan and Michel Foucault, Dreyfus examined the critical issue of the drive for rationalitè in urban planning as a form of contemporary elite ideological control that seeks to justify the existing distribution of social, economic and political power in France.

See:
Jacques Lacan, Ecrits (Paris: Seuil, 1966).

Michel Foucault, "Réponse à une question,", Esprit, 36 (5), 1968, 850-74.

4
Important biographical treatments of early urban planning in Paris can be found in:

P. M. Wolf, Eugène Hénard and the Beginning of Urbanism in Paris, 1900-1914 (1968).

Michel Z. Burke, Le Play: Engineer and Social Scientist (London, 1970).

See a new study on the development of social science and reformism within the French technocratic tradition in:

Terry Shinn, Savoir scientifique et pouvoir social: L'Ecole polytechnique, 1794-1914 (Paris: Presses de la Fondation Nationale des Sciences Politiques, 1980).

5
Jacques Amoyal, "Les Origines socialistes et syndicalistes de la planification en France," Le Mouvement sociale, 87, avril-juin 1974.

S. Lieberman, "The Ideological Foundations of Western Economic Planning," Journal of European Economic History, 10 (2), 1981, 343-71.

6
Frédéric Le Play, L'Organisation de la Famille (Paris, 1871).

Frédéric Le Play, La Réforme Sociale 2 vols. (Paris, 1864).

Ebenezer Howard, To-Morrow: A Peaceful Path to Real Reform (London, 1898).

Le Corbusier, Urbanisme (Paris: Editions G. Crès et Cie., circa 1925).

Fredrick W. Taylor, Principles of Scientific Management (New York: Harper, 1911).

See also the perceptive essay:

Charles S. Maier, "Between Taylorism and Technocracy: European Ideologies and the vision of industrial productivity in the 1920s," Journal of Contemporary History, 5 (2) 1970, 34, 35.

7
Le Corbusier, Urbanisme, preface.

W. Boesiger and W. Girsberger (eds.), Le Corbusier, 1910-1960 (Zurich: Girsberger, 1960), 17, 35-45.

8
Le Corbusier's activist management philosophy dominated the inter-war Movement for Modern Architecture in France as well as being the foundation in his charge to the post-war generation of urbanistes. See his preamble in:

France Conseil Économique, *La Charte de l'habitat français* (Paris: Presses Universitaires de la France, 1950), 200.

9
Louis Chevalier, *La Formation de la population parisienne au XIX siècle* (Paris: Presses Universitaires de France, 1950), 212.

This theme of working class integration within cultural framework of middle class society reappears in the post-war period. For example, compare Chevalier's findings with those of Hamilton.

Richard Hamilton, *Affluence and the French Worker in the Fourth Republic* (Princeton: Princeton University Press, 1967), 158-85.

10
Michel Crozier, *Le Phénomène bureaucratique* (Paris: Editions du Seuil, 1970).

Michel Crozier, "Pour une analyse sociologie de la planification française," *Revue française de sociologie*, VI, 1965, 147-63.

Stephen S. Cohen, *Modern Capitalist Planning: The French Model* (Berkeley: University of California Press, 1977), 253-55.

11
Léon Walras (1834-1910) observed the financial gyrations of the Saint-Simonian policies of the Second Empire while working in one of the more conservative Parisian financial houses. This experience left him with a strong faith in the optimizing powers of the unregulated market in which he followed the lead of his father who also had been an economist and associated with the doctrines of Jean Baptiste Say. Léon Walras, as an advisor to the *patronat* recommended the creation of HBM as a gesture of goodwill towards the *classes dangereuse*. He thought the program held little significance for either the operation of the housing market or the fiscal policies of the State. As a staunch supporter of balanced State budgets, Walras made his contribution to economic theory in the area of econometrics. Walras helped translate the assumptions

of Classical theory into what he called "pure economics," and as a social scientist of the late nineteenth century he saw his work as providing the vehicle for the modeling, testing and confirming of the critical assumptions of existing body of political economy.

Léon Walras, *Etudes d'économie sociale* (Rome: Bizzari, 1969), 63-5.

Léon Walras, *Elements of Pure Economics: The Theory of Social Wealth*, translated by William Jaffé (London: Allen and Unwin, 1954), 399.

In 1936, Keynes pointed to the same narrow philosophy of the Classical school on finance as being at the root of the world wide depression. He argued for a divorce between the management of a household or a business, and the conduct of State fiscal policy. In the *General Theory*, he angrily denounced this fundamental assumption, when he wrote "we are so sensible, have schooled ourselves to so close a semblance of prudent financiers, taking careful thought before we add to the 'financial' burdens of posterity by building them houses to live in, that we have no such escape from the sufferings of unemployment. We have to accept them as an inevitable result of applying to conduct of the State the maxims which are best calculated to 'enrich' an individual by enabling him to pile up claims to enjoyment which he does not intend to exercise at any definite time."

John M. Keynes, *The General Theory of Employment, Interest and Money* (New York: Harcourt, Brace and World, 1964), 131.

12
Anthony Sutcliffe, *The Autumn of Central Paris* (London: Arnold, 1970), 262-70.

Louis Girard, *La politique des travaux publics de Deuxième Empire* (Paris, 1952).

13
Roger Guerrand, *Les Origines du logement social en France* (Paris: Editions Ouvrières, 1967), 283, 293, 319, 320.

Lescure, 460-80.

Henri Sellier, *La Crise du logement et l'intervention publique* (Paris: l'Office publique de HBM, 1921), 152, 183, 184, 293.

Henri Sellier, *Le Problème du logement: son influence sur les conditions de l'habitation et l'aménagement des villes* (Paris: Carnegie Foundation, 1927), 84, 85, 95, 97.

L. Ferrand, *L'Habitations à bon marché* (Paris, 1906).

14
Henri Sellier, "Essai sur les évolutions comparées du logement et de la population dans la Seine, 1896-1911," *Vie Urbaine*, 1921.

Lescure, 363-485.

15
Jean Gaillard, *Paris: la Ville 1852 à 1870* (Lille: Université de Lille III, 1979).

16
Guerrand, 280-300.

Lescure, 422-423.

17
J. E. Godchot, *Les Sociétés d'économie mixte et l'aménagement du territoire* (Paris: Berger-Levrault, 1958), 12-13.

Godchot was the head of the departmental liaison series in the Construction Ministry (and its successors) under the Second and Third National Plans in the mid-1950s.

18
France. *Récueil des Lois*, 30 novembre - 1 décembre, 1894, "Ouvriers-Maisons à Bon Marché." Article 17670.

19
Jules Siegfried, who sponsored the housing reform law of 1894, began his political career under the Third Republic as the assistant mayor of La Havre, which suffered from serious housing shortages in the 1870s and 1880s when mining and refining industries in the northeast expanded. In a small tract on social reform, written in 1877, Siegfried asked "What can we do to increase order and morality in politics and society? Build workers' cities." General Boulanger, the plotter against the Republic, also defended the dual interests of the workers and the Caisse de Dépôts et Consignations in these housing reform debates. From La Misère, son histoire, ses causes, ses remèdes (Paris, 1877). Guerrand, 283, 293.

Lescure insists that even the legislation under the Siegfried reform of 1894 was insufficient to entice large amounts of new capital into residential construction--for either luxury or modest homes--and the market remained stagnant until 1908. Instead of investment in housing, French capital found its way into the development of mining, chemicals, import-export trade, and Russian bonds. Lescure, 363.

Christian Topalov takes an even more pessimistic stand on this issue, and believes that capital shied away from housing until the 1950s. See:

Christian Topalov, Les promoteurs immobiliers (Paris: Mouton, 1974).

20
France. Récueil des Lois 1889, 5-6 janvier.

In January of 1889, for instance, a decree transferred public health responsibilities from the Ministry of Commerce and Industry to the Ministry of the Interior. Yet control of contaminated and structurally dangerous buildings remained with the Ministry of Commerce and Industry. Guerrand, 320, 321.

21
David Stafford, From Anarchism to Reformism (London: London School of Economics and Political Science, 1971), 186-90, 200-01.

Also see:
Jules Guesde, Services publics et socialisme (Paris, 1883).

Peter Sterns, Revolutionary Syndicalism and French Labor: A Cause without Rebels (New Brunswick: Rutgers University Press, 1971).

22
Howard (1898), preface.

See:
Lewis Mumford, "The Garden City Idea and Modern Planning," in Ebenezer Howard, Garden City of To-Morrow (London: Faber and Faber, 1946), 29-30.

23
Many studies have been made of the Garden City idea throughout the world, but among the clearest and most novel accounts of Howard's actual successes and failures in England is found in the official records of his Garden City Association at the turn of the century.

See:
G. J. H. Northcroft (ed.) The Garden City: The Official Organ of the Garden City Association (London, 1905) 1 (3).

24
Howard, 149-60.

25
Howard, 19.

26
Howard, 12.

27
Howard, 67.

28
Howard, 74-75, 78.

29
Georges Benoît-Lévy, La Cité-Jardin: Art et coopération dans les cités-jardins (Paris: Cité-Jardins de France, 1911), 172-74.

Georges Benoît-Lévy, Paris s'étendu (Nice, 1927), 1-25.

30
Bastié, 1-8.

Le Corbusier, Urbanisme, 159-60, 190-98.

René Magan, Conception et instruments de la planification urbaine (Paris: CRU, 1973), 7-12.

31
Lescure, 363-65.

32
Albert Thomas, La Politique socialiste (Paris: Rivière, 1913).

Albert Thomas, Bolschevisme ou Socialisme (Nancy-Paris: Berger-Levrault, 1919).

33
Louis Loucheur, Carnet secrets, 1902-1932 (Bruxelles: Brepols, 1962), 144-45.

E. Beau de Lomenie, Les Responsabilités des dynasties bourgeoises v. 3 (Paris: Noël, 1963), 5, 65, 150, 173-75.

The second chief officer of the Commissariat Général du Plan, Etienne Hirsch also began his career as an engineer at Kuhlmann.

34
Jean Monnet, Memoirs, translated by Richard Mayne (London: Collins, 1978).

35
Pierre Napoléon Taittinger, Notre dernière chance (Paris: Flammarion, 1937), 9, 10, 11, 63.

36
Edmond Giscard d'Estaing, "Neo-capitalism," Revue des Deux Mondes, August 1, 1928.

See:
J. R. Frears, France in the Giscard Presidency (London: Allen and Unwin, 1981), 3-4.

According to Frears' account: "In the 1930s Edmond Giscard d'Estaing, a leader of the rightwing Action Française, was a member of the Parti Social Français and even president, in the 8th arrondissement of Paris, of the near fascist Croix de Feu league. He wrote a lot of anti-parliamentary articles under the name of Valéry de Mories but . . . he was no supporter of Hitler . . . . He supported Pétain in the war, though not in a fanatical or pro-German fashion, and was awarded the Francisque, the order of Maréchal Pétain." Also see the account of Edmond's business activities in:

Patrick Allard et al, Dictionnaire des Groupes industriels et des finances en France (Paris: Seuil, 1978), 100-01.

37
In his recent study of the economic policies of the inter-war period, Richard Kuisel has preferred to use the term "neo-Liberals" to describe the position of figures like Giscard. This phase is highly inappropriate, since these figures stood squarely in the old traditions of the aristocratic French right, with its profound distain for the bourgeois values of Liberalism, Parliamentarism and Republicanism. What made rightists like Giscard "new" in the 1920s and 1930s was their attraction to the new economic Authoritarianism of Mussolini.

Richard Kuisel, Capitalism and the State in Modern France (Cambridge: Cambridge University Press, 1981).

38
For an early treatment of these problems see:

J. B. Vergeot, Le crédit comme stimulant et régulateur de l'industrie. La conception saint-simonienne. Ses réalisations (Paris: Jouve et Cie., 1918).

39
Pierre Joseph Proudhon, Carnets de Proudhon v. 4 (Paris: Rivière, 1974), 244, 337.

No clearer Proudhonian statement can be found than in the following passage of Howard's classic To-Morrow on the Garden City idea. Howard believed that "the true remedy for capitalist oppression where it exists, is not the strike of no work, but the strike of true work, and against this last blow the oppressor has no weapon . . . . most socialistic writers appear to me to exhibit too keen a desire to appropriate old forms of wealth, either by purchasing out or by taking out the owners, and they seem to have little conception that the truer method is to create new forms and to create them under juster conditions." Howard, To-Morrow, 108, 131.

Silvo Gesell, who foreshadowed Keynesian economic theory, supported the same position and candidly attributed the essence of the argument to Proudhon when Gesell wrote in 1919 that "the author [Gesell] of this book [The Natural Economic Order] was led into the path pursued by Proudhon and came to the same conclusions . . . . No one, except Proudhon, was able to conceive that the preponderance now manifestly on the side of property can be shifted to the side of the dispossessed (the workers), simply by the construction of a new house beside every existing house, of a new factory beside every factory already established. Proudhon showed socialists over fifty years ago that uninterrupted hard work is the only method of successfully attacking capital."

Silvio Gesell, The Natural Economic Order (New York, 1958), 31.

Also see:
Pierre Joseph Proudhon, L'Organisation du crédit (Paris, 1848).

Henri Sellier, Réalisations de l'Office Publique d'habitations du département de la Seine (Strasbourg: Office Publique d'habitation, 1934).

41
Georges Lefranc, Le Mouvement Socialiste sous la Troisième République (Paris: Payot, 1963), 177. 205, 221-23, 257, 329.

42
Sellier, _Le Problème_.

Sellier, _La Crise_.

Henri Sellier, _Les Banlieues urbaines et la réorganisation administratif de département de la Seine_ (Paris, 1920).

Henri Sellier and A. Bruggeman, _Paris pendant la Guerre_ (Paris: Carnegie Foundation, 1926).

43
BN, Section géographique. Carte no. Ge s 759, circa 1928.

44
Sutcliffe, 239-42.

Peggy Anne Phillips, "Neo-Corporatist Praxis in Paris," _Journal of Urban History_ 4 (4), 1978, 397-419.

45
Sellier, _La Crise_, 135-36.

46
Georges Lefranc, _Histoire du front Populaire_ (Paris: Payot, 1965), 90-5.

47
Sellier, _Réalisations_.

48
Pierre Lhande, _Le Dieu qui bouge_ (Paris, 1930), 176.

Pierre Lhande, _La Christ dans la banlieue_ (Paris, 1927).

49
Journal de la Société de Statistique de Paris (Paris, 1929), 118.

Stanley Grossman, "Neo-Socialism," (Ph.D. Dissertation, University of Wisconsin, 1969), chapters 5, 6.

Martin Fine, "Towards Corporatism," (Ph.D. Dissertation, University of Wisconsin, 1968).

50
Sellier, *Réalisations*, 77.

51
In the case of Paris, Maurice Halbwachs' study of property values before the First World War confirmed Howard's prediction of declining central city values in the face of peripheral development. For example, Halbwachs found the following relationships:

Price of Vacant Lots
per square meter
(Index 100 = 1860)

	Central Arrondissements	Outer Arrondissement
1860	100	100
1900	87	416
1908	76	925

Maurice Halbwachs, *Les Expropriations et le prix des Terrains à Paris (1860-1900)* (Paris, 1909), 240.

Howard, *To-Morrow*.

52
Sutcliffe, 257.

53
François Marnata, *Les Loyers des bourgeois de Paris, 1860-1958* (Paris, 1961).

54
Lescure, 481.

55
See note 39.

56
Maxime Leroy, _Les Tendances du pouvoir et de la liberté en France au XX siècle_ (Paris, 1937), 3, 6, 7, 147-60.

Leroy correctly perceived the ideological character of "la France depuis qu'elle a été dotée pas la loi du 19 août 1936 d'un Conseil nationale économique, est, en partie, un Etat corporatif . . . . Ce n'est pas la classe ouvrière qui a inventé l'idée d'un gouvernement économique: l'honneur de cette invention revient sans douté à Henri Saint-Simon et Proudhon à beaucoup contribué éclairer son principe."

57
Fine, 296-311.

Maxime Leroy, "Le Socialisme," _Institut d'Etudes politiques_ (Paris, 1947), 9, 16, 27, 80, 81, 185.

In a guarded passage of his post-war lectures on the ideological connection between Socialism and neo-Corporatism, Leroy firmly argued that the "old" Capitalism of the Robber Baron era had passed in France. The new era was dominated instead by engineers, architects, designers and professional managers, in a word, technicians who replaced the owners in the direction of enterprises. These new managers of industry and commerce took their authority, according to Leroy, from "la révolution," though he was ambivalent over whether it was the national revolution at Vichy or the electoral one of the left on the heels of the Liberation.

58
Maxime Leroy, _La Ville française_ (Paris, 1927), 11-15, 27, 32, 37, 79, 170, 173.

59
Leroy, _La Ville_, 170, 173.

60
Benoît-Lévy, Paris, 42, 43.

61
Lhande, La Christ, 60.

Also see Lhande on corporatism in:

Lhande, Le Dieu, 36-40.

62
Benoît-Lévy, Paris, 22, 23.

63
Leroy, Les Tendances, 6.

Leroy, La Ville, 32, 37, 170, 173.

CHAPTER TWO

1
Le Corbusier, Urbanisme, 167-68, 263-84.

In a pamphlet, Benoît-Lévy denounced "M. Lecorbusier-Sanguier offre, avec ce qu'il appelle le plan voisin, de démolir le centre de Paris et d'en loger les occupants dans l'immense tours de Babel." Benoît-Lévy failed to recognize the significance of Howard's prediction that the large scale development of suburban Garden Cities would bring central city land prices down to the point where redevelopment would occur there also. Howard, To-Morrow, 119, 149.

2
Le Corbusier, Urbanisme, 157-85.

W. Boesiger, ed., Le Corbusier et Pierre Jeanneret: Oeuvre complète de 1929-1934 (Zurich: Les Editions d'Architecture Erlenbach, 1948), 17, 199.

In this sketch book, Le Corbusier saw the connection between modern methods of mass construction in the development of housing and his own architectural designs. He wrote "INDUSTRY MUST CONQUER BUILDING."

Le Corbusier believed that the "question d'économie générale: le marché français du bâtiment est formé pour moité des grandes chantiers où peuvent se réaliser l'industrialisation et la taylorisation par des machines et par l'organisation du chantier." The first group of "Maisons Loucheur" were designed by Le Corbusier in 1929 to take advantage of these economies of mass production in housing.

3
Le Corbusier, La Charte, 210.

4
Max Bill, Le Corbusier et Pierre Jeanneret: oeuvre complète, 1934-1938 (Zurich, 1939), 104.

5
Bill, 1934-1938, 42.

Philippe Boudon, Le Pessac de Le Corbusier (Paris: Dunod, 1969).

Michel Conan, "Notre critique sur Pessac de Le Corbusier," Bulldoc, 20-21 (1969), 33-39.

6
Willy Boesiger et O. Sturnov, Le Corbusier et Pierre Jeanneret: Oeuvre complète de 1910-1929 (Zurich: Les Éditions d'Architecture Erlenbach, 1948), 109, 110, 115, 118, 119.

7
Boesiger, 1910-1929, 109-119.

8
Bill, 1934-1938, 17, 188-93.

9
France, Charte, 210.

10
Boesiger, 1929-1934, 17.

11
Congrès Internationaux d'Architecture Moderne (CIAM), Livre du 5 Congrès (Boulogne/Seine: Editions d'Architecture d'Aujourd'hui, 1937).

12
Shepard B. Clough, a contemporary observer of the rise of fascist economic policies gave a highly perceptive summary of the system's political principles in 1932, when he wrote "this [economic] theory is based upon four principles: first, that the welfare of the State is superior to the welfare of the individual; second, that labor in all its forms is a social duty, because production is the basis for national economic strength and welfare; third, that private initiative is preferable to State Socialism; and fourth, that the State must control and plan the production of the nation by means of the Corporative system."

Shepard B. Clough, "The Evolution of Fascist Economic Practice and Theory, 1926-30," Harvard Business Review, April 1932, 302-07.

13
Alain, Eléments d'une doctrine radicale (Paris, 1925).

14
John M. Keynes, "A Short View of Russia," Collected Works, vol. 9 (New York: MacMillan, 1972), 355.

15
John M. Keynes, The General Theory of Employment, Interest and Money (New York: Harcourt, Brace and World, 1964), 353-55.

16
Keynes, General, 349.

See:
Albert Thomas, L'Etat et les compagnies de chemins de fer (Paris: Dunod et Pinat, 1914).

Silvio Gesell, The Natural Economic Order 2 vols. (San Antonio, Texas: Free-Economy Publishing Co., 1934 & 1936).

In the General Theory Keynes described Gesell as "a successful German merchant in Buenos Aires who was led to the study of monetary problems by the crisis of the late eighties, which was especially violent in the Argentine, his first work Die Reformation im Munzwesen als Brücke zum Socialen Staat, being published in Buenos Aires in 1891. . . and many books and pamphlets followed until he retired to Switzerland in 1906. . . . In 1919 Gesell joined the short-lived Soviet cabinet of Bavaria as their Minister of Finance, being subsequently tried by court-martial . . . [Gesell] became the revered prophet of a cult with many thousand disciplines throughout the world . . . . The movement's main strength lying to-day in the United States, where Professor Irving Fischer, alone amongst academic economists, has recognized its significance." Fischer played an important part in formulating the economic foundations of the American New Deal.

Keynes, General, 353, 354.

Silvio Gesell, Karl Marx in Error (Huntington Park, California: Free-Economy Association Inc., 1952).

17
John M. Keynes, The End of Laissez-Faire (London: Hogarth Press, by Leonard and Virginia Woolf, 1926), 41-42.

18
Pierre Joseph Proudhon, Selected Writings, translated by Elizabeth Fraser (New York: Anchor Books, 1969), 91.

19
Also see:
Assar Lindbeck, Swedish Economic Policy (London: MacMillan, 1974), 22-36, 94-98.

Törg Palander, Beitrage zur Standortstheorie (Stockholm: Academisk avhandling, 1935).

Bertil Ohlin, Monetary Policy, Tariffs, Subsidies and Public Works (Stockholm; 1934).

20
Cahiers de Révolution constructive: I. *Pour un plan d'action*, par Henri de Man. V-VI. *Eléments d'un Plan français*, par G. Albertini, P. Boivin, J. Itard, G. Lefranc, A. Monteil, VIII. *Le socialisme devant la crise*, par Henri de Man. 8 vols. (Paris: Valois, 1932).

Lefranc, *Le Mouvement*, 286-302, 420-421.

21
Patrick Fridenson, *Histoire des usines Renault* (Paris: Seuil, 1972), V. 1, 250-57.

Robert O. Paxton, *Vichy France* (New York: Norton, 1972), 266-67, 343.

Lehideux took over control of the Renault autoworks as his uncle's health faded in the early 1930s. Renault himself had been an innovator in the field of mass production and had sought the friendship of fellow automaker Henry Ford in the years before the First World War. Both industrialists adopted Taylorite ideas about organizing work and both became deeply involved in the question of raising the material standard of life for their work force as a means of more effectively dominating it. Ford built his Greenfield Village outside of Detroit for that purpose, and Renault, who was one of the "men of great probity" on the oversight council for HBM in the Department of the Seine, created a similar hamlet across the moat from his factory complex at Billancourt. Renault was more skeptical of the French attempts to regulate the economy in the 1930s under the economic planning commission than his nephew. Lehideux and Renault, however, fully embraced the mature corporatist formulas of Vichy, in addition to producing tanks and trucks for the Nazi Army at the direction of the Pétain regime. After the war, Lehideux was executed for his collaboration. Louis Renault died in prison before coming to trial.

22
Keynes, *General*, 349.

23
Fine, 296-311.

Grossman, ch. 5.

Paris-Demain: organe de la Démocratie Socialiste du XX Arrondissement, directeur politique Marcel Déat, August 5, 1933, 1; December 30, 1933, 3, 5; February 3, 1934, 1; June 16, 1934, 6.

24
Etat Français. Région de Nancy. Conférence sur l'urbanisme (Nancy: Prefecture de Nancy, 1943), 615-23.

Sutcliffe, 223.

Paxton, 266-67.

25
Yvonnig Gicquel, Le Comité consultatif de Bretagne: Un essai de décentralisation au milieu du XX siècle (Rennes: Simon, 1960).

26
CELIB, Bretagne: Une ambition nouvelle (St. Brieuc, 1971), 1-16.

27
August Lösch, subscribed to Walrasian theory, which, of course, emerged in the 1870s in France, during the period of sharp rejection of Saint-Simonian economics. In his chief study, The Economics of Location (published after his death in Germany at the hands of Nazi persecution in 1945) Lösch wrote that "the advantages of a free economy operating under ideal conditions lie in the individual and self-regulation of the whole or, briefly, in freedom and equilibrium. But, say its opponents [Keynes in "Nationale Selbstgeniigsamkeit," Schmollers Jahrbuch 1933] this need not be reasonable; it may be 'any kind of equilibrium.' There is much truth in what they say: it remains to be proved whether a free economy also provides, as a third advantage, the greatest social product. Its critics might well reflect, however, that economic freedom is a good in itself, and as such constitutes a part of the national income." He went on to stress "[economics] would degenerate into a contemptible or even destruction science if it were to

consider tolerable and degenerate mass phenomena in the same way [as has been the case] . . . most radically, perhaps, through the widespread tendency in the United States, and most dangerously through Keynes, whose General Theory of Employment, Interest and Money (London and New York: 1936) is really based on the phenomena of decadence in the economy."

August Lösch, The Economics of Location, translated by William Woglom (New Haven: Yale University Press, 1967), 363.

CHAPTER THREE

1
Jean Monnet, Memoir, trans. Richard Mayne (London: Collins, 1978), 240, 264-70.

Sidney S. Alexander, The Marshall Plan (Washington, D.C.: National Planning Association, 1948), 23, 25, 54.

Maurice Thorez, Paix et démocratie ne vaincourt qu'au prix d'une lutte populaire soutenue (Paris: PPI, 1960).

2
Richard F. Kuisel, Capitalism and the State in Modern France (Cambridge: Cambridge UP, 1981), 4-6.

Adolf Sturmthal, "The Structure of Nationalized Enterprises in France," Political Science Quarterly, LXVII, 1952.

J. E. Godchot, Les Sociétés d'économie mixte et l'aménagement du territoire (Paris, 1958), 12, 13.

Jacques Amoyal, "Les origines socialistes et syndicalistes de la planification en France," Le Mouvement sociale, No. 87, Avril-juin 1974.

John Sheahan, Promotion and Control of Industry in Postwar France (Cambridge: Harvard, 1963).

Raymond Vernon and Yair Charoni, State-owned Enterprises in the Western Economies (New York: St. Martin's, 1981).

3

Darryl Holter, "Miners Against the State: French Miners and the Nationalization of Coal Mining 1944-49," 2 vols. (Ph.D. Diss., Wisconsin, 1980).

France. Ministère de Reconstruction et Urbanisme, *Pour un plan national d'aménagement du territoire*, (Février, 1950), 8.

France. Ministère Reconstruction et urbanisme, *L'aménagement du territoire, Premier rapport* (Paris: Imp. national, 1950), 3.

France. Conseil Supérieur de l'Économie Industrielle et Commerciale, *La Politique économique et les problèmes du plan* (Paris, Douchet, s.d.), 60-61.

France. Ministère des Finances, *Aide intérimaire et plan Marshall* (Paris: Imp. nationale, 1948), 1-2.

4

France. Congrès nationale de l'APMED (Action des élus municipaux et départementaux). *Elus municipaux et départementaux face à l'aménagement du territoire* (Paris: APMED, 1954).

France, *Charte*, 122, 133-4, 122, 133-4.

5

Charles P. Kindleberger, *Post-War Growth in France* (Cambridge: MIT, 1967), 10-15.

6

David Singer, *Prelude to Spring* (New York: Praeger, 1969).

Dreyfus, 245-47.

7

See chapter 2.

France. Commissariat Général du Plan. *Plan et Prospectives* (Paris: A. Colin, 1970), vol. 2.

Centre de Recherche d'Urbanisme, "Propriété privée et réalisation des plans d'urbanisme," *Etudes et Essais* (Paris: CRU, 1965).

Magan, 1-8.

8
Pierre Lauga, *La Révolution urbaine* (Paris: Le Sens, 1946), 57.

Annie Kriegel, *Le Pain et les roses* (Paris: PUF, 1969).

9
"Nomenclature des Etablissements publics et semi-publics, des sociétés d'économie mixte et des fondations et associations subventionées d'intérêt national," *Assemblée nationale*, No. 6107 (Annexe) (Paris: Imp. national, 1957).

Jacques Attali, *La nouvelle économie française* (Paris: Flammarion, 1978).

France. Commissariat Général du Plan d'Équipement et de la Productivité, *Le Développement Industriel* (Paris: Reunies, 1968), 15-21, 35, 61.

France. Ministère Reconstruction et Urbanisme, "Deuxième rapport d'ensemble présente par la Commission de Verification des Comtes des entreprises publiques en exécution des prescriptions de l'article 58 de la loi du 6 janvier 1948," *Journal Officiel* (Annexe), 26 janvier 1951, 17-46.

10
Alfred Sauvy, *L'Économie français entre les guerres* (Paris: PUF, 1954).

11
France. *Le Développement Industriel*.

France. Commissariat Général du Plan. Commission de la Main-d'oeuvre, *5e Plan, 1966-70*, (Paris: Doc. française, 1966).

France. Ministère de l'Industrie et de la Recherche du Groupe de Travail, "L'industrie en milieu rurale," _Etudes de politique industrielle_ (Paris: Doc. française, 1975).

G. Beijer, _La Main-d'oeuvre rural nationale son adaptation à l'industrie_, (Paris: Organisation de Cooperation et de Développement économiques, 1965).

12
Monnet, 260-75.

13
Jean Monnet (1888-79) was a businessman in the cognac industry before the First World War. After the war, Monnet served as an assistant to the General Secretary of the League of Nations on the mission to correct the Austrian financial crisis of 1923. He reorganized the Chinese railways in 1932. During the Second World War, he worked with Keynes and others in the organization of the financial aspects of war production. He created and lead the CGP from 1946 to 1952. After the Plan, he participated in setting up the Common Market and similar international economic groups from 1955 until 1975.

14
Association Auxilliare d'Action Sociale et Familiale (AAASF), _Un grand dessin: le plan d'aménagement du territorie_ (Lille: AAASF, 1951), 2-4.

George Bensaid, _Le Culture planifié_? (Paris: Seuil, 1969).

Suzanne Berger (ed.) _Organizing interests in Western Europe: Pluralism, Corporatism and the Transformation of Politics_ (Cambridge: Cambridge UP, 1981), 83-102.

Colette Bosquet, _Planification urbaine et propriété privée_ (Paris: Libraries techniques, 1967).

15
Stephen Cohen, Modern Capitalist Planning: The French Model (London: Weidenfeld and Nicolson, 1969).

France. Conseil Economique, Etudes et travaux, No. 7, Annexe, 29-32.

16
See Chapter One.

17
Jacques Julliard, La IVe République (Paris: Colman-Lévy, 1968), 280-282, 292-295.

Gerard Adam, CGT-FO (Paris: Fondation nationale des Sciences politiques, 1965).

18
Jacques Fauvet, Les Forces politiques en France: de Thorez à de Gaulle (Paris: Le Monde, n.d.).

19
Julliard, 302.

20
Gilles Ebriq et Pierre Barjac, Le Logement dossier noir de la France (Paris: Dunod, 1970), 21-25.

Jean Duquenes, Vivre à Sarcelles? le grand ensemble et ses problèmes (Paris: PUF, 1975), 3-5.

Bastié.

Paul Clerc, Les Grandes ensembles: banlieues nouvelles (Paris: CRU, 1967).

21
François Marnata, Les Loyers des bourgeois de Paris: 1860-1958, (Paris: A. Colin, 1961).

22
Henri Albert, De Babylone aux HLM (Paris: Scorpion, 1963).

Lucien Flaus, *Les Fluctuations de la Construction d'habitation urbaines* (Nancy, 1949).

Nicole Haumont, Henri Raymond et Antonie Haumont, *La Copropriété* (Paris: CRU, 1971).

23
Congrès Internationaux d'architecture moderne, *Livre du 5e Congrès* (Boulogne: L'Architecture d'aujourd'hui, 1937).

France, *Charte*, 50-60.

24
For the Vichy period see:

Pierre Délore, *Cité, Civisme, Civilisation* (Lyons: Livre français, 1941).

Monique Dagnaud, *Le Mythe de la qualité de la vie et la politique urbaine en France: Enquête sur l'idéologie urbaine et de l'élite téchnocratique et politique*, (Paris: Mouton, 1977).

Pierre Dufau, *Non à l'urbanisme* (Paris: Flammarion, 1964).

Also see Chapter four on regional elites.

25
Philip William, *French Politicians and Elections, 1951-1969* (Cambridge: MIT, 1970).

Hamilton.

26
France. Ministère de Reconstruction et Urbanisme, *L'Aménagement du territoire, Premier rapport* (Paris: Group national, 1950).

France. Ministère de Construction. *Rapport général de 1959*, (Paris, 1959), 24, 35, 38.

27
Etienne Hirsch (1901-   ) began his career in 1924 as a design engineer for the Kuhlmann corporation. Under Monnet, he was the chief of the technical services division of the CGP in 1946. He joined Monnet as assistant chief commissaire in 1949 and became Chief Commissaire for the final years of the Fourth Republic (1952-1959). Hirsch participated in the shadow government of Mitterrand as a technical advisor on planning. After 1975, he joined the European federation movement.

28
Claude Pönsard, *Historie des theories économiques spatiales* (Paris: A. Colin, 1958).

Henri Aujac, "La hiérarchie des industries dans un tableau des échanges interindustriels, et ses consequences dans la mise en oeuvre d'un plan nationale de centralisé," *Revue Economique*, XI, May 1960, 169-238.

George Dawson, *L'Evolution des Structures de l'administration locale déconcentration en France*, (Paris, 1969), 129-40, 440-480.

France. Commissariat Général du Plan. Commission des transports et communications, Section des transport intérieurs, *Rapport en vue de l'établissement du troisième plan de modernisation et d'équipement, 1951-61*, Transports urbains et voies ferrées d'intérêts locals mars, 1957.

29
Bruno Revesëz et Bruno Joubert, *Représentation sociale et planification* (Paris: Fondation Nationale des Sciences Politiques, 1972), pp. 41, 63-4.

This plan for the restraint of Parisian growth was strongly opposed by Valéry Giscard d'Estaing on the grounds that it created severe diseconomies of expansion by interfering with the migration of labor. The first Parisian land use plan was created in 1936, but never implemented. Between 1955 and 1960, most French regions, including Paris, enacted some form of master plan, though actual implementation schedules varies considerably across the country.

Délégation general au District de la Region de Paris, Schèma Directeur d'aménagement et d'urbanisme de la région de Paris (Paris, 1965).

Valéry Giscard d'Estaing (1926-) held a series of important policy making posts from the mid-1950s until his election as President of the Fifth Republic in 1974. The contours of the Fifth Plan were clearly foreshadowed in his policies in these posts. Giscard was directeur adjoint in the cabinet of Edgar Faure from June to December 1954, Secretary of State in the Debré cabinet of 1959, also Minister of Finances from January to April 1962, continuing in that post under the first Pompidou cabinet until November 1962, in the second Pompidou cabinet from December 1962 to January 1966, as President de la commission des Finances, de l'Economie général et du Plan de l'Assemblée nationale from April 1967 to May 1968.

See:
Valéry Giscard d'Estaing, French Democracy (New York: Doubleday, 1977); and the prophetic essay by his father:

Edmond Giscard d'Estaing, "Le Néo-capitalisme," Revue des Deux Mondes, August 1, 1928.

30
See the summary arguments raised on new town development strategies in the following works on the debate over public vs. private management or urban growth.

Magan, 8-12.

France. Ministère de l'Équipement, Région de Haute-Normandie, Ville nouvelle du Vaudreil: la planification des villes nouvelles (Février, 1971).

Chambre de Commerce et d'Industrie de Paris, La Ville (Pantin: Rélais parisiens, 1964).

Jean Larteguy, La Grande aventure de Lacq (Paris, 1961), 154-9.

31
Roger Priouret, La Caisse des Dépôts (Paris: PUF, 1966), 384-394, 404-407 and 416-420.

Also see:
François d'Arcy, Structures administratives et urbanisation: la SCET (Paris, 1968).

SCET, Dix ans aux services des collectivités locales (Paris, 1966).

32
Priouret, 384-94, 404-07, 416-20.

With $26 billion in assets in 1971, the Caisse was the world's second largest bank.

Société Centrale d'Aide au Développement des Collectivités, Annual Report: 1970 (Caisse des Dépôts et Consignations 1970).

François Bloch-Lainé (1912-) like Giscard, began his career as a civil servant in the finance bureaucracy and became head of the Treasury. From 1952 to 1967, he was president of the Caisse, SCIC, SCET, FDES, a member of the Conseil général du Banque de France (1947-1967) and president of the Fifth Plan's commission on urban development. His writings on economic management include:

François Bloch-Lainé, La Zone Franc (Paris, 1953), Le Trésor public (Paris, 1961), Pour une réforme de l'entreprise (Paris, 1963), and Profession: Fonctionnaire (Paris, 1976).

Mendès-France played a key role in the promotion of national economic planning among moderate and Radical political factions. In 1954, he formed an economic braintrust which included figures who would come to direct the French economy under the Fifth Republic as well. The braintrust included (age in 1954):

Paul Délouvier (40)	Claude Gruson (43)
Etienne Hirsch (53)	Simon Nora (33)
Gabriel Ardant (49)	Jacque Duhamel (30)

François Bloch-Lainé (?) Valéry Giscard d'Estaing (28)

Pierre Besse (39)

A contemporary observer of the Mendès-France brain-trust, Alexander Werth, underscored the apparent contradictions in this group. "Was this 'Keynesian' Council as Mendesiste as Mendès? Was there complete harmony between him and these Inspecteurs des Finances--that super aristocracy of the French civil service, with their powerful *esprit de corps*, their traditionalism, their Big Business contacts, their inevitably divided loyalties?"

Alexander Werth, *France, 1940-1955* (London: Hale, 1956), pp. 713-4.

33
Dawson, 440-480.

34
See Chapter Four.

35
Monnet, 270-5, 483-4.

36
See note 32.

37
Charles S. Maier and Dan S. White, eds., *The Thirteenth of May* (New York: Oxford Press, 1968), 1-12.

CHAPTER FOUR

1
Monnet, 429.

2
Among the best treatments:

Jacques Dreyfus.

3
Monnet, 484-5.

Etienne Hirsch, "Necessité d'un Certain Pragmatisme," Les Cashiers de la République, no. 45, Juin 1962.

4
Louis Leroy, Exode ou Mise en valeurs des campagnes (Paris: Flammarion, 1958), 8, 11, 78.

France. Ministére de la Construction, Rapport général de 1958, prospectives de 1959 (Paris, 1958), 38, 83.

5
Pönsard.

Claude Pönsard, et al, Travaux sur l'espace économique (Paris: Gauthier-Villar, 1966) no. 4, 1-24, 64.

Alfred Sauvy, Historie économique de la France entre les deux guerres, v. 1 (Paris: Fayard, 1965).

Alfred Sauvy, Dépeuplement rural et peuplement rationale (Paris: PUF, 1949).

Törg Palander, Beitrage zur Standorts theorie (Stockholm: Academisk avhandling, 1935), 1-5.

Bertil Ohlin, Monetary Policy, Tariffs, Subsidies and Public Works (Stockholm: Academisk avhandling, 1936), 2-8.

7
Sauvy, Dépeuplement, 119-20.

8
France. Ministère de l'Industrie et de la Recherche du Groupe de Travail, L'industrie en milieu rurale (Paris: Etudes de politique industrielle, 1975).

9
France. Commissariat Général du Plan de Modernisation et d'Équipement, Plan intérimaire: 1960-61 (Paris, 1960), vii.

10
Valéry Giscard 80, 77, 79.

11
Annie Kriegel, Les Communistes Français Essai d'éthnographie politique (Paris: Seuil, 1968).

12
Dawson, 482, 452-3.

Joseph Martray, La région pour un État moderne (Paris: France-Empire, 1970), 85-91.

13
Dawson, 482.

David North Kinsey, "New Town in Normandy: Planning, Politics & Participation in France, in Study of Héronville-St. Clair," (Ph.D. Diss., Princeton, 1975), 310-5.

14
Hamilton, 158-185.

15
Sauvy, L'Economie, 55, 56.

16
France. Commissariat Général du Plan, Concentration et Politique des structures industrielles (Paris, 1974), 43-45.

17
Concentration, 42.

18
Sauvy, *Dépeuplement*, 10.

19
Concentration, 42.

20
J.C. Dutailly et D. Burlan, *Les Conditions de logements des ménages en 1970* (Paris: INSEE, 1973), 38.

21
Allard, 95-105.

22
Allard, 100-101.

Giscard's father Edmond was an honorary chairman of the board in one of the banking subsidiaries of Suez.

André Granou, *La Bourgeois financière au pouvoir et les luttes de classes en France* (Paris, 1970), 237.

23
Allard, 101.

24
Allard, 102-103.

Public Works:	*La Hénin*:
Cie, pour la construction du Conseil de l'Europe.	La Hénin Banque, crédit foncier et immobilier.
Apel, Concessionnaire des autoroutes Paris est Lorraine.	Snism, Nouvelle immobilier des des supermarchés.
Autoroute Rhône-Alpes.	Silh, Immobilière La Hénin.

Quille, bâtiment travaux financière et publics.

Gefic, Générale immobilière.

Constructions La Hénin.

Cocéfi, Centrale de crédit et de placement immobilier.

Aric, Aménagement et realisation immobilière et commerciale.

Allard, 227.

Giscard has had a special insight into the strategies of the French in the field of high technology since his brother Olivier is a member of the board of directors of IBM-France.

25
Allard, 224, 226.

26
Valéry Giscard, 77, 109.

27
Jean Duquesne *Vivre à Sarcelles? Le grand ensemble et ses problèmes* (Paris: PUF, 1975), 122-8, 138-40, 109-20.

Paul-Henri Chombart de Lauwe, *Paris: Essais de sociologie 1952-1964* (Paris: Editions Ouvrières, 1965), 37-55, 45-50.

Also see the excellent study:
J. Jenny, *Problèmes psychologiques concernant les équipements socio-culturels pour les jeunes dans les nouveaux groupes d'habitation* (Paris, 1961).

28
Chombart de Lauwe, 45-50.

29
Ebriq, 6-7.

30
Granotier, 94-97, 77, 89.

31
In 1964, the turnover rate in industry was:

French workers	12.8%
North African workers	33.6
Italian workers	17.6
Spanish workers	86.0
Portuguese workers	44.5

Concentrations of immigrant labor by sector in 1962 were as follows:

Construction	32.5%
Metal working	22.9
Agriculture	11.9
Domestic help	9.8
Mining	5.4
Other	17.5

Granotier, 99, 110, 102-3.

32
Granotier, 99.

33
Ebriq, 29-30.

CHAPTER FIVE

1
France. Commissariat Général du Plan d'Équipement et de la Productivté. Commission de l'Equipement urbain. Ve Plan 1966-1970: Orientations de la politique urbaniste (Paris, 1965), 1, 3, 37.

2
Monnet, 245, 261, 319, 322. The report declared that "in the matter of rendering town plans operational it is necessary to appeal to alternative sources of financing as the number of goals grow and the amount of public credits remains insufficient," and then went on to endorse the creation of private Zones d'urbanisme prioritaire (ZUP) and company towns.[2]

Edmond Maire et Jacques Julliard, La CFDT d'Aujourd'hui (Paris: Seuil, 1975), 12, 163-165, and 169.

Julliard notes that by 1970 the CFDT had developed a critique of both capitalist and Soviet planning. The union advanced as a possible alternative the concept of "socialisme autogestionnaire." Julliard also reported the results of the election of labor representatives to the factory comités (a quintesential expression of corporate organization) in the early 1970s. Membership in organized labor during the 1960s produced the following ranking:

CGT	40.8%
CFDT	19.6
CGT-FO	7.7
CGC	5.1
(remainder scattered)	

3
Jean-Pierre Oppenheim, La CFDT et la planification (Paris: Tema action, 1973), 17, 18.

4
Oppenheim, 18.

5
Oppenheim, 24.

6
Jean-Claude Poulain, La Transformation de la CFTC en CFTD (Paris: Revue marxiste d'économie, 1965), 7, 1, 13.

7
Oppenheim, 1.

8
Ve Plan, 5, 9, 20.

9
Jobert, 41-45, 63, 68-75.

France. Ministère de la Construction. Inspection Générale, Récapitualtion des Principales Statistiques Annexées au Rapport Général d' Information (Années 1960 à 1964) (Paris, n.d.), 3.

10
Ebriq, 45.

Granotier, 95-96.

11
See Chapter One.

12
France. INSEE, Enquête sur les Budgets Familiaux 1963-64 (Paris: Documentation française, 1964).

The results of this survey were considerably different than the findings of the 1962 census, and both sets of records have been the subject of much technical controversy.

13
Haumont, 15-26.

14
Hamilton, 158-185.

The Hamilton study of the Fourth Republic also identified a certain tendency for the working class to purchase automobiles. His study also found a greater likelihood for Socialist workers to own automobiles than for Communist workers.

15
This regional direction of urban development policy is treated more extensively in the case study of Brittany in Chapter Six.

16
David North Kinsey, "New Town in Normandy: Planning Politics and Participation in France, a study of Heronville-St. Clair," Ph.D. Dissertation, Princeton University, 1975, 310.

17
Kinsey, 311-312.

Commissariat Général du Plan. Comité d'habitat. Préparation du 7e Plan: Rapport du Comité Habitat (Paris: Documentation française, 1976), 15, 42.

18
Valéry Giscard, 79.

19
France. Commissariat Général du Plan d'Équipement et de la Productivité, Le Développement Industriel (Paris, 1968), 51.

20
Le Développement, 61.

CHAPTER SIX

1
Congrès 37: Rapport (Paris: CGT, 1967), 3-4.

Cohen, (1969).

2
See Chapter Seven.

3
Pierre, Massé, Planification nationale et programmes professionnels Paris: ATIT, 1961.

'X' (Une groupe d'Anciens Elèves de l'Ecole Polytechnique), "Considérations sur la Planification Démocratique", Homes et Techniques, no. 218, janvier 1963.

4
Beau de Lomenie, 5, 65, 150, 173-5.

Allard.

5
Suzanne Berger (ed), Organizing interests in Western Europe: Pluralism, Corporatism, and the transformation of politics, Cambridge, Cambridge Univ. Press, 1981.

Manuel Castells, La question urbaine (Paris, Maspero: 1972).

Monique Dagnaud, Le Mythe de la qualité de la vie et la politique urbaine en France: enquête sur l'idéologie urbaine de l'élite technocratique et politique 1945-1975 (Paris, La Haye Mouton, 1977).

Dreyfus

7
Paul-Henri Chombart de Lauwe, Paris: Essais de sociologie 1952-1964 (Paris: Ed. Ouvrières, 1965).

Ebriq.

Bastié.

J. Jenny, *Problèmes psychologiques concernant les équipements socio-culturels pour les jeunes dans les nouveaux groupes d'habitation* (Paris, 1961).

8
Jacques Dreyfus, "Les ambiguités de la notion d'environement," *Bulldoc*, 25-26, 1970, 3-13.

Raymond Fichelet, *et al.*, *Pour une approche écologique de l'utilisation des moyens de transport: contribution à une psycho-sociologie des comportements urbains*, Paris, Min. Equip. Log. (D.A.F.U.), 1970.
(étude réalisée par la S.E.R.E.S. pour la D.G.R.S.T.).

9
Jean Bégué, "Projections Tendancielles de Besoins français en main d'oeuvre par professions (1968-1975-1980), *Les Collections de L'INSEE*, no. 8D, Juin 1970, 12F.

Jean-Jacques Bonnaud, *Le Ve Plan, une stratégie de l'expansion* (Paris: Ed. de l'Espargne, 1967).

France. Ministère des Affaires Sociales, Fonds national de l'emploi études spécifiques, *Le Marché du Travail* (Echelon regional de l'emploi de Lyon: 1967).

10
J. Bourgeois-Pichat, "Recent Demographic Change in Western Europe: An Assessment," *Population Development Review*, March 1981, 7 (1), 19-42.

Sabine Gley, *Evolution géographique du commerce en France de 1966 á 1971*, (Paris: les collections de l'INSEE, 1976), No. 39, séries E.

J. P. Puig, "La migration régionale de la population active," *Annales de l'INSEE*, October-December 1981 (44), 41-79.

11
Peggy Anne Phillips, "Mitterrand's Wage Strategy and Women's Labor Force Participation Rates in France

during the 1980s," (Omaha, European Studies Conference, 1982), 3.

12
See Chapter Three.

13
Roger Kain, "Conservation Planning in France: Policy and Practice in the Marais, Paris," _Urbanism Past and Present_ (Winter 1978), No. 7, 22-35.

Sutcliffe.

Jean Boulet, _L'Industrialisation de la banlieue Nord-Ouest de Paris: évolution des localisations industrielles et facteurs de localisation_ (Paris: C.R.E.D.O.C., 1964).

Délegation Générale au District de la Région de Paris, _Schéma Directeur d'Aménagement et d'Urbanisme de la Région de Paris_ (Paris, 1965).

14
Henri Décugis, _et al_, _Urbanisation et Désurbanisation_ (Paris: Plon, 1945).

Michel Beaud, "Analyse Régionale-Structurale et Planification Régionale," _Revue Economique_, mars 1966.

F. Bloch-Lainé, "Sept Années d'Incitation à l'Expansion Régionale: Bilan et Leçons," Annales de la Faculté de Droits et des Sciences Economiques de l'université de Bordeaux: _Revue Juridique et Economique du Sud-Ouêst_, no. 4, 1964.

V. Briquel, "Les comptes régionaux des branches industrielles en 1970," _Les Collections de l'INSEE_ (#179), Série R, no. 21, Dec. 1975.

Industrialisation régionale: l'exemple de Rhône-Alpes, Doc. realisé pour les professeurs de géographie par la Chambre régionale de commerce et d'industrie "Rhône Loire" (Lyon: 1972).

15
See Chapter Seven.

16
Georges Marchais, Programme Commun de gouvernement: du Parti Communiste Français et du Parti Socialiste (27 juin 1972), (Paris, 1972).

17
Peggy Anne Phillips "French Town Planning since 1946: An Experiment in Corporatist Economics," (Ph.D., Diss. Wisconsin, 1981), ch. 5.

G. Beijer, La main-d'oeuvre rurale nationale son adaptation à l'industrie (Organisation de Coopération et de Développement économiques, Paris, 1965).

18
Sylvie Biarez, Pierre Kukawka, Christian Mingasson, "Planification globale, politiques urbaines et institutions locales," in Aménagement du Territoire et Développement régional, vol. IV (Grenoble, Institut d'Etudes Politiques; Paris, Documentation française, 1971) 127-43.

Marc Tessier, Les Groupes d'Action municipale, (Paris: Editions universitaires, 1971).

Kinsey.

19
Centre de Recherche d'Urbanisme, Etudes et Essais (Paris: CRU, 1965).

Hyacinthe Lena, Acquisitions immobilières publiques et maîtrise urbaine: aspects de l'interventionisme foncier urbain (Paris: CRU, 1976).

20
François D'Arcy, Structures administratives et urbanisation, la Société centrale pour l'équipement du territoire: SCET (Paris: Berger-Levrault, 1968).

Société Centrale d'Aide au Développement des Collectivités, 1970 (Annual Report) (Paris: Caisse des D., 1971).

SCADC, "La Situation des zones opérationnelles d'Habitat," Le Moniteur des Travaux Publics et du Bâtiment, no. 31, Aug. 3, 1968, 27-35.

SCIC, "La Participation des Conseils de Résidents à la gestion des Grandes Ensembles," Urbanisme, no. 119, 1971.

21
Roger Aubin, Communes et Démocratie (Paris: Ed. Ouvrières, 1965).

Gaston Bardet, L'Urbanisme (Paris: PUF, 1972).

George Bensaid, La Culture planifiée? (Paris: Seuil, 1969).

Claude Blumann, Droit et l'urbanisme (Paris: Dallez, 1977).

Colette Bosquet, Planification urbaine et proprieté privée (Paris: Libraires techniques, 1967).

Pierre Corbel, Le Parlement français et la planification (Paris: Edition Cujas, 1969).

Jacques Dreyfus, La Ville disciplinaire: essai sur l'urbanisme, (Paris: Ed. Galilée, 1976).

Pierre Dufau, Non à l'urbanisme (Paris: Flammarion, 1964).

Fondation Nationale des Sciences Politiques, Paris (Centre régional, Grenoble), Jobert, Bruno et Revesz, Bruno, Representation Sociale et planification (Paris, 1972).

Denis Lacorne, Les notables rouges: La construction municipale de l'union de la gauche (Paris: Presses de la Fondation Nationale des Sciences Politiques, 1980).

Magan

22
France, *Charte*.

Genéviéve Marco, *Le Corbusier ou les mythes des urbanistes* (1969).

23
Dawson.

CHAPTER SEVEN

1
Dreyfus, v. 1, ii.

2
Michel Foucault, *L'histoire de la folie* (Paris: Plon, 1961) and "Réponse à la question," *Esprit*, 36 (5) 1968, 850-874.

Louis Althusser, *Pour Marx* (Paris: Maspero, 1965).

Herbert Marcuse, *L'homme unidimensionnel* (Paris: Minuit, 1968).

Manuel Castells, *The Urban Question: A Marxist Approach* (London: Arnold, 1977).

3
Dreyfus, v. 1, v.

4
Petr Kropotkin, *Khleb i volia* (London, 1893), rpt. Moskva 1919, and *Fields, Factories and Workshops* (London, 1898), 2nd ed.

5
The same vision viviated Giscard's election pamphlet in 1976, where he wrote "a united society is the necessary end result of the long evolution of the Christian West. . . . Our society will not be completely reconciled with itself until the old divisions have been removed." Giscard continued "Is a more unified society a utopia? Not at all. The

gradual ending of class differences is one of the fundamental results of the historical evolution of Western style societies."

Valéry Giscard, 25-26.

6
Dreyfus.

7
Keynes, 217-221.

Georges Marchais, Pour gagner et changer vraiment un seul moyen votez communiste le 12 mars: Rapport de Georges Marchais à la conférence nationale 7-8 janvier 1978 (Paris, 1978), 7.

Marchais denounced the inequalities in contemporary France where "les 10% de familles les plus pauvres possédaient 0.5% de la fortune particulière en France, alors que les 10% de familles les plus riches possédaient 50%. . . . Un foyer d'industriels ou de gros commerçants achète une fois et demie plus viande qu'un ménage d'ouvriers et c'est une viande de meilleur ouvrier sur dix possède une télévision couleur contre près d'un foyer de patrons ou de professions libérales sur trois."

8
See the popular analysis of French bureaucracy by Crozier and the counter argument by Suleiman.

Crozier, Le Phénomène.

Ezra N. Suleiman, Elites in French Society (Princeton: PUP, 1978).

9
France. CGP. Plan et Prospectives (Paris, 1970), essai par R. Fraisse, 9-18.

10
Fraisse.

France. Conseil Economique. La charte de l'habitat (Paris, 1950), 121-134.

11
Magan, 6.

12
Magan, 7.

13
In 1972, an especially acute analysis of norms and deviance in urban social planning was offered by Joubert and Revesz. They saw "une fonction fondamentale de la société est d'établir des normes, des pointes de référence, cet ordre objectif est intériorisé par le processus de son expérience. La relation au monde social donne sens à la rèalité et à l'identité de l'individu."

Joubert, 100-101.

For example, that socialization process was precisely what rural migrants reports, such as M. Cailleux at the age of 35, living in a ZUP and working at the new Citroen plant near Rennes. He recalled "je suis né dans une famille de onze grosses, mon père possèdait 14 ha en Vendée. Jusqu'à vingt-et-un ans, j'ai toujours dormi à même le sol. . . . Passionné par la mécanique je suis allé suivre un stage de formation de réparateur de machines agricoles à Limoges . . . à l'époque, j'étais catholique, je le suis toujours. En Vendée, être catholique cela signifiait être de droite. L'homme de gauche à mes yeux (à nos yeux) c'était le partagneux, delui qui commettait l'adultère. Je votais à'Indépendant et Paysan'. Puis je me suis marié avec une fille d'agriculteur."

Claude Glayman, Liberté pour les Régions: Bretagne et Rhône-Alpes (Paris: Flammarion, 1971), 72.

14
France. CGP. Rapport du Comité de l'Habitat: Préparation du 7e Plan (Paris: Documentation française, 1976), 15.

15
Yves Mény, "Urban Planning in France: Dirigisme and Pragmatism, 1945-80," in David H. McKay, Politics and Planning in Western Europe (London, 1982), 21.

By the 1960s, the pejorative term "Sarcellite" referred to the residents of the grands ensembles, who were plagued by juvenile delinquency, isolation, overcrowding, foreign neighbors and generally represented the lowest income groups, in addition to recently arrived country folk: The non-Parisians.

16
Magan, 7.

Magan indicated "l'urbanisme total suppose une conduite volontariste du processus d'urbanisation à partir d'un centre de décision unique. Il est secrètement le rêve de tout urbaniste. Ce genre d'urbanisme est celui qui serait pratiqué dans une économie de type socialiste à planification autoritaire centralisée. Mais c'est aussi d'une cité industrielle ou minière dépendant totalement d'un puissant groupe capitaliste qui possèderait les terrains, prendrait en charge les constructions, contrôlerait les emplois . . ."

17
Suleiman, Chapter Four.

18
Ella Searls, "Ministerial cabinets and elite theory," in Jolyon Howorth and Philip G. Cerny, eds. Elites in France (New York: St. Martin's, 1981), 162-180.

19
Giscard concluded "alone among the advanced democracies . . . the mood is not that of citizens discussing their affairs, but rather that of a religious war barely tempered by the fact that the protagonists live side by side. . . . Our political divisions arise less from unavoidable sociological factors, as is sometimes claimed than from historical traditions and the temperment of the individual."

Valéry Giscard, 109.

20
Valéry Giscard, 75-83.

21
Pierre Massé, *Le Plan ou l'anti-hasard?* (Paris: Gallimard, 1965).

22
See Chapter Two.

23
France. CGP. *Ve Plan*, 1-2, 37.

The CGT specifically denounced the ZUP privées, an early form of contract planning for urban land use.

24
Logement et la gauche (Paris: Utopie, 1967).

Michel Rocard, *Plan intérmimaire: stratégie pour deux ans 1982/1983* (Paris: Flammarion, 1982), 62-66.

25
Rocard, 276-287.

26
Rocard, 277, iv-xi.

Mény, 40.

See Chapter Two.

27
Rocard, 283.

28
Juxtapose the arguments of Gravier and Sauvy in the early years of the Fourth Republic.

Jean Gravier, *Paris et le désert français* (Paris, 1947).

Sauvy, *Dépeuplement*.

29
Rocard, 31.

30
France. INSEE, "Une représentation de l'économie française: le modèle DMS," *Revue économique*, 32 (5) 1981, 930-981.

"DMS: Premières explorations macroéconomiques pour la France à l'horizon 1985," *Economie et Statistique* 115, 1979.

31
Andrew Shonfield, "L'VIIIe Plan: Hypothèses et Constraints," *Revue économique*, 32 (5) 1981, 829-833.

Pierre Massé, "Repenser le Plan," *Revue économique*, 32 (5) 1981, 817-819.

32
Rocard.

CONCLUSION

1
Paul Boury, *Comprendre l'urbanisme* (Paris: Moniteur, 1977).

2
Jean Marczewski, *Cours de planification et aménagement du territoire* (Paris: Les cours de droit, 1966).

3
Pierre Massé, "Repenser le Plan," *Revue Economique* (1980) 31(5), pp. 813-19.

Andrew Shonfield, "Who Controls the Planners?" *The Listener*, December 13, 1962.

4
Stephen S. Cohen, *Modern Capitalist Planning: The French Model* (Berkeley: University of California Press, 1977).

5
Denis Lacorne, *Les notables rouges: La construction de l'union de la gauche* (Paris: Presses de la Fondation Nationale des Sciences politiques, 1980).

Hyacinthe Lena, *Acquisitions immoblières publiques et urbaine: aspects de l'intervention foncier urbain* (Paris: CRU, 1976).

6
P. A. Klein and G. H. Moore, "Growth Cycles in France," *Revue Economique* (1981), 32(2), pp. 468-89.

APPENDIX

THE PATTERN OF CONCENTRATION IN INDUSTRIAL EMPLOYMENT IN LARGE BUSINESSES

Strength of the mergers	Region	Rate in 1970 as ratio of the 1961 rate	Key sectors involved
Weak	Nord	-2.4%	Textiles; clothing; metals
Deconcentration	Lorraine	-1.7	Metals; automobiles
Stable	Alsace	0.4	Textiles; automobiles
	Picardie	0.4	Automobiles; mechanics; chemicals
	Auvergne	0.6	Chemicals; automobiles
Weak	Hte Normandie	1.6	Automobiles; electronics
	B Normandie	2.4	Automobiles; electronics
	Pays de Loire	2.4	Automobiles; mechanics; electronics
	Languedoc	3.2	Mechanics; services
	Midi Pyrénées	3.6	Electronics; clothing; mechanics
Average	Rhône-Alpes	5.0	Mechanics; automobiles; electronics
Concentration	Franche-Comté	5.1	Automobiles; mechanics
	Paris	6.7	Chemicals; electronics
	Aquitaine	7.0	Chemicals; clothing
	Centre	7.5	Electronics; autos; chemicals
	Bourgogne	8.1	Electronics; autos; chemicals
Strong	Champagne	12.1	Mechanics; chemicals
Concentration	Poitou-Charente	14.2	Electronics; automobiles
	Provence-C d'Azur	16.6	Electronics; chemicals
	Limousin	18.0	Automobiles; elect; clothing
	Bretagne	21.0	Automobiles; foods; electronics
AVERAGE		5.0	Automobiles; elect; chemicals

Source: Michel Hannoun et Philippe Temple, Les implanations industrielles et l'emploi régional en France (Paris: INSEE, 1976), series E, No. 40, 16.

A COMPARISON OF THE RATES OF JOB CREATION AND WAGE LEVELS BY REGION

Regions	I 1960-1970* Rate of Job Creation	II Distribution of wages (French average = 100)
Basse Normandie	49.3%	82
Bretagne	37.6	76
Poitou-Charentes	37.6	80
Centre	35.0	83
Pays de la Loire	34.0	85
Haute Normandie	29.5	95
Auvergne	27.7	88
Picardie	26.0	91
Bourgogne	25.6	85
Franche-Comté	18.5	96
Aquitaine	14.6	91
Midi Pyrénées	14.2	90
Champagne	12.7	85
Languedoc	12.6	90
Limousin	12.3	78
Alsace	10.7	92
Rhône-Alpes	8.9	96
Provence-Corse-Côtes d'Azur	8.0	105
Lorraine	3.5	94
Nord	2.6	91
Paris	-3.1	126
AVERAGE	30.0%	100 (in 1970)

Sources: Michel Hannoun et Philippe Temple, _Les implantationsindustrielles et l'emploi régional en France_ (Paris: INSEE, 1976), séries E, No. 40, 13. (I)

V. Briquel, _Les comptes régionaux des branches industrielles en 1970_ (Paris: INSEE, 1975), séries R, No. 21, 29. (II)

*Enterprises with more than one hundred employees.

CHANGE IN THE VACANCY RATE FOR HOUSING
(1954-1962 = 100)

Region	Amount of Change in 1962-1968
Paris	204
Champagne	126
Picardie	97
Haute Normandie	80
Centre	138
Basse Normandie	72
Bourgogne	100
Nord	101
Lorraine	160
Alsace	99
Franche-Comté	111
Pays de la Loire	300
Bretagne	110
Poitou-Charente	121
Aquitaine	127
Midi-Pyrénnées	97
Limousin	85
Rhône-Alpes	129
Auvergne	73
Languedoc	121
Provence-Côtes d'Azur	116
Corse	96
AVERAGE	123

Source: P. Durif et N. Séligmann, *l'Estimation des Besoins régionaux en logement au cours du VIe Plan* (Paris: INSEE, 1973), 29.

THE CONFIGURATION OF MAJOR CONGLOMERATES IN THE WAKE OF THE MERGERS OF THE 1960S
(circa 1975)

	Working Capital (thousands of francs)	Gross Revenues (thousands of francs)	Gross Return on capital Investment	Employees	Productivity Index
Paribus				160,000	
RP-PRICEL	8,940	17,875	199.9%	115,800	83
PUK	6,263	18,741	299.2	102,700	100
Thomson-Brandt	1,717	12,556	731.2	94,500	72
DNEL	3,798	17,529	461.5	84,000	111
BSN-GD	2,298	9,987	434.5	62,900	83
CFP	11,690	39,168	335.0	44,300	488
Total/Average	34,706	115,856	333.8	664,200	94
Suez				116,000	
SGPM	7,910	21,164	267.5%	146,000	77
CGE	2,463	17,440	708.0	131,000	72
Wendel	3,896	7,399	189.9	42,000	94
Total/Average	14,269	46,003	332.3	435,000	55
Private Groups					
Peugot	5,000	26,000	520.0%	172,000	83
Empain-Schneider	-----	21,300	-----	129,000	88
Michelin	7,000	15,000	214.2	126,300	61
Total/Average	12,000	62,300	519.1	427,300	77
State Owned					
SNCF	2,000	20,340	711.1%	300,000	33
Renault	3,000	33,539	1117.9	222,436	83
GDF	2,193	12,000	547.1	100,000	66
EDF	32,143	25,906	-19.5	98,300	144
ELF-Aquitaine	8,617	30,687	356.1	38,000	444
SNIAS	1,186	6,440	543.0	42,000	83
Total/Average	49,999	128,912	257.8	800,736	88
GRAND TOTAL/AVERAGE	110,974	353,071	318.1%	1,935,736	100

Adapted from: Patrick Allard, *et.al.*, *Dictionnaire des Groupes industriels et finances en France* (PARIS: Seuil, 1978), p. 7.

Characteristics of "Swing" Voters

(Regional Level)

Dependent Variable: Population Change 1946-68

Multiple R = .9774
R^2 = .9553
F ratio = 64.125 d.f. 5/15

(1)	Left votes 1946-68	-.4076	-.2619
(2)	Farmers	-.9105	-.2170
(3)	Welfare Transfer Payments	-.8890	-.7319
(4)	HLM rentals	.1092	.1877
(5)	Housing Starts 1948-68	.0825	.0712

Relationship of Agricultural Income to
Housing Investment

Multiple R	=	.903
Multiple R^2	=	.815
F ration	=	6.630 (8/12 d.f.)
N	=	21

State Regulated Investment	R =	Beta =
HLM Rented Units	.498	1.001
HLM Purchased Units	-.204	-.130
Standard Mortgage	.200	.289
Differed Payment Mortgage	-.174	-.273
Non Regulated Investment		
without Mortgage	-.479	.433
without state guaranteed mortgage	.101	.631
Other Factors		
Population Change 1948-68	-.581	-.513
Left Vote Change 1946-68	-.574	-.061

Relationship of Industrial Income
to Housing Investment

Multiple R	=	.911	
Multiple R^2	=	.831	
F ration	=	7.400	(8/12 d.f.)
N	=	21	

State Regulated Investment	R =	Beta =
HLM Rented Units	.504	-.961
HLM Purchased Units	.139	.215
Standard Mortgage	.112	-.224
Differed Payment Mortgage	.384	.690
Non Regulated Investment		
without Mortgage	.510	-.686
without state guaranteed mortgage	-.058	-.686
Other Factors		
Population Change 1948-68	.524	.484
Left Vote Change 1946-68	.541	.164

Change in the Active Population

Since 1946

BIBLIOGRAPHY

Urbanisme:

Albert, Henri. De Babylone aux HLM. Paris: Scorpion, 1963.

Allard, Patrick et al. Dictionnaire des Groupes industriels et finances en France. Paris: Seuil, 1978.

d'Arcy François. Structures Administratives et Urbanisation: la SCET. Paris: PUF, 1968.

Aubin, Roger. Communes et Démocratie. Paris: Ouvières, 1965.

Bastié, Jean. La Croissance de la banlieue parisienne. Paris: PUF, 1964.

Baude, Pierre. Les Communes et la question de l'habitation. Paris, 1932.

Benoît-Lévy, Georges. La Cité-Jardin: art et cooperation dans la cité-jardin. Paris: Cités-Jardins de France, 1911.

Benoît-Lévy, Georges. La Formation de la race. Paris: Cités-Jardins de France, n.d.

Benoît-Lévy, Georges. Paris S'étendu. Nice: Cités-Jardins de France, 1927.

Caerléon, Roman. Au Villages des condamnes à mort. Paris: La Table Ronde, 1970.

Cahiers du Centre économique et sociale de perfectionnement des Cadres de la Fédération Nationale des Syndicats d'Ingenieurs et de Cadres. Les Grands problèmes de l'urbanisation à fin du siècle. Séries d'Elites et Responsabilités. Bordeaux: Bellenef, 1966.

Castells, Manuel. *City, Class and Power*. London: MacMillan, 1978.

Castells, Manuel. *La question urbaine*. Paris: Maspero, 1972.

Castells, Manuel. *Sociologie de l'espace industriel*. Paris: Anthropos, 1975.

Chambre de Commerce et d'industrie de Paris. *La Ville*. Pantin: Ateliers Rélias Parisiens, 1964.

Chombart de Lauwe, Paul-Henri. *Paris: Essais de sociologie, 1952-1964*. Paris: Ouvrières, 1965.

Clerc, Paul. *Les Grandes Ensembles: Banlieues nouvelles*. Séries Travaux et documents. Paris: Centre de recherche dúrbanisme, 1967.

Cohen, Stephen. *Modern Capitalist Planning: the French Model*. London: Weidenfeld and Nicolson, 1969.

Dawson, Georges. *L'Evolution des structures de l'administration locale déconcentration en France*. Paris: PUF, 1969.

Délégation Générale au District de la Région de Paris. *Schèma directeur d'aménagement et d'urbanisme de la Région de Paris*. Paris: Prefecture Région de Paris, 1965.

Délore, Pierre. *Cité, civicisme, civlisation*. Lyon: Livre français 1941.

Dessus, Gabriel *et al*. *Matériaux pour géographie volontaire de l'industrie française*. Paris, 1949.

Dollinger, Philippe *et al*. *Bibliographie d'histoire des Villes de France*. Paris, 1967.

Dreyfus, Jacques. *L'urbanisme comme idéologie de la rationalité: le réfus de l'ordre de la difference*. Prais: CREDOC, 1974.

Duplouy, Joseph. *Le Crédit aux collectivités locales*. Paris: Seuil, 1967.

Duquenes, Jean. *Vivre à Sarcelles? le grand ensemble et ses problèmes*. Paris: PUF, 1975.

Durif, Pierre et N. Séligmann. _L'Etimation des besoins régionaux en logement au cours du VI Plan_. Paris: INSEE, 1973.

Dutailly, Jean-Claude et D. Burlan. _Les Conditions de logement de ménages en 1970_. Paris: INSEE, 1973.

Ebriq, Gilles et Pierre Barjac. _Le Logement dossier noir de la France_. Paris: Dunod, 1970.

Flaus, Lucien. _Les Fluctuations de la construction d'habitations urbaines_. Nancy, 1949.

Fondation Nationale des Sciences Politiques. _L'Experience française des villes nouvelles_. Paris: Colin, 1970.

France. Conseil Economique. _La Charte de l'habitat_ Paris: PUF, 1950.

France. Ministère de Construction. _La Vie des ménages de quartre nouveaux ensembles de la Région parisienne, 1962-1963_. Paris: CINAM, 1963.

France. Commissariat Général du Plan. _Plan et prospectives_. Paris: Colin, 1970. 2 vols.

France. Ministère de l'Equipement. Région de Haute-Normandie. _Ville nouvelle du Vaudreil: la planification des villes nouvelles_. 1971.

Godchot, J. E. _Les Sociétés d'économie mixte et l'aménagement du territoire_. Paris: Berger-Levrault, 1958.

Gravier, Jean. _Paris et le désert français_. Paris, 1947.

Gravier, Jean. _L'Espace vital_. Paris: Flammarion, 1984.

Hackett, John and Anne-Marie. _Economic Planning in France_. London: Allen and Unwin, 1963.

Hansen, Nils. _French Regional Planning_. Bloomingdale: University of Indiana, 1968.

Haumont, Nicole _et al_. _La Corpropriété_. Paris: CRU, 1971.

Jenny, J. Problèmes psychologiques concernant les équipements socio-culturels pour les jeunes dans les nouveaux groupes d'habitation. Paris: PUF, 1961.

Jobert, Bruno et Bruno Revesz. Représentation sociale et planification. Paris: Fondation Nationale des Sciences politiques, 1972.

Keynes, John Maynard. The End of Laissez-Faire. London: Hogarth, 1926.

Larteguy, Jean. La Grande aventure de Lacq. Paris: Gallimard, 1961.

Lazarde, Jean. Les Grandes Ensembles douze ans après. Paris: Urbanisme, 1968.

Leroy, Maxime. La Ville française: institutions et libertés locales. Paris: Rivière, 1927.

Lhande, Pierre. La Christ dans la banlieue. Paris: Plon, 1927.

Le logement et la gauche. Paris: Etudes socialistes, 1967.

Magan, René et al. Conceptions et instruments de la Planification urbaine. Paris: CRU, 1973.

Marnata, François. Les Loyers des bourgeois de Paris: 1860 à 1958. Paris: Colin, 1961.

Merlin, Pierre. Les Villes nouvelles. Paris: PUF, 1972.

Mondellini, Rino. Etre urbaniste. Paris: L'école de Rochefort, 1941.

Ponsard, Claude. L'Histoire des théories économiques spatiales. Paris: Colin, 1958.

Prefecture de la Région parisienne. Cinq villes nouvelles en Région parisienne. Paris: MAPE, 1974.

Priouret, Robert. La Caisse de Dépôts. Paris: PUF, 1966.

Raiga, Eugene et Maurice Félix. Le Régime administratif et financier du Département de la Seine et de la Ville de Paris. Paris: Rousseau, 1935.

Rival, Ned. Déjà Paris demain "Beaubourg-les Halles". Paris: La Table Ronde, 1974.

Société Centrale des Immobilières Collectives. La Participation des Conseils de residents à la gestion des grandes ensembles. Paris: Urbanisme, 1971.

Sutcliffe, Anthony. The Autumn of Central Paris: The defeat of town planning. London: Arnold, 1970.

Sweet, Morris and S. George Walters. Mandatory Housing Subsidies: a comparative international analysis. Washington: HUD, 1974.

Tessier, Marc. Les Groupes d'Action Municipale. Paris: PUF, 1971.

Thoenig, Jean-Claude et Erhard Friedberg. La Création des directions départementales de l'equipement. Paris: CRU, 1970.

Tilly, Charles. An Urban World. Boston: Little and Brown, 1974.

Topalov, Christian. Les Promoteurs immobiliers: contributions à l'analyse de la production captialiste du logement en France. Paris: Mouton, 1974.

Walsh, Anne-Marie H. Urban Government for the Paris Region. New York: Praeger, 1968.

Le Corbusier:

Besset, Maurice. Qui était Le Corbusier? Geneva, 1968.

Boudon, Philippe. Pessac de Le Corbusier. Paris, 1969.

Daria, Sophie. Le Corbusier, sociologue de l'urbanisme. Paris, 1964.

Evenson, Norma. Le Corbusier: The Machine and the Grand Design. New York: Braziller, 1969.

Le Corbusier. Précisions sur un état présent de l'architecture et de l'urbanisme. Paris, 1930.

Le Corbusier. L'Unité d'Habitation de Marseilles. Souillac, 1950.

Le Corbusier. L'Urbanisme. Paris, 1925.

Le Corbusier. La Ville Radieuse. Boulogne, 1935.

Turner, Paul V. The Education of Le Corbusier. New York: Garland, 1977.

INDEX